Paprika
A Spicy Memoir From Hungary

Joanne Sasvari

Copyright © 2005 by CanWest Books Inc.,
a subsidiary of CanWest MediaWorks Publications Inc.

All rights reserved. No part of this book may be reproduced, stored in a retrieval system or transmitted, in any form or by any means, without prior written consent of the publisher or a licence from the Canadian Copyright Licensing Agency (Access Copyright). For a copyright licence, visit: www.accesscopyright.ca or call toll free to 1-800-893-5777.

Published by CanWest Books Inc.
A subsidiary of CanWest MediaWorks Publications Inc.
1450 Don Mills Road
Toronto, ON
Canada, M3B 2X7

Library and Archives Canada Cataloguing in Publication

Sasvari, Joanne
    Paprika : a spicy memoir from Hungary / written by Joanne Sasvari.

ISBN 1-897229-05-4

    1. Sasvari, Joanne. 2. Hungary—Description and travel. 3. Cookery, Hungarian.
I. Title.

DB956.6.S27A3 2006   914.3904'53   C2006-900009-3

Edited by Barbara Hehner
Book Design by Mad Dog Design Connection Inc.
Cover Illustration by Nina Berkson

Printed and bound in Canada by Friesens

First Edition

10 9 8 7 6 5 4 3 2 1

For Aranka Wintermantel
(1902 to 1989)
who survived two world wars, imprisonment, exile and a revolution,
who escaped from the fascists, the Allies and the communists,
who lived through great poverty and great wealth,
who lost her mother, her daughter and her country,
who stayed married for nearly 60 years to a charming rascal,
and who not only made the best plum dumplings in the world,
but also fixed her own roof each winter.

"Ne nézz hátra, csak elöre."

Table of Contents

PROLOGUE	The New Hungarian Revolution	1
CHAPTER 1	Sweet, Strong, and Sometimes Bitter	6
CHAPTER 2	Not the Hungary I Remember	21
CHAPTER	A Potted History	45
CHAPTER 4	Flowers in the Chimney	63
CHAPTER 5	What to Eat When You're in Jail	85
CHAPTER 6	"Help! Help! Help!"	107
CHAPTER 7	Oh-oh Canada	123
CHAPTER 8	1989	140
CHAPTER 9	Roux the Day	147
CHAPTER 10	Lakeside	159

CHAPTER 11	Modern Magyar	172
CHAPTER 12	The Family at Dinner	185
CHAPTER 13	Take Me Down to Spicy Town	197
CHAPTER 14	Wine-o-rama	207
CHAPTER 15	The Wine of Kings	226
CHAPTER 16	About That Dead Russian	238
CHAPTER 17	The Goulash Bash	245
THE RECIPES:	Go On, Try It Yourself	254

Pronunciation Guide 276

Thanks, Sources, Credits, and Other Debts of Gratitude 278

PROLOGUE
The New Hungarian Revolution

Somewhere, the ghosts of the ancient warrior-princes Áttila and Arpád are having a great big laugh. When I first decided to write a culinary memoir about Hungary, I thought it would be fun – and easy, too. After all, I had a wealth of family anecdotes and generations of recipes to draw on. And, I discovered, it's a marvelous destination, a beautiful country of elegant cities and charming countryside. Its people combine the courtliness of the Old World and the edginess of the New with their own spicy personalities. It has everything from high culture to low, from opera to Soviet pop kitsch. Best of all, its cuisine and its wine industry are undergoing a deliciously remarkable renaissance.

Heck, I thought, I'll take a few notes, read a few books, try a few new recipes, and we'll have a lively tale just in time for the fiftieth anniversary of the Hungarian Uprising. I must have forgotten I was dealing with Hungarians. And whenever they're concerned, everything is much more complicated than it needs to be.

The complications begin with language. Hungarian is widely considered to be the world's most difficult language to learn, yes, even harder than those written in different scripts and those that were last spoken thousands of years ago. It's part of a tiny language group known as Finno-Ugric: in other words, the only other language to which it bears any resemblance is Finnish. It's purely phonetic and purely logical, but that doesn't help when you're all entangled in diphthongs and cases and accents and umlauts and double consonants and that weird backwards sentence structure. Luckily, Hungarians realize that no one else in the world can speak their tongue, so most seem to speak at least a little English. That, combined with the fact that I still remember some Hungarian from childhood, got me through two visits and countless unintentionally hilarious interviews.

Of course, that was after I actually managed to get to Hungary, which also proved to be a challenge. Hungary may be right smack in the middle of Europe, but it has spent much of its 1,100-year history isolated from the rest of the world. That's partly the result of geography – all those mountain ranges – and partly the result of geopolitics, but it also has a lot to do with the Hungarians' determined sense of independence. Even now, flights from North America are not cheap and not frequent.

Thanks largely to that same isolation, finding Hungarian recipes also presented an unexpected problem. I'd never cooked a single Hungarian dish in my entire life, but I figured I could teach myself in the same way I'd already taught myself how to cook French, Italian, Thai, and all sorts of other cuisines. I thought this, that is, until I opened a recipe book compiled by one of my aunts and read the following incomprehensible (at least to me) instructions for *almas pité* (apple squares), which is supposed to be an easy dessert:

> *12 pupos evökanál lisztet 1 csomag sütoporral 15 deka zsirrel eldolgozunk, hozzáadunk 6 evokanál porcukrot és 1 egész tojást. Azután annyi tejfellel vagy tejjel összeállitjuk, hogy nyujtható legyen, két egyenlö részre osztjuk. Felét tepsibe téve cukorral fözött almapéppel megkenjük, törött fahéjat is hinthetünk ra, a másik fele tésztát kinyujtva rátesszük és tojással megkenve megsütjük.*

Well, *that* clearly wasn't going to work, so off I went in search of a Hungarian cookbook written in English. There, where it should have been – between the Greek and Italian cookbooks – there was nothing. Hungarian cuisine, it seemed, was out of fashion in a world that prized fast, easy, healthy food rather than recipes that started with a cup of lard and ended with three or more hours of cooking time. Still, I kept coming across hints of Hungarian flavors in unexpected places, and the more I explored the cuisine, the more I realized that real Hungarian food — not the stodgy thing it had become during nearly five decades of Soviet hardship — was everything that we crave from modern food. It's fresh, regional and seasonal, at once simple and complex, and it's refreshingly honest. It combines a true *cucina povera* — simple food made by home cooks on a budget — with a richness based on game, foie gras, and deeply flavorful sauces. It goes far, far beyond the old standbys of goulash and paprikash.

For a year, I checked every bookstore I could find in every city I visited. Sometimes there'd be a dusty copy of George Lang's *Cuisine of Hungary* from 1994 or *The Art of Hungarian Cooking*, originally published in 1954. Mostly, though, I was simply out of luck. Still, I managed to find some recipes — some handed down from my family, some from other cooks, some from books, and some I simply created myself — and they are included at the back of this book.

But the biggest challenge I faced was trying to reconstruct my own family history. For that I had to rely on the memories of my mother, my aunt, and other family members, as well my own fuzzy recollections of half-understood stories I had been told — or overheard — as a child. I swear, there was not a single story, anecdote, quotation, or piece of history that didn't come to me in at least two wildly different versions. Uncomfortable events would simply disappear, only to reappear, repackaged as acts of heroism or hilariously bad luck. Entire decades of family history would vanish in the telling of some event. Rakes and reprobates would become devoted family men and vice versa, criminals would become heroes, people would be sent to prison for the wrong reasons or no reasons at all. Mystifying statements would be tossed out in the middle of a story: "And that's when we lost your great-grandmother."

"What do you mean, lost? You can't just lose someone!"

"No, we just lost her."

No one came from just one place. Borders moved, names were obliterated from church records, uncomfortable family connections were severed. No one had just one name, either — each had a formal name, a casual name, a nickname, and often a North American name, too. Some had no names at all, just "your cousin Tommi" or "good grandmother" (as opposed to "mean grandmother").

On my wall hangs my mother's family coat of arms. The Wintermantels' origins have been traced back to 1410, more than four centuries before my great-great-grandfather Ludwig left the Black Forest and moved to a village called Perjámos, which was then in Hungary but has been part of Romania since 1919. The coat of arms features a shield divided horizontally with a gold unicorn on a blue background in the top half and on the bottom a bearded man in a red cape – a "mantel," of course – on a white "winter" background. Though my mother assures me that it's accurate, it's so much the kind of coat of arms you'd make up for yourself that I still have my doubts. But it's a great story, and a great image, and I love it.

That goes for so many of the stories I heard while I was trying to research this book. They may not always be strictly accurate, but they're emotionally true, and isn't that the most important thing?

So often those stories began or ended with food. From its earliest days when the military might of the nomadic Magyar tribes was nourished by their bottomless soup pots, Hungary's history has always been flavored by its food, its wine, and its most famous spice. Paprika arrived with the Turkish occupation. It became a symbol of national pride when the Austrians ruled the land. And, during the dark years of the Soviet regime, its bright color and lively flavor offered hope where little was to be found. As recently as 2004, paprika was at the center of a scandal that some alarmists believed might bring down the government.

In fact, paprika is sprinkled throughout Hungary's turbulent history. But perhaps it has never been more important than today, when the country's latest, greatest revolution is taking place, not on the battlefield, but in its kitchens and wine cellars.

I traveled to Hungary twice in the last couple of years and found a revitalized country. Fifteen years after the end of communism, the economy, the cuisine, and the hope of the people all seem to be flourishing. But some things haven't changed, and never will. It is still a country where the past always sits at the dinner table with the present. It is also a country whose people have a flair for dramatic storytelling.

And it is a country as obsessed with food as any other, and quite a bit more than most.

So there you have it. It's customary for writers to say that any errors are theirs and not their sources', but I am confident in stating that while any mistakes you find may be my fault, they're just as likely to be someone else's. So, choose the stories you find most entertaining, and the recipes that sound most enjoyable. That's what any true Hungarian would do.

CHAPTER 1

Sweet, Strong, and Sometimes Bitter

The funny thing is that until just recently, I never really liked paprika. Oh, I know — other people yearn for the food their mothers made when they were young. They get that soft, sentimental look in their eyes when they think of perogies or gnocchi or mushy peas or congee. They rhapsodize about this traditional food or that; they reminisce fondly about the flavors of their youth. Not me. For years, I loathed the exotic red spice that flavored the *gulyás* (goo-YASH) and *paprikás* (puh-pree-KASH) we grew up on.

Perhaps it was too hot or too sweet for my sister's and my North Americanized palates. Perhaps the dishes our parents made with it were too oily, too fattening, too apt to stain our best clothes. Or perhaps it was because paprika's peppery sweet smell was a constant reminder of being different, of being foreign. When its perfume clung to our clothes it was as if we carried with us a whiff of the old country, not the soapy-clean scent of the new. And when we opened our front door, it was a pungent blast of Hungary that greeted us, not the mild Canadian smells of margarine and air freshener that lingered in our friends' houses.

It took me a long time to recognize paprika for what it really is to me — the scent of home. It took even longer to admit that home was a place where I'd actually like to spend some time, even though the family who lives there — that is, my family — is a bit more eccentric and their history a bit more troubled than most. And perhaps, too, they've decorated with just a few more embroidered doilies than is strictly necessary. I guess sometimes you grow up, look back, and suddenly start to long for all the things you spent your youth trying to escape.

Take paprika. For as long as I can remember, its dusty aroma flavored every meal and hung in the air alongside every conversation, every crisis, every celebration, every moment of joy or argument. It was there during the good times – those long, leisurely Sunday lunches at my parents' place, lively backyard parties at my aunt's, and the marvelous Christmas feasts where my grandmother, Nagymama, would produce platter after platter of roasts and ragouts and strudels and other sweets.

Paprika was also there during the bad times. There were those hurried weekday dinners when we'd eat in tight-lipped silence, my father's anger over some imagined insult simmering like the pot of soup steaming on the stove. There were those parties when the combination of wine and politics and bad memories proved hotter than even the spiciest paprika in the cupboard. Then voices would rise, insults would be exchanged, and within minutes someone would be putting on their coat and leaving early, slamming the door on the way out. There were countless times when, with no warning at all, one wrong word meant the paprika would hit the fan and either my sister or I, and sometimes both of us, would be sent to our room with no dinner at all.

Paprika, you see, isn't quite like other spices. On its own, it has no flavor and very little aroma. Sprinkle it on, say, salad or deviled eggs and all it adds is a pretty splash of color. But if you mix it with liquid and turn up the heat, you have something quite different, a peppery flavor that ranges from mild and sweet to searingly hot, so hot, in fact that it can make you cry. Similarly, you can take the gracious Hungarians I know, pour a few glasses of wine down their throats, introduce an incendiary topic or two (and frankly, those are the only ones they like to talk about) and then watch as they dazzle with wit or explode with rancor and rage.

Paprika also makes me think of all the cooks in my family, and the way they'd dish out love along with all those rich, spicy sauces. No one confuses love and food the way Hungarians do, and when a Magyar cook places in front of you a steaming bowl of *gulyás*, what she or he is really offering you is comfort and affection and a safe refuge from the harsh realities of life. And who would know better about those harsh realities than a people who've been invaded and occupied, who've marched to battle and fled from their homeland as many times as the Hungarians?

Mind you, that heaping serving of love and paprika is a dish generally served with a great big pinch of guilt as well. "If you don't eat it, I know you don't like it. And if you don't like it, I know you don't love me!" is the subtext of many a meal, a sentiment that can induce indigestion as effectively as a too-hot helping of Csipes Pista paprika paste.

Indigestion is often associated with Hungarian food for other reasons, too, or at least with the traditional dishes we know so well. It's rich, fattening, deep-fried and frequently loaded with sour cream, potatoes, lard and lots and lots of onions, an utter disaster for anyone trying to follow an even remotely low-fat diet. On the plus side, it is cheap and hearty and flavorful. While there is a gourmet Hungarian cuisine as fine as any you'll find at a French feast – Tokaji wines, wild game, forest mushrooms, foie gras, rich pastries – most Magyars, even the rich, even the aristocrats, have been poor enough at some point to appreciate how to make a single sausage and a pound of potatoes feed an entire family *and* all their argumentative friends.

Certainly, that was the case for my family when they first came to Canada. They arrived here in 1957, shortly after the disastrous Hungarian Uprising of the previous October, when the great, grumpy bear to their east squashed their naive little rebellion with a disdainful swat. Some 200,000 Hungarians escaped, ending up in whatever country would give them refuge.

The Sasváris and Wintermantels who left (some stayed behind, either too afraid of the authorities back home or too unwilling to start over in a new place) chose Canada. By the 1960s, they were living in a big old house at the down-at-heels end of a once-genteel neighborhood in Toronto.

The house was a dark and gloomy Edwardian three-story, with creaky wooden floors and windows that stuck, and it was decorated with brocade draperies and the formal, old-fashioned European-style furniture Nagymama bought with the discount she got from working at Sears. That old place provided a refuge for my grandparents, József and Aranka Wintermantel; my Aunt Luizi; my parents, Joe and Madge Sasvári; and, when we were born several years later, me and my sister Fran.

My parents, sister, and I lived on the second floor. Upstairs, my mother's only sister, Luizi, lived in the attic, which she'd transformed into a charming little suite. My grandparents – our landlords, really, since everyone helped with the payments – lived on the main floor. In the basement was the paying tenant, a mysterious stranger we rarely saw but whom we all revered, because without him we would have had no money for my father's books and my grandfather's brandy.

On our floor, the aroma of paprika would burst from the kitchen in sharp little explosions. My mother was an impatient cook whose culinary forays were accompanied by slamming cupboard doors, the clatter of dropped pot lids, and occasional angry shouts. Still, she dutifully prepared the basics of Hungarian cuisine: *gulyás*, the paprika-scented soup of the Hungarian plains; *pörkölt* (PURR-kult) its stewier cousin; and, when she was in a very good mood, *lángos* (LAN-goesh) a salty, garlicky fritter that we all loved but got to enjoy far too seldom.

My mother, Magdolna – whose name was changed to Madge by immigration officials when she landed in Canada – much preferred sitting at the table with a martini and a cigarette, wearing her trim career girl's white shirt and pencil skirt, a patent pump swinging from one toe, joking with the men. She was a flirt and a tease and a bit of a tomboy, with short, dark curls, and a pale complexion that had been ravaged by the sun during the years she'd had to work in the cotton fields. That was one experience she didn't like to talk about, although she would spend hours telling outrageous anecdotes about life back home and hilarious stories about her series of hapless jobs in Toronto. She was, variously, a diner waitress who could speak no English, a secretary who could not take shorthand and, eventually, an insurance claims adjuster who wasn't all that great at math. She could find humor in anything, it seemed, and she could turn almost any awful memory – watching her father get first shot and then arrested, losing the family home, walking through streets filled with dead and mutilated bodies – into a merry tale with a punchline that made you forget that what you were laughing about was actually something that should have made you weep. What she couldn't turn into a *jo vicc* (YO veets), a good joke, she simply pretended didn't exist. The Queen of Denial, we called her, in later years.

One thing she could never make light of was my father's black moods. Back home, József Sasvári had trained to become a diplomat or an ambassador, but in Canada, "Joe" was simply a stock boy at Sears. What upset him most was how the very anglo Torontonians made fun of him. Even the worst-educated employees mocked his accent, ordered him around, and called him a DP, a displaced person. It was a crushing comedown for the star student of the foreign languages school, so he worked feverishly to change his circumstances. After his shift in the stock room, he would come home and study. He worked on his accent, took political science courses at the university, and even became a minister by mail. When he wasn't studying, he was writing bleak short stories and apocalyptic poetry, some of which actually got published. (Well, it *was* the sixties.)

When he wasn't in one of the unpredictable moods that had us all tiptoeing around the apartment, Joe had an almost childlike sense of fun. And one place he could always find some cheer was in the kitchen. He not only loved to eat, but unlike his wife, Joe loved to cook. He brought a remarkably innovative spirit to the task. No recipes for him: he'd toss whatever he could find into a pot, throw in a handful of paprika, and hope for the best. He was usually pretty successful when he made fish soup, or *halászlé* (huh-LASS-lay) though it was so spicy you feared it would tear the roof off your mouth. His other creations, which he uniformly called "Chinese soup," were not always so great, since they involved dumping everything in the crisper into a pot all at once, then adding a whole whack of paprika. Since he always left behind a mess that looked as if Áttila and the boys had just marched through our tiny kitchen, my mother greeted his culinary adventures with a look of dread and a quick nip of brandy.

When things got too intense on our floor, I'd escape upstairs to my aunt's quiet apartment and gentle conversation. Her name was Allojza, but her friends and family knew her as Luizi; Canadians called her Louise; and I knew her as Luli. Every Hungarian I've ever met has a seemingly endless supply of names and nicknames, and once a name has been given to you, you have it for life. My mother, for instance, was Magdolna, Magda, and Madge, but no one in the family ever called her anything but Pintyi (PEENT-yee), the nickname her father gave her when she was a baby. (Actually, it was originally Pintyuke, but shortened to Pintyi, and it means "Little Finch.") Later on, her sons-in-law, who couldn't quite pronounce that "tyi" sequence, renamed her "Pinky.") Nagypapa was the great bestower of nicknames in our family: he was the one who called me Csibike (CHEE-bee-keh), which means Little Chick, or at least I hope it does. At any rate, that's better than my cousin who's called Süni, which means Hedgehog, or a most unfortunate friend of mine whose dad nicknamed him Kis Ló Faszikám: My Little Horse's Dick.

Luli's nickname didn't really mean anything, but it was a perfect fit, for it sounded as lilting and lovely as she was. She was in her late thirties and unmarried, although she always had a fiancé hanging around. She was the family beauty, tall, slender and elegant, with masses of dark hair all piled up like a woman in a Gustav Klimt painting. She had the grace and the sort of education one might expect of a girl who'd been brought up to marry an aristocrat, which had been her expected role in life before all the chaos disrupted it. What she really should have been, however, had she been born in different, less war-torn times, was a chef, specifically, a pastry chef.

Of everyone in the family, Luli had the lightest hand in the kitchen. I loved to sit at her kitchen counter, listening to the snick-snick-snick as she chopped a pound of walnuts into fine crumbs in no time at all. She'd cream sweet butter and sugar by hand and always let me taste a spoonful of it before she spun it magically into a fancy, multileveled torte. All the while, she'd tell me stories of life back home, of cousins I'd never met who lived in houses I'd never get to visit. And when she used paprika, it would waft in the gentlest of breezes as she deftly folded up a batch of Hortobágyi *palacsinta* (Hore-to-BAD-yee puh-la-CHEEN-ta) – crêpes with a paprika-flavored meat filling – or stirred together a delicate paprika-cream sauce.

The real cook in our family, though, was my grandmother, Aranka. The scent of paprika would bloom in great rich clouds from the first floor, where she made the same hearty, sour-cream-laced dishes she'd once prepared at the restaurant her family ran back in the resort town of Siófok on the shores of Lake Balaton. Nagymama was a quick and stern cook. From our suite upstairs, we could hear the thunk-thunk as she chopped the onions, the hiss as they hit the hot grease in the pan, the rattle of the wooden spoon as she stirred in the paprika, the sharp rise and fall of her voice as she berated my grandfather, whom she adored, when he poured himself yet another glass of red wine.

Nagymama was tiny and peppery. Even if she stretched tall, she barely reached five feet, but she was by far the biggest presence in that house and, indeed, in all our lives. It was at her table we gathered for holiday dinners, in her living room we sipped wine on snowy evenings, in her garden we lounged on sunny afternoons. She was the most down-to-earth and practical person we knew, yet she was also the sort of woman who never left the house without her hair done, who always wore her diamonds, who always had beautiful furniture and furs, even if she had to eat nothing but potatoes to be able to afford them.

Back home, she and Nagypapa had been rich, then poor, then rich again. And then they lost everything. They had been, at different times, the toast of Hungarian society and outcasts who were arrested, jailed, tortured, and exiled. In Canada, though, they were just another pair of foreigners.

They were both in their fifties when they left Hungary – Nagypapa was nearly fifty-seven; Nagymama two years younger – and ill-prepared to start over in a new place where they spoke barely a word of the language. Nagypapa, who had never really recovered from his terrible experiences at the hands of the Soviet police, didn't go to work, but became our babysitter. A most indulgent one he was, too. He was an elegant older gent with swept-back hair and a proud beak of a nose. He always wore dapper suits and proper hats and his years in the secret police cells had left him in need of a cane. Each day, he'd take us for a walk to the park and would somehow always "find" pennies and dimes on the sidewalk. He told us silly stories and, although he was no cook, he would make us soft-boiled eggs mashed in a cup, buttery fingers of toast and, when we were sick, tea with lots of sugar and a splash of rum in it.

Nagymama was made of sterner stuff than her husband. Despite her heavy accent and the fact that she knew approximately three words in the entire English language, she promptly got a job making sandwiches in the Sears cafeteria, where she worked until she could retire with a decent pension. From that menial job, and with contributions extorted from the rest of the family, she managed to save enough money to buy the house in Toronto, to provide herself with a fur coat, and to feed her clan. To help pay the bills, she put up preserves, made her own clothes, did her own repairs and rented out rooms in her house.

She was brilliant when it came to transforming cheap, filling food into heavenly meals that could feed a crowd. She'd add a few chunks of spicy sausage to a mound of potatoes and make it into enough *paprikás krumpli* (puh-pree-KASH KROOM-plee) to feed us all until we were bursting – and she'd still have enough leftovers for the next day. Or she'd toss egg noodles with sizzling, salty bacon, cottage cheese, and sour cream to make *túros csuzsa* (too-roesh CHOO-suh); or she'd mix those noodles with cooked cabbage, or ground walnuts, or poppy seeds, for what seemed like an endless variety of cheap and delicious noodle dishes. Then again, she really shone when she made fancy food, like the rich creamy lobster ragout we loved so much at the annual Christmas feast, or the fanciful layers of chestnut purée and whipped cream called "Monte Bianco" that was the finale of the holiday meal.

On Sundays, she'd spend the day in the kitchen. In the evenings, our other Hungarian relatives and friends would come over, drawn to Nagymama and her cooking as if she were some sort of tiny magnetic force. Among them were the Czumpfs, my dad's sister Frances, whom we called Franci néni, and her husband Frank, aka Feri bacsi. ("Néni," pronounced NAY-nee, and "bacsi," pronounced BA-chee, are the polite titles children give their elders; they mean something like, though not exactly, "uncle" and "auntie.") The Sasváris, like the Wintermantels, supposedly came from a wealthy family – or at least it had been wealthy until some ancient ancestor gambled away the family fortune, leaving future generations to make their own way in the world.

My dad's sister was something of a glamour girl. I was aware that she'd had a particularly rough time of it back home, not that anyone would ever talk about what actually happened. She was especially determined to make things work in Canada, and she did, becoming one of the first women executives in Toronto and a member of all the right clubs and volunteer boards of directors. She was the first person in our family who really figured Canada out, and she had the most determined sense of style: she decorated her house all in white, bought nothing but white flowers, drove a white Lincoln Continental, and had a tiny white poodle called Bijou. (Her husband, a dedicated tennis player, was also nearly always in white and treated her as if she were made of the most delicate porcelain.) She was funny and high-strung, dyed her hair platinum blonde, dressed in icy shades of silk and floor-length furs, and always wore heaps of jewelry.

Among the other regulars on Sunday nights were my godparents, Kati néni and Dezsö bacsi ,and my Aunt Luli's on-again, off-again fiancé Miska bacsi, the dentist. For entertainment we had our family friends, Mara néni and Nori bacsi, who were always in the midst of financial shenanigans. Laughing and telling impossible stories, they'd knock back harsh red wine while Nagymama kept the platters of roast meats and salads and pastries appearing like some Magyar version of the loaves and fishes.

There would always be cheese straws and the salty, bacon-studded biscuits called *pogácsa* (poe-GACH-uh) for us to nibble on before dinner. Then we'd begin with a soup, a clear broth with liver dumplings, perhaps, followed by a cucumber salad. The main course might be roast pork stuffed with Debrecen sausage or *vagdalt hús* (VUG-dalt hoosh), a fancy meatloaf stuffed with boiled eggs, or maybe a roasted duck. There would be a buffet laden with side dishes – a mayonnaise salad, deviled eggs, red cabbage, potatoes, gratinéed cauliflower, and platters of cold cuts. We'd always have cheese to follow, and then, depending on the season and what Nagymama could find at the market, cherry squares, plum dumplings, poppy seed strudel, jam-filled crêpes, or walnut cake.

Even years later when I was a teenager, desperate to fit in and wishing that my family came from some normal place with boring food – England or Scotland would have been good, especially if the family had left several generations ago so that we didn't have to care so much about the current political situation – I still knew that no one, but no one, ate as well as we did when the family put on a feast.

It was an odd period in our lives, when we all lived in that old house. On the one hand, the family had been through so much turmoil and pain and loss that it was a rather sad time; on the other, they'd all survived, and that made them almost giddy with joy: everyone was together, building a new life, safe, comfortable and eating well. But perhaps the restless genes of the nomadic tribes that first settled Hungary had been passed down through the generations, because it didn't last. Not even Nagymama's famous walnut strudel could keep her family there. First one couple left and then another, and it wasn't too long before the family was dispersed all over Canada. First to go were my godparents, who moved to, of all places, Baffin Island. The Czumpfs and Miska the dentist stayed put in Ontario, but the rest of us headed west, one couple at a time, all of us ending up eventually in various parts of British Columbia.

The house in Toronto became a distant memory. Within a few years, the neighborhood was taken over by another wave of immigrants, who would themselves move on and then the next group of newcomers washed in. Overnight, it seemed, aromatic jerk spices and steel drums replaced the sound of gypsy violins and the scent of paprika.

The paprika that flavored my childhood is the spice that flavors nearly all Hungarian cooking. There is no other nationality so intrinsically associated with a single spice – not the cilantro of Mexican food, the tarragon of French, the basil of Italian, the fish sauce of Thai, or even the turmeric and coriander of South Asian cuisine. Like everything else about Hungary, its people, its history, and its cuisine, there are countless different versions of the story of paprika. Just about the only thing that is indisputable is that paprika is the dried, ground pod of the sweet red pepper (*Capsicum anuum*). Pretty much everything else is up for debate.

Legend has it that the fierce Magyar warriors who swept across Europe in the Middle Ages fired their fearsome rampages with paprika. It's a vivid image: the wild horses, the men with their sweeping moustaches and exotic costumes, drawing their swords as they descended on helpless villagers, ending their bloodthirsty battles with a pot of *gulyás*. Sadly, though, it's not likely to be a true one.

Paprika – along with coffee and strudel – was probably introduced to the Magyars by the much-loathed Turks, who occupied the country for 158 long years. Paprika originated in South America, and was reportedly brought to Europe by the doctor on Christopher Columbus's journey to the New World. However, it should perhaps be noted that there are also indigenous Asian peppers similar to paprika. Since the Magyars sprang from the Mongolian plains and roamed bloodily throughout Asia before settling along the shores of the Danube, it's entirely possible that they nibbled on hot local peppers before the good doctor made his voyage.

One theory has it that the occupying Turks brought the first pepper plants to Hungary in the seventeenth century, but grew the plants only for their own use. In fact, the story goes, any Hungarians caught with paprika would be summarily executed. The threat of prompt decapitation by an Ottoman blade would surely have discouraged even the most foolhardy gourmand from plundering the occupiers' gardens. Another theory claims that Balkan tribes fleeing the dreaded Turks brought the seeds in their luggage. They used the spice for flavor, and eventually this practice caught on with the locals, too.

It isn't until the late eighteenth century that records in Hungary show the "heathen pepper" first being used in cooking. Until then, it was likely used mainly for decoration. It became popular throughout Europe when Napoleon's blockades prevented black pepper, which was used as a preservative as well as a flavoring agent, from getting through. People may have started using paprika out of necessity, but soon began to enjoy it for its own unique flavors. It became so popular that eventually paprika replaced the other herbs and spices traditionally used by the Hungarians – tarragon, rosemary, basil, thyme, aniseed, juniper, saffron, and ginger – until it reached the point where a Hungarian kitchen would only have three seasonings in the cupboard: salt, pepper, and paprika.

Paprika comes in six or seven different types, but they split into two main varieties: sweet, which is called *édes*, and strong, *erös*. The same can pretty much be said about the Hungarian people. On the one hand, you have marzipan blondes like the famous Gabor sisters, Eva, Zsa-Zsa and Magda, all sweet and charming and gently witty. On the other, you have the descendants of the Magyar warriors, with their high cheekbones, strong noses, and violent opinions on just about anything. Those two opposites combine to form the national character. It is a lively and entertaining mix, but not one that leads to peaceful coexistence, neither among the Hungarians themselves nor with anyone else.

Just like the Hungarian people, even the sweetest paprika has a bit of heat and the hottest paprika has a bit of sweetness. Paprika's high sugar content is the reason you always have to take a pot off the stove before you add paprika, and why you can't put it back on the flame until you've added something to temper it. If you don't, paprika burns and becomes inedibly bitter.

"Bitter," unfortunately, also describes too many Hungarians, both those who left and those who stayed. And who can blame them, really? They once lived in one of the most beautiful places on Earth, a land of mountains and plains and vibrant cities with graceful boulevards filled with lively discussion, where the fields and orchards produced exquisite food and lovely wine, where the universities produced poets and musicians and artists. When the 1956 Uprising failed so spectacularly, it was not only as if they'd been driven out of Eden, but as if Eden itself had been taken over by a bunch of joyless thugs intent on uglifying every aspect of life. Even the food and wine, always a Hungarian's greatest source of joy, became tainted by the Soviet occupation. In a land that had always been a place of limitless bounty, the scarcity of foodstuffs and the long lineups came as a shock. Yet even that wasn't nearly as depressing as the way the Soviets destroyed the small old family-owned farms and vineyards and replaced them with collective-style cabbage plantations and wine factories that produced cheap, plentiful, and horrid plonk.

I learned young that bitterness is not a palatable dinner companion. It can turn sweet wine to poison in your mouth. Many were the toxic meals I can recall with someone – or indeed, everyone – spitting blame like venom at some group or individual for everything from the high price of wine here in Canada to the loss of the family's properties back home. The trajectory of blame could go from the soup to the roast to the cheese to the after-dinner Bénédictine, tracing history right back to the days of the Turks. Russians and communists or even faintly pink socialists would usually come in for the roughest time, however, since the Soviets' crimes were so much more recent and so much more deeply resented.

How I longed to be part of a family that would sit around the table and talk about, say, mortgage rates and celebrity gossip. I was pretty sure my friends weren't having long discussions about how unfair it was that the Americans had helped Czechoslovakia in 1968 after snubbing Hungary in 1956, or about how those sneaky Romanians pulled a fast one at the Versailles talks in 1919, or about how they would love to have their cousins visit if only they could convince the KGB to let them out of the country, or about how difficult it was to find sour cherries, decent sausage, and delicate Hungarian peppers in their new country.

It wasn't just the endless political conversations that had me wishing that I came from a different background. There was also that whole sense of being an outsider, indelibly different from the Canadian kids we went to school with – and what little girl ever wants to be different from her peers? When our friends came to visit, they'd wrinkle their little noses at the weird smell in the air. They would always take care to ask what was for dinner before accepting an invitation to stay. They'd laugh at our accents and the excess of embroidery around the house. And when their parents found out that we'd always get a splash of wine in soda water for dinner, some of them forbade their offspring to visit.

I suppose it's not that odd that my sister and I turned our backs on Hungarian culture. We turned it into a bit of joke, rolling our eyes and laughing at the silly quaintness of it all. It wasn't just the history and the accents and the resentments and the stupid peasant blouses we rejected, either. More than anything, it was the food.

Whenever a friend or relative visited Hungary, they'd bring back little sacks of paprika because, frankly, there wasn't much else they *could* bring back, there being little to purchase under the communist occupation. I don't think either of us ever opened a single packet of that paprika; certainly we never actually cooked with it. It would sit unopened in the spice drawer for months or years until the next time we changed apartments and threw it out.

Still, despite rejecting their culture and their cuisine, I must have inherited something from all the cooks in the family, because over the years I became a respectable home cook and, variously, a food writer, a restaurant reviewer, a food stylist and even (during a brief period of apparent insanity) a caterer. But while I cooked Italian, French, Spanish, Moroccan, Thai, Chinese, and almost any other cuisine you can think of, I never cooked a single Hungarian dish.

Then one day I was leafing through *Gourmet* magazine and made two life-changing discoveries. The first was that the editor and my idol, Ruth Reichl, came from a Hungarian background. How cool is that, I thought? The second was the idea that there might actually be a *modern* Magyar cuisine emerging from the old. The magazine had a recipe for a zippy update on the classic chicken paprikash: Instead of the traditional dish of chicken pieces stewed with paprika and sour cream, Cornish game hens were brushed with paprika oil and roasted with root vegetables.

It looked, well . . . good. Like something I'd make. Like something I'd serve my friends. I suddenly wondered: What else are those clever Hungarians cooking up? And with that, three decades of disdain ended, rapidly to be replaced by an almost insatiable hunger for something I'd never tasted before. I hungered to learn the story of paprika, the story of the Hungarians, the story of my family – the story, finally, of me. I'd spent my life on the move, trying to escape the past and the paprika and the places that connected us. Now I wanted it all back.

I decided to spend a year exploring all that is Hungarian. A year is reasonable, I thought. A year gives me time to travel and read books and meet long-lost family, and even to spend some time in the kitchen.

I determined that I would learn to cook the traditional dishes like *gulyás* and *lángos* and *Dobos torta*. I would also learn how the revolutionary young chefs back home are creating a brand new cuisine for a country full of brand new possibilities – for there is a revolution going on in Hungary, and this one features flavors and culinary techniques rather than gunfire and tanks in the streets. I'd wander the replanted vineyards of a land that once produced a third of the world's wine. I would learn about the country's history and what it's like today. I'd explore its graceful streets with their bullet-pocked Art Nouveau buildings and relax in its thermal spas and Turkish baths. I'd learn the story of my family, the Sasváris and the Wintermantels, yes, even the bad bits, the bits we sometimes tried to pretend never actually happened.

And I'd learn all I possibly could about that most mysterious and exotic of spices, paprika.

CHAPTER 2
Not the Hungary I Remember

Just a few weeks later, I was on a big old Malév airliner from Toronto to Budapest. I remembered that the last time I traveled on Malév, twenty or so years before, they had brought the wine around in gallon jugs and served us platters of spicy cold cuts and wonderful rye bread. This time it was the same soggy pasta and microwaved chicken that you get on every other airline in the world.

"You shoulda seen it," I was saying to my partner, Lionel, who had joined me on the trip. "There were all these drunk Hungarians partying like mad and yelling and singing." I thought about it for a moment. "At least they were partying on the way back to Canada – I can't remember too much celebration on the way over."

Just then the little plane on the screen at the front of the cabin changed position, and with a whine and a bit of clunking from the undercarriage, we began our descent into Budapest's Ferihegy Airport. Below us, the gray clouds began to give way to flashes of green. Then there was a flicker of silver from the Danube River and the first red-roofed houses began to appear. As I peered out the window, I thought back to that earlier visit and hoped that this one would go a whole lot better. You see, the last time I was in Hungary, I almost ended up in a gulag in Siberia.

OK, OK, so they probably wouldn't really have sent us to jail. Even the old-school communists knew it would be bad optics to imprison a bunch of western teenagers who were visiting their country on a UNESCO-sponsored cultural trip. But the threats certainly seemed real at the time. (And the way we were grounded when we got home – that was definitely real.)

It all happened a few years before the Berlin Wall came down and the Iron Curtain went up. I was fifteen, my sister was thirteen, and my parents had decided that we were *not* going to waste our summer hanging around with boys and partying out at the lagoon in our suburban West Coast town. Instead, we would attend summer school in Hungary. That way they could go on an extended trip around Europe while Fran and I would learn a little Hungarian, connect with our past and, most importantly, stay out of trouble. Or so they thought.

The school was in a village called Sárospatak in the northeastern corner of the country. Sárospatak is known, variously, as the Cambridge of Hungary or Athens on the Bodrog River, and features a famous Calvinist high school, the Sárospataki Református Kollégium. For 450 years, the offspring of Hungary's elite have attended the school to become thinkers, leaders, and generally useful members of society. That summer, though, it was the site for a six-week-long program hosted by UNESCO for kids whose parents had fled Hungary after the 1956 Uprising.

We ranged in age from twelve to eighteen and we came from France, England, Scandinavia, the United States, Canada — in fact, pretty much everywhere the escaping Hungarians had ended up in the fifties and sixties. None of us was all that excited about the academic focus of our summer, especially since it involved a lot of folk-dancing classes. How loserville. We were, however, happy to learn that Hungarians have relaxed views about teenage drinking. Woo-hoo, we thought, bring on the palinka!

The boys were housed on one side of the building and the girls on the other. In between us were the classrooms, the cafeteria, and the shower rooms where the hot water ran out each day by 6:45 a.m. Fran and I shared our dorm with a couple of raunchy English girls, a crazy Swede named Valli, and a perky American named Judy, who promptly became my best friend even though she was a couple of years older than me. Maybe it was because we were both pining for boys that summer, me for a guy back home, she for the love of her life up in Czechoslovakia.

A few weeks earlier, while visiting relatives across the border, she had fallen hopelessly in love with Paul, a young minister in the

Reformed Church. Even though she was only eighteen, she was talking seriously about running away and marrying him or getting him to escape from Czechoslovakia and marry her. It had caused a huge scandal with her family back home in New Jersey. They had always thought their brilliant daughter would one day become president or win the Nobel Prize, and now she seemed determined to shatter their hopes by becoming a hausfrau to an impoverished cleric. So they begged the school administrators to keep a stern eye on Judy, which meant they kept a stern eye on the rest of us in the dorm, too. On weekends, when he visited her, the two of them would walk sadly around the grounds, knowing they were always being watched. I never saw them kiss or even touch hands. They were a very serious couple, unlike my friends back home, who were always being sent to the principal's office for necking in the hallways.

Our dorm may have been the school's center of romance and intrigue, but the epicenter of cool in our little world was the dorm occupied by the four California boys: Tom, Tom, Mike, and John. One of the Toms had gone to school with Susan Olsen, the girl who played Cindy Brady on *The Brady Bunch*. The other Tom was a geeky-cool super-brain who was into computers before the rest of us had even figured out how to work our Texas Instruments calculators. Mike and John were two cute brothers from Modesto, with tousled curls, blinding white smiles, and perma-tans shown to great advantage by their Ocean Pacific shorts and surfer shirts.

Nowadays, with the current wave of Eastern European cool, it's hard to remember what it was like in the old days of the Soviet Bloc. Back then, countries like Hungary and Czechoslovakia were cut off from the West. Things we took for granted – multiple TV channels, McDonald's, Bonne Bell lip gloss, the freedom to say what's on your mind – simply didn't exist there.

For instance, our teachers warned us never to use the Hungarian expression for "fuck off" – *baz meg* – because it also means "fuck me." The local men were poor, bitter, and angry, the teachers said, and would be happy to take us up on the offer, especially since everyone knew that girls who shaved their legs were prostitutes. But we all ignored their advice, especially the English girls, who dropped the

F-bomb the way we Canadians would mumble "excuse me, I'm sorry" all the time. They were always telling someone to *baz meg*, and sure enough, they were always running into the dorm, panting and gasping, having just run away from some pervy guy who'd chased them across the park beside the school, hoping to *baz* them indeed.

We were a bunch of naïve, spoiled western teenagers, and we didn't understand why everyone whispered all the time, or why there didn't seem to be any color anywhere, or why there was hardly anything to buy in the stores. We were shocked when the local gypsies would sneak into the school and wander the hallways looking for drugs, money, and blue jeans. We didn't really understand that there were things we weren't supposed to talk about and things we weren't supposed to do. And we certainly didn't understand how different our lives were from those of the people with funny hairdos, dorky clothes and tacky, plastic shoes. So we complained about the music (all Boney M all the time), we complained about the lack of hot water, we complained because our hair dryers and curling irons didn't work, and above all, we complained about the food.

At school, we were fed gallons of greasy *gulyás* and mountains of rubbery dumplings. The eggs were fried till they were crispy and the vegetables cooked until they were nearly liquefied. The milk had a funny taste to it, and so did the mystery meat and the margarine, which came in a white, lard-like block. Naturally, we spent night after night moaning on about how we'd kill for a Big Mac or a slice of pizza.

Luckily, though, our program involved plenty of road trips and each time we got on the bus, we found some wonderful food. On an excursion to Debrecen, for instance, we discovered Hungarian hot dogs. Debrecen is the second biggest city in Hungary and such an important center for the Reformed Church that it is known as "the Calvinist Rome." It is home to darkly beautiful Transylvanian Art Nouveau buildings, thermal spas, and the famous Debrecener sausage (which our family friend Nori bacsi claims his ancestors invented).

After we'd spent a long, boring morning visiting churches and museums, we found the hot dog stand in a shady square where we were waiting for the last of the stragglers to meet us. The vendor used a special machine to drill a big, long hole lengthwise into a *kifli* (KEE-flee), a crusty roll that's roughly crescent-shaped and sprinkled with coarse salt. Into the cavity he stuffed a steaming European wiener, a *virsli* (VEER-shlee), slathered in brown mustard. The English girls found it hilariously rude, but oh, it was so delicious.

Lángos was something else we enjoyed whenever we could. Luckily for us, there was always a *lángos* stand at all the big tourist attractions, the parks and baths and zoos and such. Basically, a *lángos* is a chunk of yeasty dough, flattened into a disc and deep-fried, sort of like a big, flat, savory beignet. We'd eat it sizzling hot with a healthy sprinkle of salt and some fresh garlic rubbed all over it, but you can also find it with toppings of sour cream, cheese, dill, even sweet stuff – if you can find it at all. These days it's easier to find Big Macs and pizza than it is to find *lángos*, at least outside of old-fashioned farmer's markets.

On another side trip we stopped at a *halászcsárda* (huh-LASS-char-duh)– a fisherman's tavern – by the Tisza River and had *halászlé*, the spicy Hungarian fisherman's stew. It was far too hot for our wimpy palates, but the California boys decided to tackle it as a test of manliness. While we girls promptly decided it was a good time to start our diets, the boys spooned up the fiery soup with determination, their faces getting redder and redder and redder, and beads of sweat rolling down their faces like salty marbles. When their spoons finally clattered in the bottoms of the empty bowls, the staff, amused and impressed in equal measure, brought them a round of beer in congratulations.

Closer to home was the neighborhood *cukrászda* (tsook-RAZ-duh), the sweets store. It's a funny thing that even when you couldn't buy toilet paper and milk in Hungary, you could always buy pastries and fancy cakes. We'd head down to the *cukrászda* every day when our classes were done and we'd learned all we could stand about Hungarian grammar and history and geography and folk dancing. There we'd have a *fagylalt* (FUDY-lult), a delicious sort of Hungarian gelato, or a slice of cake, or a pastry stuffed with apricots. There being no Pepsi available, we'd wash down the goodies with soda water sweetened by a splash of raspberry syrup.

Not far from the *cukrászda* was the Borostyán restaurant. I can't remember if it was our teachers who took us there or if we just went on our own, but I do remember going there a couple of times and enjoying the *fa tál*, the Transylvanian wooden platter. A traditional wooden platter has all manner of mostly fried things on it, sausages and battered mushrooms and wiener schnitzel and red cabbage and potatoes. It's meant to be shared, so it was a perfect choice for us student types who, while rich by local standards, were on a limited budget by North American ones. I remember that the Borostyán's *fa tál* was a very fine one indeed. What I don't remember is who had the bright idea that almost got us all sent to Soviet jail.

One night we arrived at the Borostyán just as a very loud and very drunk party of Soviet worthies, including several in military uniform, was leaving. For most of us, this was our first close-up view of the species, aside from the airport soldiers who trained their submachine guns on the crowds at all times. Although we were too young and too dumb to know much about world politics, we had all grown up listening to our parents talk about the Soviets, how cruel and evil they were, how they'd destroyed their country and their lives. And suddenly, here they were, Soviet soldiers in the flesh, looking remarkably like anyone else, though perhaps a bit redder of cheek and more bloodshot of eye. A strange little frisson of fury ran through the group.

In honor of the Soviet delegation, the Borostyán staff had decorated each table with a small wooden staff bearing a Soviet pennant in blood-red velveteen, with a gold hammer and sickle, and the letters CCCP embroidered in gold. Then they foolishly left those fancy little flags out on the tables, within easy reach of a bunch of teenagers suddenly eager to avenge the wrongs done to our families. One of us, I don't recall who, marched over and picked up one of the flags along with its staff, tucked it in a pocket, and walked right out of the restaurant with it.

When we got back to the school, we decided to burn the flag. We gathered in the California boys' room as the fading purple light of dusk fell through the windows. We spoke in whispers and kept the lights low. Someone produced a lighter; someone else held the flag; a third person lit the thing on fire. It took a minute to catch, then it smoldered a little bit, and finally burst into flames along with a big cloud of foul-smelling smoke. Someone pulled out a camera, and we all posed with the flaming flag, great big grins on our faces. Take that, Lenin! And you, too, Stalin! Yeah, that'll show them.

When all that was left was the slightly charred wooden staff the flag had hung upon, crazy Valli took it and chucked it out the window. The distant clatter as it fell to the ground brought us to our senses. Suddenly it dawned on us that the bit of wood wasn't simply the souvenir of a clever prank, but evidence of a crime. Two of the boys ran outside and searched for what seemed like hours, digging through the shrubs and flowers in the shadows of the courtyard below. No matter: they simply couldn't find it. Sadly for us, the military police had no such difficulty the next morning.

A terrible quiet fell over the school as, one by one, we were called in for questioning. As these stern, gray men in their gray uniforms threatened us with an extended holiday someplace rather chilly, we all cleverly lied our faces off. A what? A flag? From the Borostyán? Never saw it, never heard of it, wouldn't do such a thing. Nope, no way, uh-uh. Must have been the gypsies, they've been hanging around the school a lot looking for Levi's and controlled substances.

Although it may seem ridiculous now, when they talked about sending us to a work camp in Siberia, they sounded serious. Really serious. So we were getting pretty worried when, thankfully, Charlie bacsi was brought in.

Charlie was my mother's cousin by marriage, and he was some sort of big shot involved with the school system, Hungarian heritage, and UNESCO. He spoke several languages fluently, and years later, he got the contract to write the Hungarian-French dictionary, which allowed him to spend several years at the Sorbonne in Paris. While we were at Sárospatak, he'd drop by every couple of weeks to take Fran and me out on a little excursion to Lake Balaton, along with his wife Maju and their two young sons, Gábor and Támas, better known to us as Gubby and Ke-ke, poor things.

It was in a conversation with Charlie that I issued my famously dismissive verdict about all Hungarian food: "It's nothing but grease, onions, and paprika," I scoffed with all the rudeness but none of the wit of an A. A. Gill or other feisty critic. Charlie thought that was pretty funny, and after that we got on like a house afire. Good thing, too, because when he got the call about our little flag-burning fiasco, he just started laughing and drove right up from Budapest to set things right. He arrived late at night, and by the next morning Charlie had pulled a few strings, had a few words with the right people, and somehow made the problem go away. He never told anyone exactly what he said or did, just smiled mysteriously and said something about grease, onions, and paprika.

After that, things got back to normal at the school. Even though we all dreaded dealing with the wrath of our parents – because we knew they'd find out eventually, and we were right – we were pretty happy to go home to our friends and beach parties and food that wasn't made with paprika.

For a few years after Sárospatak, my sister and I kept in touch with Judy and the two Toms, but eventually we all lost track of each other. One year we visited one of the Toms in California and spent a fun week going to Disneyland and Universal Studios and Rodeo Drive. Another time, three or four years later, we visited Judy in New Jersey, where she was getting ready to enter her last year of university and, believe it or not, preparing for her wedding to Paul. Her parents had sponsored the young cleric's move to the United States and they were finally ready to start their life together.

Eventually, all of us moved on, and I lost touch with everyone except Charlie, Maju, and the boys. We saw more of them than anyone else in the family. Maju and Gábor visited us in Canada; I visited Charlie and Maju in Paris; Mom and Dad visited them all in Budapest. In 1996, the same year my father died, Charlie also passed away, taking with him the secrets of how he saved our lives in Sárospatak. But even though Charlie was gone, his family was still around and still coming to my rescue. In fact, two decades after my last trip to Hungary, it was Charlie's widow, Maju, who hosted us in Budapest, and his son Gábor – still known as Gubby in some circles – who came to greet us at the airport.

I was traveling with Lionel, the guy I've been happily living with for the past decade. Travel is our passion, and between us we've visited a fair chunk of the globe. This trip was different, though. It wasn't just a trip to a specific destination, but a voyage into the past – my past.

As the plane landed and rolled to a stop, I found myself unusually nervous, and it wasn't the usual worries about lost luggage and passport inspection, or even the extra stress of arriving with no money because we hadn't been able to exchange our Canadian dollars for Hungarian forints back home.

Right away, I could tell how much things had changed. The guys at passport control were young, cute, and flirtatious, and they didn't carry guns, or at least not that I could see. The soldiers I remembered so well from last time with their hard stares and their AK-47s were nowhere to be seen, either. There were actual shops in the airport and well-dressed business travelers rushing through carrying expensive leather briefcases. The airport is a small one, and on my previous trip had seemed to be nearly empty. Now it was crowded with people. And these people weren't quiet and subdued, but happy, passionate, and vibrant. They wore bright colors and hugged and kissed each other and cried out with delight when the electric doors swooshed open and their aunt, or son, best friend, or nagymama walked through.

We got to check out the scene for a good long time because Gábor was late. I began to worry that I wouldn't recognize my cousin in the crowd. After all, it had been six or seven years since I'd last seen him, and a lot can change in that time. I was acutely aware that I had no cash, could barely speak Hungarian, and wasn't entirely sure what Maju's address was.

Then suddenly, there he was, a pale, youngish man with a shy grin on his face and his young daughter Bianca in tow. The last time we'd seen him, he'd been a skinny kid visiting us in Vancouver, a trip remarkable mostly for the huge phone bill he ran up calling his then-girlfriend from our place in the middle of a party (much wine had been consumed) and for the word *torna csipö*, or running shoe, which he insisted on teaching us (again, after much wine had been consumed). Since then, though, he'd grown up quickly. He had a responsible job in the Budapest planning department and he was married (though not to the girlfriend he'd been so desperate to call), with two little kids and third one on the way. He was no longer skinny, and he was wearing a shirt and tie even though it was a Saturday. But he was still, unmistakably, Gubby. We hugged and kissed a little awkwardly, then made our way across the cracked pavement to his car, and began our journey of Hungarian rediscovery.

The drive from the airport to the Budapest *centrum* is a brisk introduction to the many ways the city is changing now that the communist era is over. In places, it looks as if three Budapests exist: the graceful old turn-of-the-century Budapest, the bleak and shabby communist one, and the brand new metropolis that's being created by billions of forints (Hungarian currency) of foreign investment.

The road from the airport is only two lanes wide and a bit bumpy, but with high-tech directional lights and constant improvements going on. There are still occasional police patrols by the side of the road, but they're mostly just hanging out in case a driver needs assistance, not hassling people and demanding bribes as they once did. Along the road, there are cellphone towers, and football stadiums and enormous billboards advertising everything from politicians to ice cream. At the same time, there are rusting old railway sheds and old country houses covered in crumbling red and ochre stucco. It seems to go on like this forever, then suddenly you turn a corner and you're on a wide, graceful boulevard with elegant buildings on either side. Ahead of you is a treed hill with a big statue on top and the points of a bridge below. This is Budapest, one of the most beautiful cities in the world, a city that has risen from the ashes of countless wars and rebellions to become with each incarnation just a little bit more lovely than the last time.

Budapest is actually three cities in one. Buda sits on the hills to the west of the Danube. It is leafy and green and dotted with elegant apartment buildings, villas, hotels, and thermal spas. Further north and west is the suburban Óbuda with its Roman ruins. Pest is on the other side of the Danube, linked by a series of graceful bridges: Margit; Széchenyi, which is also called the Lanc Hid or Chain Bridge; Erzsébet; Szabadság or Freedom Bridge; and further along, the Petöfi and Arpád bridges. Pest is the business center of town, where most people live and work and play, and where most of the hotels and restaurants are. Although the three cities were linked in 1873 to form Budapest, most Hungarians, when they talk about the city, still call it simply Pest.

Like Paris with its arrondissements, Budapest is defined by a series of twenty-two *kerülets*, districts usually abbreviated as *ker*.

District I, for instance, is the Castle District in Buda, while the *belváros*, the inner city, is District V in Pest, although people take it to mean VI and VII as well. Budapest is designed as a series of wide boulevards like spokes radiating from the city center, joined by a number of ring roads called *korut*. The subway and tramlines follow all the main roads, so getting around is simple, as long as you're not driving. (Budapest not only has the narrow side streets typical of any European city, it also has, I swear, the tiniest, most impossible-to-read street signs in the world, as well as a dire shortage of both parking spaces and left-hand turns.)

My mother's cousin Maju lived in the old family apartment on Rákoczi Út, the main street on the border of District VII, right near the center of all the action. This was where we would be staying over the next few weeks. As we got closer to her place, ugly new buildings – proletarian, Soviet-style structures – gave way to beautiful old ones, mostly apartment blocks with a ground floor of stores and restaurants. Many of these buildings dated from the late nineteenth century and were designed in the Belle Époque, neo-Gothic, or Art Nouveau style, with graceful proportions and whimsical ornamentation. Some of the older buildings were beautifully restored, others were fading genteelly, while still others were crumbling rapidly into rubble. All were liberally decorated with graffiti. It seemed that after nearly five decades of being forbidden to express themselves, Hungarian youth were taking every opportunity to do so now by tagging anything that didn't move.

All these old apartment buildings in Budapest follow a similar design. There is a gate, or *kapu*, that opens onto the street. Inside is a cavernous foyer, a dark, cool space that leads to an open-air courtyard. The ground floor is called the *földszint*, while the first floor is what we in North America would consider the second floor. The apartments are built around the courtyard, with a little walkway that goes all around each floor. There will often be Art Nouveau ironwork along the walkway, or decorative tiling, a bit of sculpture or fancy molding, and here and there an explosion of plants. Rumor has it that during the Uprising of 1956, when blood ran in the streets and people cowered on the floors of their apartments in fear of stray bullets flying through the windows, families buried their dead in those courtyards. Practical, perhaps, but kind of creepy, too.

On one side of the building, there is always a grand staircase that sweeps from floor to floor, often in utter darkness, and a tiny, slow-moving elevator that inevitably smells of urine. At Maju's, we crammed ourselves into the elevator with all our many suitcases and, with a lurch, headed up the one floor to her place.

As the elevator came to a stop, we could hear the sound of locks being laboriously opened one after the other. Over the next few weeks we would become all too familiar with Maju's baroque system of locks and bolts and chains, not to mention the fistful of enormous keys we'd have to carry with us everywhere we went, like keepers of some medieval dungeon. (This, it would turn out, was typical in Budapest – its older residents vividly remembered the days when a jackbooted home invasion could happen any time.) Finally, she emerged into the gloom of the landing, still blonde and youthful-looking despite all the terrible events that had taken place during her sixty-odd years. "*Csillagom!*" she cried, which translates roughly as "my little stars." We kissed politely and went inside, stepping suddenly into the past.

The apartment had been in the family since the turn of the last century, and it had once been quite a bit bigger. That was before the government expropriated a large part of it for a more deserving – read: communist – tenant. Until 1945, when the war and the communists put them out of business, the family gold and jewelry store had been conveniently located downstairs in the back on Dohany Utca, the border of Elizabeth Town, the Jewish part of the city. In fact, Maju's most impressive neighbor was the new Nagy Zinagóga. It's the largest synagogue in Europe, built in the 1990s on the site of a much older synagogue desecrated by German Nazis and the Hungarian Arrow Cross thugs during the Second World War. Because anti-Semitism continues to thrive in Europe, there was always a large assortment of security personnel back there. Maju said it made her feel very safe, though it made us wonder if our sleep would be shattered by a large blast some night.

I looked around the apartment curiously. At one time, my great-grandparents lived here, and the halls still seemed to echo with their hopes and heartbreaks. It must have been my great-grandmother Alujzia who chose the ornate dark bronze chandeliers that hung from the twelve-foot-high ceilings in each room. Over the years, though, most of the electrical connections had burned out and were too expensive to fix, so the light they provided was a fickle thing at best. Alujzia must also have commissioned the family portraits that glared down from the walls, their massive frames separated by skinny water pipes that ran from room to room. Old-fashioned lace curtains draped the tall, shuttered windows just as they must have done in Alujzia's day, and her heavy, dark furniture still filled the rooms.

But Maju had put her own stamp on the place, too. She'd filled her grandmother's antique cabinets with a whimsical collection of curios, bits of crystal and china, travel souvenirs, photographs, and the myriad little treasures every family collects. She'd added practical new furniture, like the daybeds we'd be sleeping on in the guestroom, which clashed oddly with the heavy old pieces. And she'd modernized the ancient marble bathroom with a melamine storage unit and a sink stand. She'd also installed a brand-new shower stall fueled by a diabolical gas heater that ran boiling hot or freezing cold, in a pitiful trickle or a scouring deluge, often switching from one extreme to the other within seconds.

This would be our home base for the next few weeks, and almost as soon as we dropped our bags, Maju welcomed us in the traditional Hungarian way, by offering us a shot of hard liquor. We sat on sagging velvet-covered chairs under one of the flickering chandeliers as Gábor fetched a small silver tray and tiny silver cups, and with a gentle pop, Maju opened a bottle of palinka. "*Egészségére!*" (eg-ACE-shay-ger-eh) — to your health — she cried, clinking glasses. "Cheers," we said in reply, and knocked back the harsh liquid.

Palinka is the Hungarian version of grappa or schnapps. Given that it has an alcohol content higher than 40 per cent, most non-Hungarians, upon encountering it for the first time, are left sputtering, their eyes watering, their throats burning. It's not uncommon for hosts to offer it as a little wake-me-up at breakfast; it's also drunk as an aperitif, an afternoon refresher, a digestif, or a nightcap. No wonder Hungarians have a reputation for what one guidebook calls "death wish drinking habits."

Palinka comes in a variety of flavors, though if you drink the cheap stuff you may be forgiven for thinking they all bear a remarkable resemblance to nail varnish. Apricot is probably the most typically Hungarian flavor, and there are versions made with honey that are much smoother and easier to drink. Apricot palinka also forms the basis of the only real Hungarian cocktail, the Puszta cocktail. Careful, though – a couple of glasses of this cocktail will knock you as flat as the Great Hungarian Plain for which it's named.

Palinka is a fermented fruit drink. As well as apricots, it is also made with cherries, plums, mixed fruit, or even hot paprika. Artisanal palinka is becoming very fashionable these days, much more so than the gasoline-like commercial beverage whose only purpose is to get you drunk as quickly as possible. It's also a regional drink – Szatmár is famous for its plum palinka, while Kecskemét is known for apricot. There are a number of famous palinka makers, and none other than the Duke of Windsor was a huge fan of apricot palinka from Kecskemét. Although Hungarians have been making palinka at home since the seventeenth century, it is no longer legal to do so. They can, however, take their fermented fruit to a distillery that will produce it for them.

Should you be inspired to try your hand at making your own palinka, here's how it's done: To begin the process, the fruit is fermented in large barrels where the fructose converts naturally to alcohol. For apricot and cherry palinka, the seeds are included in the mash to add a subtly bitter flavor. Next the mash is washed and distilled, heated until vapors rise and cooled until they return to liquid form. The process is repeated until the aroma and the alcohol reach the desired level. The spirit is placed in oak barrels to age until the flavor mellows, when the drink is bottled and the partying can begin.

Indeed, "mellow" is how we felt after a couple of shots of palinka, luckily for us. Because that's when Maju announced that my Aunt Frances had a surprise planned for us that night. She had invited all the Wintermantels over for a dinner party, and we were expected, oh, in an hour or so.

For years, my glamorous Aunt Frances had been spending half the year in Toronto and half in Budapest. At first it was because her husband, Frank, had decided he wanted to come back home for the last few years of his life. They kept the apartment in Forest Hill and bought another one in the hills of Buda and she began her twice-yearly trips back and forth. Then Frank, who was quite a bit older, died. While Frances was trying to decide what to do with her life, a friend of Frank's came calling to offer his sympathies.

Somewhat unusually for a Hungarian, Pál was a quiet man. When everyone else was arguing about politics or history or religion, he'd just sit there watching the action, occasionally making a wry comment. He was a cosmopolitan gent and an urbane gourmet. He loved his kids and adored Frances, though he never made the mistake of letting her emotions get out of control. In fact, he was the one person who could always joke her out of a bad mood. They made a great pair, and after a while, what had started as good manners turned to friendship and then to romance. So she continued traveling back and forth for years, until just before our arrival, when Pál had convinced her to move to Hungary full-time.

As well-suited as they were, it didn't stop some people on the other side of the family from criticizing the relationship. Pál, you see, had been a big shot in the old communist government, which upset certain people who couldn't stop themselves from making digs that never failed to get under Frances's admittedly thin skin. For her part, Frances fought back unsuccessfully with comments about my right-wing grandfather's dubious antics leading up to and during the war.

Although there were more differences than similarities between the Wintermantels and the Sasváris, they both started off the same way. Both families were Swabian; Germans imported into Hungary to replenish the population after it was decimated by the war with the Turks. But that's just about where the resemblance ends.

My mother's family arrived in the nineteenth century and was rich, conservative, Catholic and pro-German right through the Second World War. My dad's family, on the other hand, arrived in the sixteenth century. Even though they'd had money at one time, by the mid-twentieth century, they were firmly middle class or even proletariat. They were also liberal, agnostic, and so anti-German that, repelled by the rise of the Third Reich in the 1930s, my grandfather Marton changed the family name from the very Deutsch "Stock" to the very Hungarian "Sasvári." The Wintermantels hated the communists; the Sasváris hated the fascists. The Wintermantels liked to reminisce about the past; the Sasváris looked to the future, my father going so far as to discourage us from learning to speak Hungarian. The Wintermantels were as tough as the gristle at the bottom of a pot of *gulyás*; they were opinionated and outspoken, with a habit of dishing out breathtakingly blunt insults. The Sasváris were sensitive, moody, and inclined to take offence even where none was intended, and where it was intended, obsessing over it for days, months, even years.

Unfortunately for the Sasváris, they were vastly outnumbered by the Wintermantels. After my dad died, the only Sasváris left were my Aunt Frances, my sister, me and some distant cousins we'd never met. As for the Wintermantels, as Lionel and I were soon to discover, there were plenty of them kicking around, including a whole new generation growing up.

For Frances to host them all was a gesture of great, if somewhat foolhardy, kindness. It also promised to be a tough social event. I'd never met most of them, didn't even know who they were, and could speak very little Hungarian. Lionel, of course, could not speak Hungarian at all. That called for another round of palinka, a quick exposure to the eccentric plumbing, and off we went.

Maju went ahead with Gábor, while we got a ride with her younger son, Támas, a.k.a. Ke-ke. I'd first met Támas when we visited Hungary the very first time, when I was just eleven and Fran was eight. I hardly remember that trip at all – like so many preteens, I was moody and self-obsessed – but Támas was a memorable bright spot. He was only four years old, but he was magnetically drawn to trouble. I remember one scrape involving chewing gum, which was our fault, for chewing gum was an exotic thing in Hungary and the boys couldn't quite get the idea of not swallowing it, which led to panic and tears. Then there was another little fiasco when Ke-ke tried to climb into the lion pit during our visit to the zoo. As a young man, Támas floated from job to job, always searching for that career that would give him the freedom and adventure he yearned for and at the same time a big enough paycheck to help him support his son Süni, from an earlier relationship. Most recently, he had been traveling around Hungary selling New Age souvenirs like dreamcatchers and panpipe CDs to shops.

The sun was beginning to set behind Gellért Hill as we made our way down Rákóczi Út, which became Kossuth Lajos Út, and across the Erszébet Bridge, one of the more modern bridges slung across the Danube. As we crossed it, the legendary river shimmered in the rosy light. All along its banks, lights began to flicker on. A long time ago, someone made the brilliant decision to show off this city at night by lighting up every one of its most beautiful buildings and monuments – the castle on the hill, the great statues, the dome of St. Stephen's, the bridges, the roadways along the river. Today it is one of the most gorgeous urban nightscapes in the world.

To our left, the statue of Bishop Gellért stared morosely from his grotto on the hill. Gellért was the Italian bishop who helped King Stephen (Ístvan I, the first of the country's saint-kings) convert the Hungarians to Christianity in the eleventh century. For his trouble, he was reportedly packed into a barrel studded with spikes and rolled down the hill that now bears his name. The top of that hill offers the greatest views of the city, especially at sunset. Támas decided that we needed to begin our Hungarian journey with the most spectacular vista in the country, and for that we could afford to be a few minutes late for dinner.

Instead of turning right toward Frances's place on Áttila Út, he swung left and joined a steady convoy of tour buses up the hill. He parked a little haphazardly and we got out to walk the short distance around the walls of the Citadella to the Freedom Statue, or Susie with the Fish, as she's called by disrespectful locals, or Susie with the Kifli. It's a robust, 14-meter-high, Soviet-style depiction of Lady Liberty holding an acanthus branch over her head. It looms over the entire city. It is widely believed that the statue was actually designed to be a memorial to the son of Admiral Horthy, the ultra-right-wing general who led the country between the two world wars. The way the story goes, the grieving Horthy commissioned the statue, which originally held a propeller in her hands, to commemorate his pilot son's death in a plane crash. Then when the Soviets marched in at the end of the Second World War, they simply adapted it to their own purpose. Not so, say the experts. It was always designed as a symbol of Soviet triumph. At one time it even had a bunch of other jaunty Soviet statuary around its base. Those works have since been exiled to Statue Park, where all the bad Soviet artwork is sent to die.

We stood there for a while, enjoying the cool breeze drifting off the river below and marveling at the way the setting sun played on the buildings of downtown Pest. To our left was the city's other big hill, Castle Hill, topped by the sprawling 203-room Royal Palace, commissioned by the Austrian Empress Maria Theresa in the eighteenth century. There has been a castle on this spot since the thirteenth century, but it has been demolished so many times in so many wars that hardly an original stone remains. Throughout the castle district, you can spot bits of Gothic, Baroque, Renaissance, and Turkish stonework, but few, if any, entirely original structures. Even Maria Theresa's palace was badly damaged by the 1848 War of Independence, then rebuilt in a neo-baroque style at the end of the nineteenth century. Those buildings in turn were damaged during the numerous battles of the twentieth century. Reconstruction is ongoing.

The castle district is jam-packed with museums, shops, restaurants, churches, and the Budapest Hilton. A little funicular takes foot passengers from Clark Adam Tér below up to the castle, while a tiled tunnel takes cars from the busy streets of Buda underneath the hill and onto the Chain Bridge to downtown Pest.

To the left of the Chain Bridge, which is the greatest of the many achievements of "the Greatest Hungarian," Count Ístvan Széchenyi, is the Parliament. The Országház, as it's known in Hungarian, is the country's greatest monument to optimism. It is an enormous neo-Gothic structure with a neo-Renaissance dome that was inspired by Westminster in London. Indeed, its reflection shimmers in the waters off the Danube's left bank much as the English parliament does in the Thames. Construction on it was begun in 1885, and it took a thousand workers until 1902 to complete it. Designed to be one of Europe's largest public buildings, it has 691 rooms, ten courtyards, twenty-nine staircases, and an enormous dome encircled by statuary, with slender towers, graceful arcades, and hundreds of statues throughout. It was meant to symbolize Hungary's new place in the world at a period when the future seemed bright in the Dual Monarchy. But as it turned out, only one democratically elected government actually sat here until the fall of communism in 1989.

To the right of the Parliament, right at the foot of the Chain Bridge, is the newly renovated Four Seasons Gresham Palace. The Gresham is a perfect Art Nouveau building with a giant peacock motif woven into its three massive black iron gates. For decades it had been an overcrowded and run-down apartment block. It took five years to renovate the building to its former beauty, but the time was well spent, for it is now one of the most remarkable buildings in Budapest. It certainly puts to shame the ugly, modernist hotels that line the Danube to its right.

A few blocks behind the Gresham is St. Stephen's Basilica. This, too, was built in the latter half of the nineteenth century in a neo-Renaissance style, and although the building is hidden by all the other structures in front of it, its large dome flanked by two tall spires stands above the bustle of downtown Pest.

All these wonders, old and new, were spread out below us. Along the river, brightly lit cruise ships plied up and down, the sound of merrymaking floating up to us across the hum of traffic and the whisper of the breeze in the trees. Behind them, the facades of old stone villas and the concrete and glass of new hotels shone in the last rays of the setting sun. To our right, at the foot of the green-girdered Szabadszág Bridge crowned with its flock of mythical turul birds, was the big market, a glass, brick, and iron sculpture inspired by the works of the Eiffel company of Paris.

I remembered Hungary as gray, drab, and subdued, but what lay before us was a vibrant landscape of purples, reds, and ochers, at once sophisticated and kitschy, proper and fun. This was a very different Hungary from the one I remembered, and I suddenly realized I could easily grow to love it.

By now we were running very late – in our circles, there's no such thing as being fashionably late; a habit of tardiness is considered a bigger disgrace than public drunkenness or chronic bankruptcy – and Támas urged us to get into the car. Swiftly, we swooped down the curving, tree-lined roads of the hill and along the road that runs behind the castle. Its crumbling stone walls towered above us, while at its base clustered clumps of Soviet statuary and dozens of tiny Opels, Fiats, and Trabants.

Frances's place was on Áttila Út, very close to the tunnel, which in Hungarian is called the Alagút. The entrance to her building was guarded by two white Art Deco statues. In fact, the building is such a perfect example of Central European Deco that if it hadn't been damaged by a Second World War bomb, it would be preserved as a heritage site. It was built on the same plan as Maju's place: the open courtyard, the gloomy stairs, the tiny elevator. Up we went, to find Frances and Pál on the landing outside. We went through the ritual of Hungarian greeting, the cries of hello, how are you, the kiss on each cheek, the handing over of the wine and the chocolates, the questions about the rest of the family, before we could even get in the door. And once we did, the most amazing sight greeted us.

At home, my family is very small: only Mom and Fran and me, plus our spouses and my baby niece Eva. Everyone else has either died – my grandparents in the '80s, my dad in 1996 – or moved away, not that there were many of us to begin with anyway. So when I walked into the bright living room to encounter a crowd, I wondered, "Who the heck are all these people?" before it dawned on me, "They're my family."

I don't even know how to describe the way it felt to walk into a room of strangers and walk out of it with a great big family. Well, it was lovely, of course, if slightly disorienting. At the same time, it was terribly sad. It's one thing to read about geopolitics or to share war stories over the Sunday roast. It's an entirely different thing to understand how a bunch of men in a conference room can pitilessly tear a family, an entire people, asunder; to realize how a border, which is nothing but an invisible line, can put up a barrier that is vaster and more insurmountable than the deepest ocean or highest mountain range.

It didn't help that during the communist era, some of the cousins had made certain accommodations with the party – may, in fact, have actually signed up. Other cousins refused to play along and were convinced that this was why their careers had stalled and their children's futures weren't as bright as some others. For many years, the cousins didn't talk to each other, barely even mentioned each other by name, which was why I'd never met so many of the people at Frances's place that night. Unusually for a Magyar feud, though, once communism ended, so did the hostilities – it only took a couple of years before everyone was speaking and sharing drinks again.

That night, I met my mother's quiet cousin Kálman – the one who puzzles the rest of the clan because he doesn't drink, smoke, gamble, or have any other apparent vices; how could he be a Wintermantel, they wonder? – and his kindly wife Edina. Their children were the family's biggest success stories so far: both married, both starting families, and both pursuing stellar careers. Their son Zsolt is a rising politician in Hungary and daughter Andrea a banker living in London. Kálman spoke a very erudite sort of Hungarian, which I could barely understand since my grasp of the language was very simple, at the level a little kid would speak. I smiled and nodded a lot when we talked, but I couldn't miss the warmth in his voice, especially when he gave me a copy of the family tree he'd been compiling. There we were at the very bottom, and he'd even included Lionel's name. I was truly touched.

Ístvan, Kálman's brother, had been a newspaper editor during the communist years. It must have been a terrible balancing act to maintain, weighing truth against propaganda against the possibility of messing up and spending the rest of your life in jail. "I read your stories on the Internet," he told me proudly. Tears sprang to my eyes. I was moved to think that half a world away a virtual stranger cared enough to follow my work, to follow me, especially since I figured he couldn't be all that interested in stories about fashion and food and reviews of mystery novels. He and Lionel, who is also an editor, immediately hit it off, although neither could speak the other's language. Somehow, though, they managed to communicate and soon were chatting away merrily.

Ístvan's second wife, Ildiko, is the family fashionista, with a lively and dramatic flair for clothes, especially hats. Between them, they have five children, all doing well in their various fields. A couple of them even made it to Frances's that night, including the charming and multilingual Peter. We fell on him with relief since he spoke English fluently. It turned out he was an economist and was only home for a few days from his job in Tokyo.

And then there was my cousin Tommi. My cute, flirty cousin Tommi, who looked a lot like David Cassidy when he was a teenager, back when Fran and I hung out with him during our Sárospatak days. He seemed to have not changed much in the intervening decades, except that his dark, tousled rock-star hair had gone gray and was cropped short. The roguish glint in his eye remained, as well as his naughty sense of humor.

Tommi was the great-grandson of my great-grandfather's brother Adam. His late father, Hanzi, was my mother's favorite cousin, and by all accounts even more of a rascal than his son. Tommi and his wife Jolcsi lived with his mother Cica and their daughter Szilvi, out at the old family compound in a suburb called Rákosszentmihály. That night he brought Szilvi to Frances's, and the four of us spent a lot of time laughing as we struggled to understand each other and interpret what the other was saying.

There were ghosts at Frances's apartment, too, of the ones who had died before the family could be reunited. My grandparents' generation, of course, was long gone, although their presence could be felt keenly that night. Also gone were Charlie and Hanzi and Maju's brother József, who died in 1998. His children, Balazs and Krisztina, were there, though, part of the crowd of young cousins who dropped in and out all night.

In fact, that was the most amazing thing to me, how many young people there were in the family. In Canada, Fran and I were always the only kids in our generation, growing up surrounded by older people. But here there were family members in their twenties and thirties who were starting to have families of their own. Here we were, all in one room, the country's past and its future, the people who'd survived the turmoil of the twentieth century and the people who were moving into the twenty-first with hope and determination.

At first it was awkward. Aside from the language barrier, we were all a bit shy with each other, and the conversation was subdued and stilted. But as the wine flowed and my Hungarian, bad as it was, gradually came back to me, they began sharing their stories and memories – and their love, too.

We loaded our plates with food from my aunt's luxurious buffet – platters of cold cuts and cheese, savory roasts, mayonnaise salads, and exquisite little open-face sandwiches, each a tiny work of art, a cloisonné of salami and sliced eggs, ham and tomato, or smoked salmon and caviar – drank our wine, and reminisced about our pasts, both the past we shared and the past we were forced to spend apart. My aunt and Pál kept the food and the wine and the love flowing freely despite the political ghosts that hovered in the corners of the room.

Soon – too soon – words began to fail me and Lionel was flagging, too. Our vision began to blur, and it wasn't just because of the wine. We were tired travelers, so, with regret, with kisses and hugs and a sense of wonder at this newly discovered family, we left to do battle with the complicated locks and moody plumbing at Maju's place.

Hours later, I lay awake listening to the drunks bellowing in the street below Maju's windows. As I drifted in and out of restless sleep, I realized that Hungary was no longer the country that I remembered from my teens, a country that would threaten to send a kid to jail for playing a stupid prank. There was a new country here now, filled with hope and opportunity and vibrant youth.

Yet the memory of that earlier country still existed. You could see it in the emotional scars my family bore, in the shadows behind their eyes, in the bitterness that had not quite faded away. History was not forgotten here. History lingered in every corner, at once bloody and awful, whimsical and eccentric, noble and glorious, and, at times, shameful and cruel. It was a history that had swept up every member of my family. As the first gray light of dawn crept into the room, I realized that I'd have to learn about that history to understand my family and, indeed, to understand myself.

I didn't know what I'd discover when I began my journey into the past. I didn't know how long-forgotten events could wreak emotional devastation forty, fifty, even a hundred years later. I didn't know, when I started all this, that some days I'd be left shaking with rage over a terrible injustice and that other days I'd be weeping over an unimaginable loss. I didn't know how ashamed I'd be over certain incidents in the past, events I wished I could change but knew I never could, events that left me sleepless with nausea and grief. I didn't know there would be days when I'd laugh out loud over some misadventure. I didn't know how delicious it would be, the food, the stories, the history. And I didn't know how proud I would become of my family, especially the women, survivors all, who could be knocked down time and again and jump right back up with a new recipe they just had to try right now.

There was a lot, it turned out, that I didn't know at all.

CHAPTER 3
A Potted History

The story of Hungary — its people and its food — begins with a soup kettle. The Magyars began cooking with this humble vessel hundreds of years before there even was a Hungary. They continued cooking with it long after they settled in the Carpathian Basin and they still cook with it today. From it emerged all the country's signature dishes: *gulyás*, *pörkölt*, *paprikás*, and *halászlé*.

In the Hungarian language, the kettle is called a *bogrács* (boh-GRACH) and it comes in two varieties. One has a wide top that curves slightly outward and is meant for meat dishes such as *pörkölt* and *gulyás*. It's designed so that broth will reduce quickly over a fire while absorbing as much of its smoky flavor as possible. The other style of *bogrács* has a narrow top that helps retain the delicate essence of tender fish in a *halászlé*. Both styles have bottoms that are curved in the perfect shape for flames to embrace and a handle that is hooked to a tripod standing over the fire.

The *bogrács* would hang behind a Magyar's saddle, along with bags of dried and pulverized meat that would provide an instant soup when there was nothing else available to eat. Historians believe that this ability to dine quickly and heartily on the hoof is what allowed this small band of Asiatic horsemen to traverse huge areas of land and to conquer armies that were many times bigger and stronger than theirs.

Cooking with a *bogrács* has always been a man's job. Today that Magyar cook might spend the long cooking time drinking beer and swapping rude jokes with his friends, but back then he'd have spent the time by seeing to his horse and tending to his cattle — as well as swapping rude jokes with his friends.

The Magyars originally came from the frosty and barren reaches of western Siberia, where they belonged to a gathering of tribes that spoke a language now known as Finno-Ugric. Around 2000 BC, perhaps because of bad weather or invasions by other tribes or the loss of a major food source, the Finno-Ugric tribes split up and moved out of their homeland. The Finnish tribes headed west to Scandinavia, to what would be called Finland, while the Ugric tribes headed south. They stayed in their new home east of the Ural Mountains for several centuries, leading a nomadic hunters' existence, until over-population or climate change encouraged them to move on once again. Most of them moved back up north, while a newly formed tribe, a splinter group known as the Magyars, moved south to an area between the Ural Mountains and the Aral Sea, an area that would later be known as Magna Hungaria.

By the fifth century AD, the Magyars were getting restless again. Over the next four centuries, they gradually migrated west, crossing large swaths of Russia and Khazakstan, where they learned how to make wine. They skirted the Black Sea, where they picked up words and cooking techniques from the Turks, and traversed the Ukraine until they reached the jagged range of the Carpathian Mountains. Those mountains encircled an attractive geographical landform known as the Carpathian Basin, and that's where the Magyars decided to stay. The only problem was that this area was already occupied by several major powers, including the Byzantines, the Bulgars, and the Franks. But the Magyars were undaunted. Led by their *gyula* or military leader, Arpád, the Magyars waged a merciless war until the land was theirs. It was 896, and the Hungarians had come home for the first time.

They had found a place of breathtaking beauty, lush abundance, and mellow climate. The Carpathian Mountains cradle the country from the northwest to the southeast, protecting it from the chill Nordic winds. At the same time, the Alföld, the Great Plain, opens to the warmth of the Mediterranean in the south. The climate is continental, which means the summers are long, hot, and sunny, the winters cool and damp, very much what you'd find if you continued due west and landed in downtown Paris.

Although it is a landlocked country, it is not a dry one. Two major rivers flow through Hungary, the Tisza and the Danube. In the country's west is Lake Balaton, Europe's largest freshwater lake, a pleasure playground of sandy beaches, action-packed casinos, and sailing clubs. And thanks to the volcanic nature of the surrounding mountains, the country also has 1,200 thermal springs, including the one that feeds the world's largest swimmable thermal lake, Héviz.

No wonder so many invaders, weary after traversing harsh mountains and brutal steppes, found themselves in pastoral Hungary and thought, hmm, this would be a nice place to settle down for a while. Unfortunately for its inhabitants, Hungary is about as central as you can get in Europe, as far from the Atlantic as it is from the Ural Mountains, and halfway between Scandinavia and the Aegean Islands. It is surrounded by restless neighbors: directly to the north is Slovakia; to the east are Ukraine and Romania; Yugoslavia and Croatia are due south; and to the west are Slovenia and Austria. Austria, of course, was just one of the nations to build its empire in Hungary's backyard; the other empire builders who've camped out amid the poppies and paprika are Turkey, Rome, Germany, and Russia.

While Hungary is in the middle of all these different countries, it doesn't belong to any one national group. It's not part of the Balkan states to the south, nor the Russian ones to the east, nor the Germanic ones to the north and west. It is culturally and linguistically on its own.

The Magyars, of course, weren't the first to settle in the Carpathian Basin. People had been living here for thousands and thousands of years before Árpád's army set up their soup kettles on the Great Plain. Evidence suggests that the area was first populated by prehistoric man half a million years ago, followed by migrant hunters between 80,000 and 30,000 BC. They were followed by farmers and increasingly sophisticated tool-makers, who lived in relative peace until the first century BC, when the Roman legions arrived.

The Romans named their newly conquered province Pannonia and promptly set about building walled cities, paved roads, elaborate baths, and stone buildings so sturdy that some were in constant use until the end of the eighteenth century. The remains of Aquincum, their administrative headquarters, can still be seen in Óbuda.

The Romans also brought vines and winemaking to the area. By the second century AD, they had planted grapes in Villány and around the north shore of Lake Balaton. Even today, farmers tilling the fields in the rich volcanic soil of Villány keep turning up bits of Roman artefacts. Hungarians, in fact, had vines even before the French. If only they hadn't been involved in so much unrest over the centuries, their Kékoporto (KAY-ko-port-oh) and Hárslevelú (HARSH-leh-veh-loo) might have enjoyed the kind of status that wines from Burgundy and Champagne do. Still, wine is an essential part of the culture. Even the national anthem celebrates it in these lines by the poet Ferenc Kölcsey:

Ears of ripe corn wave to us
Across Cumanian meadows,
Tokaji grapes extend to us
Honey dripping shadows.

The Romans only had a couple of centuries to settle in, though, before they faced the most brutal and determined of the barbarian invasions. Hello, Áttila.

No one seems entirely sure who the Huns were. They likely came from Central Asia, for they were Mongolian in appearance, although they spoke what sounded like a Turkish dialect. They were fierce horsemen and hardy travelers. They traveled east, where they were known as the Hsiung-nu, against whom the Chinese began building the Great Wall in 300 BC. They traveled south, where they defeated India's Gupta Empire in 500 AD and marauded their way as far as Persia. And they traveled west, fighting all the way. By 375 they had crossed the River Volga, waging battle against the Alans, the Ostrogoths, the Visigoths, and any number of Germanic tribes.

The Huns arrived in the Carpathian Basin around 420. There they set up a base from which they conducted raids throughout the region and into the Balkans and Western Europe. They were known for their brutal, punishing attacks, their victories made all the more remarkable because they fought in such small bands. They were disciplined, well-trained, and utterly without pity.

In 441, led by the warrior prince Áttila and his brother Bleda, the Huns took on the Romans. The Huns had only a few hundred horses and warriors armed with bows and arrows. The Romans had thousands of soldiers, equipped with sophisticated armor and weaponry. Yet somehow the Huns won and sent the Romans packing right out of Pannonia. Unfortunately, by the time Áttila was done pillaging and plundering, the sophisticated communities the Romans had built were little but smoldering rubble. So, while they continued expanding their empire across Western Europe, the Huns also began the slow process of rebuilding.

This would prove to be the country's template for the next 1,500 years: invasion, occupation, rebellion/uprising/war, a country in ruins, reconstruction, and doing it all over again. And again. And again.

Áttila may have been a great warrior, but he didn't leave a great legacy behind him, unless you count the lingering fondness Hungarians have for naming their offspring after him or in honor of his son, Csaba. In 453, Áttila died suddenly. The way the story goes, Áttila had just taken a somewhat reluctant Italian princess as a bride in an attempt to establish his rule over certain Roman lands. On his wedding night, presumably in the throes of passion, he developed a terrible nosebleed. It was so terrible that he bled to death while his resentful new wife looked on.

Once Áttila was gone, his followers turned against his sons and welcomed the Romans back. The Romans not only brought law and order, they also brought with them gifts of titles, land, and prestige for Huns who renounced their late leader and embraced the Roman way of life.

But the walls had been breached and the country made vulnerable to raids by other barbarian tribes and by other powers, too, such as Bulgaria and Byzantium. By the time the Magyars arrived, 400 years later, it didn't take them long to take over and settle in. They began farming and rebuilding the cities, but what they were best known for was their great herds of cattle, which they would drive across the plains to the big cattle markets in Moravia, Vienna, Nuremberg, and Venice.

The Hungarian *szürkamarha*, or gray cattle, were remarkably hardy beasts with sleek gray coats, long horns, and a lean, flavorful flesh. Because the herdsmen were away from home for weeks and weeks at a time, they learned to cook and to make their meals easily transportable. One thing they'd do was make sure there was always a "sickly" beast among the healthy herd. Partway along the journey they'd slaughter it and have enough meat to make a *gulyás* that would last them several days. So intertwined are the soup and the cowboy that *gulyás* is the word for both, and so precious is beef to the Hungarian that *marha* means not only "cattle," but also "treasure."

The Magyar cooks must have roasted many of these oxen for the celebrations of Christmas Day 1000. That was the day that Hungary became a real country. Magyar Orszag, they called it: the country of the Magyars.

On January 1, 1001, the first day of the new millennium, Ístvan I had himself crowned the country's first king. Like his father Géza, Ístvan was descended from the *gyula* Arpád. Géza had brought Christianity to Hungary, and now his son would make it the law of the land. He was crowned by the Pope and promptly began importing literate priests to educate his rustic, pagan subjects. Not all the Magyars were thrilled to be placed under the mantle of Rome, though, and they launched a series of bloody pagan revolts. Priests, easily identified by their crosses and robes, were targeted by vindictive Magyars who devised creatively cruel means of despatching them to heaven. Eventually, of course, Hungary did accept Christianity, and Ístvan become the first of the country's three saint-kings. (The other two were László I and Emeric.) Ístvan, who died in 1038, was canonized in 1083.

By the twelfth century, the country had expanded to include the Balkans, Croatia, and Dalmatia. There were advances in justice and in culture, in power and equal rights for the nobility, and in education, too. In 1301, the House of Arpád died out, and for the next 150 years, the country was led by a variety of leaders from all over Europe, including the Neapolitan Angevins Charles-Robert and Louis I the Great as well as Luxembourg's Sigismund I.

Meanwhile, to the south and the east, the Ottomans in Turkey were amassing land, power, and an unbeatable army. They began their rise in the eleventh century, and for the next 800 years expanded their Muslim empire, eventually occupying most of northern Africa, western Asia, and southeastern Europe, including, of course, Hungary.

The Turks attacked Hungary for the first time in 1456, at Nándorfehérvar (now Belgrade, Yugoslavia). The Hungarians were ready for them. Led by the great military leader János Hunyadi, they repelled the Turks soundly. Everyone breathed a sigh of relief, though it was inevitable that one day those flashing blades would return.

Hunyadi was fêted and celebrated throughout the country, and a few years later, his son, Matthias, brought back the monarchy and made himself King Matthias I. He introduced Renaissance culture to Hungary, and his reign was one of growth, culture, and fine dining. In 1475, he married one of Hungary's most beloved queens, the Italian princess Beatrice, daughter of the King of Naples, who brought with her what would become one of her people's favorite foods: pasta.

Now, it's entirely possible that the most rustic form of Hungarian pasta – the pasta pellets called *tarhonya* (TAR-hon-yuh) – came with the Magyars from Asia, although many people suspect it was yet another gift of the Turks. (There are similar dishes throughout the Balkans and Turkey.) But "real" pasta came with Beatrice. Today, there are nearly as many different types of noodle dishes in Hungarian cuisine as there are in Italian. There are thin noodles and wide noodles, short ones and long ones, square noodles, jaggedy-cut noodles called "strawberry leaves," paper-thin sheets of noodles called *lebbencs* (LEB-bench), snail-shaped corkscrew noodles, stuffed noodles, and oblong egg noodles of various widths. Each pasta dish is designed for a specific noodle. Some noodles are used in soups; others are sweet and served as dessert – noodles with nuts or poppy seeds, for instance. Still others are served as side dishes or easy main courses using cheap, vegetarian ingredients such as cabbage or wheat germ.

One of Matthias and Beatrice's other favorite foods, which they brought from Italy and which has since become the most important ingredient in Hungarian cuisine, was the onion. The onion not only is the base for the country's most famous dishes, the soups and the stews, but is also eaten cooked, raw, pickled, stuffed, or in stuffing. There are lovely, sweet purple onions that are eaten raw with goose liver. There are golden onions from Mako that are best with bacon. There are big onions and little ones, white ones, yellow ones, and green ones. So important are onions to the cuisine that it is a rare savory recipe, which doesn't start with a couple of them. In fairy tales, the adventurer always brings an onion on his journey. And Hungarians know that a man will never go hungry or his life lack flavor as long as there is one onion left in the sack.

Matthias' reign was one of abundance and peace. Until recently, it was also the only time in its 1,100-year history that Hungary was truly independent. But the good times didn't last. In 1526, the Turks attacked again, at the famous battle of Mohacs, and this time Suleiman's troops were victorious. By 1541, the country was split into three parts: the Turks ruled in the middle, the Austrian Hapsburgs ruled in the west, and Transylvania was made a semi-independent state under Ottoman rule to the east. You can still see the evidence of this three-way split in the architecture: the west has Germanic-looking structures with white walls and black roofs; the east has darker Transylvanian-style buildings with lots of wood and folkloric motifs; and the center has the bright colors, mosaics, and ornate forms of the Turkish style.

Over the 158 years of Turkish occupation, there were many skirmishes and even a few victories against the Turks. One of the most famous victories occurred in 1552 at Eger. The castle was under attack by the Turks, and those besieged within its walls were horribly outnumbered. The Hungarian forces withstood the Turkish invaders for several weeks until it was clear to their commander, Ístván Dobó, that their strength was exhausted. So he ordered that the cellars be opened. Now, underneath Eger there are miles and miles of cellars, three layers of serpentine corridors built atop each other and snaking under the city. They were used to get quickly from one place to another, and to hide from the Turks. They were also used – and still are used – to store the local wines. Eger is one of the great wine-producing regions of Hungary, best known for a hearty, spicy red cuvée. When Dobó ordered his cellars opened, he also ordered that each man be given as much of his famous cuvée as he wished. Many of the women in the castle also partook. If they were going to meet their maker, they reasoned, they might as well do it with a smile on their lips.

But the wine had an extraordinary effect. It gave the Hungarians almost superhuman powers. The Hungarian soldiers descended on the Turks in a murderous frenzy. Above them on the ramparts, the women hurled stones and poured vats of boiling pitch on the heads of the invaders below. When the Turks saw the crazed Magyars coming after them, they fled in terror. But as they scurried off, they noticed that their tormentors' moustaches were covered in red liquid. They surmised that the Magyars must have been drinking bulls' blood to have become so imbued with power. (At least, that's what they told anyone who'd listen.) The Turks were decisively routed – so badly beaten that they didn't venture another attack for forty years – and to this day that spicy red wine is known as Egri Bikavér, the Bull's Blood of Eger.

That victory was a rare exception. For the most part, the Turks defeated the hapless Hungarians again and again, and occupied their lands for a good long time. It was the most brutal period in a history filled with more than its share of bloodshed. During the occupation, more than half the Hungarian population was killed. Those who survived barricaded themselves in increasingly isolated villages and paid massive taxes and levies to their new Ottoman overlords. Worst of all, with so many men killed in battle, there were too few people left to tend the fields. What had once been the most fertile land in Europe became so barren that people began calling the Great Plain the Puszta, which means the "Devastated Land."

The Turks may have exploited the land and the people who lived on it, but they also brought with them many of what would become the country's favorite foods. They introduced paprika, which would one day flavor Hungary's most popular dishes, as well as sour cherries, corn to feed the animals, and tomatoes, which the Hungarians revere so much, they call them *paradicsom* (PUH-ra-deech-com), or paradise. They also introduced the pita, which became *lángos*, and a noodle dish that would evolve into the country's most popular pasta. *Túros csusza* (TOO-rosh CHOO-suh) is hot egg noodles tossed with sour cream, a creamy pot cheese called *túro*, and crispy chunks of sizzling hot bacon (though the latter was probably a Hungarian addition, as the Muslim Turks were unlikely to have eaten any pork).

Most importantly, though, they brought with them a new beverage that would one day fuel all the great literary, cultural and political movements of the nation: coffee.

These days many people consider coffee the true Hungarian drink, more important even than wine, palinka, or soda water, which was also a local invention. Certainly, Hungarian kávé (KAH-vay) is some of the best in the world, on a par with Italian for its dark, rich flavor. It is very much like an espresso, but meant to be drunk slowly and leisurely, ideally alongside a slice of rich, sweet torte and a generous helping of lively conversation in an ornate *kávéház* (KAV-ay-haz), or coffeehouse. But at first, coffee was not considered a good thing at all.

Coffee was discovered in Ethiopia centuries ago and gradually made its way north to the Turks. The first coffeehouse in Constantinople opened in 1554 and by 1579, coffee had arrived in the Magyar capital, a century before it arrived in Vienna. At first, the Hungarians called it *fekete leves* (FEH-keh-teh leh-vesh) or "black soup." As with paprika, for the most part they left this strange new foodstuff to the Turks, who had odd customs aplenty. One of those customs was to avoid discussing business during a meal, instead waiting until the end when the coffee was served. Then they'd announce the bad news about taxes, levies, and other financial matters. The Hungarians came up with a saying that is still used today. When faced with something gloomy and dire and expecting things to get even worse, they'll say, "The black soup is yet to come."

It took a while for the Hungarians to embrace this new beverage. But once they did, they embraced it wholeheartedly. As in other European centers, ornately beautiful coffeehouses opened up in Budapest, Szeged, and Debrecen, especially in the nineteenth century when artists, writers, reformers, politicians, and thinkers of all stripes gathered to discuss the matters of the day in the local *kávéhaz*.

One of the things people best love to eat with that coffee is strudel, or *rétes* (RAY-tesh), as it's called in Hungarian. And there certainly wouldn't have been any *rétes* without the Turks, for it was they who brought the filo pastry needed to make it.

Although the word "filo" or "phyllo" comes from the Greek word for leaf, the pastry was actually a Turkish invention, used in pies called *borek*. Because the Turks were in Hungary for such a long time, local cooks soon learned to bake with filo. Unlike the Turks and Greeks, who typically layered the filo with fillings in a dish, the Hungarians rolled the filo around the filling – usually fruit and/or nuts, although there is a toothsome version made with *túro* and raisins – to create a tender, flaky log of pastry.

As for how thick the dough should be, well, it can vary, but according to a hundred-year-old saying, "The housewife will know her strudel dough is good enough when she can take a piece of dough the size of a bread roll and work it sufficiently to wrap up a Hussar – and his horse – in strudel."

Hungarians may have invented strudel, but their neighbors to the west soon adopted it and made it their own. Austria and Hungary have always shared many traits, geography, food, boundaries, and for a long time their language, too. Austria, though, was more fortunate in location – closer to the West, farther away from the Turks and Russians – and more skilled in politics. For centuries, its ruling family was one of the most powerful in the world. Sometimes this worked out well for its smaller, scrappier neighbor; other times, less so.

The first of the powerful Habsburgs was Count Rudolf, who was elected King of Germany and Holy Roman Emperor in 1273. He annexed a number of duchies, including Austria, which became the heartland of the family's empire. In 1556, the empire was split between Philip II – who got Spain, the Netherlands, Italy, and everything overseas – and his brother Ferdinand I, who got all the rest. In 1526, the same year the Turks defeated Hungary at Mohacs, Ferdinand had become king of Hungary, although it was only a tiny bit of western Hungary that he ruled, with Pozony (today known as Bratislava, Slovakia), as its capital.

In 1686, the Habsburgs ejected the Ottomans from Buda. A year later, Austria occupied Transylvania. In 1699, the Ottomans lost Hungary entirely to the Austrians when they signed a peace treaty that ended the 158-year occupation. You might think this made the Hungarians happy, but no. What they wanted was independence and self-rule; what they got was new landlords. Like the Turks, the Austrians used Hungary primarily for its fertile lands and cheap cannon fodder, without investing in the people or the country's infrastructure. They also made German the national language, which meant the nobles and professional classes spoke the language of their Austrian masters, while the peasants and workers spoke Hungarian. While the rest of the continent basked in the Enlightenment, Hungary was left in the dark, in a poor, brutal, feudalistic society.

Still, life under Austrian rule allowed Hungary to replenish the fields and vineyards that had been devastated by the Turks. Then, when the male line of the Austrian Hapsburgs ended in 1740, Maria Theresa became empress and began a forty-year reign of enlightenment and progress. Among other things, she began a massive building scheme that included the reconstruction of Buda Castle, which the Turks had reduced to rubble. She also encouraged people from overcrowded parts of her German lands to relocate to Hungary and start rebuilding the country's population.

The culinary influence of all those Germanic newcomers can't be underestimated. For one thing, although Hungarians had been making sausage for centuries, the Germans brought with them their sophisticated smokehouse traditions. Sausages are widely considered one of the world's first convenience foods – they are even mentioned in Homer's *Odyssey* – and the Germans have more than a thousand varieties in their culinary repertoire. Soon, Hungary was producing pork sausages, beef sausages, goose sausages, game sausages, fish sausages, and sausages made with all sorts of organ meats. They were flavored with salt, paprika, garlic, and pepper, as well as more exotic things like truffles, marjoram, cumin, horseradish, and lemon rind.

While Hungarians had feasted on the local wild boar and shaggy-coated Mangalica pig since the Magyars arrived in the ninth century, with the new German smokehouses they could really develop another of the nation's great foodstuffs: bacon. There are more than twenty types of bacon in Hungary: some are cured, some salted, some smoked, some treated in a variety of ways; some have lots of meaty streaks, others have none at all; some are sweet and plain, some are intensely salty, and some are spiced up with a generous dash of paprika.

The country's vast selection of dumplings or *nokedli* also likely arrived with the Germans, or Swabians as they were usually called. The most popular dumplings are *galuska* (GA-loosh-kuh). These are the small white dumplings similar to spaëtzle that are usually served with *pörkölt* and *paprikás*, oftentimes sprinkled with fresh dill. But there are dozens of other types of dumplings, including the big, savory liver dumpling used in soups and the filled potato dumpling known as *gomboc* (GOME-boats). It is similar to – but not the same as – the perogy, which is popular in the country that lies to Hungary's east, Ukraine. The two must have shared a common parentage at some point. The perogy is a sturdy potato-dough dumpling usually stuffed with onions and cheese, fried, and served with sour cream. The Hungarian *gomboc* is also a stuffed potato dough dumpling, but the dough is lighter and the fillings more varied — fruit, *túro,* or meat. The most popular is the *szilvás* (seel-vash) *gomboc*, which is stuffed with plums and sugar, then boiled and quickly fried with bread crumbs.

In fact, because the borders in the region shifted so often, and because the people moved around and intermarried so frequently, Hungary shares many culinary traditions with her next-door neighbors. For instance, dishes with the prefix *rac* (rats) are based on Serbian cuisine; those dishes are usually made with tomatoes and bell peppers and often with smoked bacon, but never with paprika. The red spice isn't used in dishes from Transylvania, either. Transylvania, or Erdély as the Hungarians call it, is known as the "enchanted garden" of Hungary (although it has been part of Romania since 1920). Its cooking was at one time considered one of the greatest culinary achievements in the world. It relies on fresh green herbs for flavor, such as basil, dill, marjoram, rosemary, tarragon, and thyme. Hungary's large Jewish population also made a huge culinary impact, and today, while you will find few Hungarian cookbooks on bookstore shelves, you will find plenty of Jewish ones filled with traditional Hungarian recipes.

One dish that seems to pop up in every cuisine in Central Europe is the cabbage roll or stuffed cabbage. The dish is so closely associated with Hungarian cuisine that there used to be a saying back in the eighteenth century: "Meat and cabbage are the coat of arms of Hungary." While some countries make cabbage rolls with a tomato-based sauce, Hungarians traditionally serve them with sour cream, while Transylvanians make them with dill and savory. (Cabbage also shows up in the sauerkraut that is sold by the bucketful at the country's many farmer's markets; the art of making sauerkraut most likely came from the Slovaks.) Meanwhile, the meat filling for the cabbage rolls and countless other stuffed dishes came from the Balkans, and these cultures in turn learned it from the Turks.

As for the Austrians, they gave Hungary the *virsli* (wiener), the wiener schnitzel, which in Hungary is called *bécsi szelet* (BAY-chee

SELL-et), and best of all, the fine art of pastry making. The Austrians are notorious for their love of sweets, and the Hungarians are not far behind them. Both countries love a sort of toothsome torte made with eggs and nuts and very different from airy North American layer cakes. Both have taken this base and made their own national cakes – Sacher torte in Austria, for instance, and *Dobos torta* in Hungary.

By the beginning of the nineteenth century, Hungary was beginning to come into its own again. It all began with the language reform movement that made Hungarian the national language again. That was followed by a huge literary movement and the publication of dozens of books and poems in Hungarian. The country underwent a culinary renaissance, too. "National" dishes such as *gulyás*, which until then had only ever existed in the cooking kettles of the peasantry, appeared on the tables of the nobility. What had once been eaten only out of a communal metal pot was now served on the finest china. Folk dances and traditions were woven into the fabric of the everyday. Paprika became a popular condiment.

For the first time, the five elements of Hungarian cuisine came together. It had started with the culinary techniques of Hungary's Asiatic ancestors, then it grew with the Italian Renaissance influences of King Matthias and Queen Beatrice. It expanded with the ingredients brought by the Turks, from corn to cherries to coffee and strudel. It developed a unique richness from the traditions of nearby cultures. And, finally, the French chefs arrived via Austria to give it a subtlety and finesse that made it into one of the greatest, most interesting cuisines in the world.

Austrian noble families had begun importing French chefs to raise the quality of their cuisine to grand new heights at the end of the eighteenth century. Soon, the Hungarians followed suit, and by midcentury, the French lightness of touch and sophistication of approach had begun to transform the many separate styles of Hungarian cooking into a real national cuisine.

It was that French-Austrian tradition that influenced, for instance, the legendary Gundel family. In 1857, Johann Gundel had left his family home in Bavaria and eventually made his way to Pest, along the way befriending Eduard Sacher, son of the Franz Sacher who invented the famous Sacher torte in Vienna. In Pest, Johann bought his own restaurant and hotel and adapted the somewhat rough-around-the-edges Hungarian cooking to the standards of bourgeois Viennese – that is, French – cuisine. His son Károly inherited the business and his father's gifts as a host. Károly trained in Paris at the Ritz and Adlon hotels, and in 1910, he opened Gundel near the Budapest Zoo in Városliget (City Park). This was a little Art Nouveau paradise where the food was always made from the freshest and best ingredients, invariably chosen by Károly himself each morning at the market. Gundel became Hungary's most famous eatery. It has fed kings and queens and famous actresses and its wine cellars were even featured in an episode of *The Amazing Race* television show.

Another man who made an impact on Hungarian cuisine was József Marchal, born Joseph Maréchal in France. After he had cooked for Emperor Napoleon III and for the Russian tsars, Prince Pál Eszterházy made him chef de cuisine at the National Casino in Pest. In 1863, this was the most exclusive club in town, and the young Frenchman revolutionized Hungarian cooking. While still using traditional seasonings and ingredients, he gave everything a French flair. Even today you will see many dishes on Hungarian menus served "á la Marchal."

The third man who put a French accent on the rugged Hungarian cuisine was József Dobos, who owned a remarkable fine food shop in Budapest. He imported dozens of cheeses, wines, and delicacies from all over the world. He was as well known for his showmanship and he was for his delicious foodstuffs and the four famous cookbooks he wrote. But he is best-known for inventing the famous Dobos torta in 1887, six exquisite layers of fine torte with a chocolate crème in between them and a hard layer of caramel on top. (In 1962, the city of Budapest hosted a full-scale festival to celebrate the seventy-fifth anniversary of the cake. Now that's a city that takes its sweets seriously.)

Meanwhile, in France itself there was a growing interest in *la cuisine á la hongroise*. In 1879, the great French chef Georges Auguste Escoffier introduced Hungarian paprika to the West when he had it shipped from Szeged down the River Tisza and eventually to the Grand

Casino at Monte Carlo. At the casino, he put *Poulet au Paprika* and *Gulyás Hongroise* on the menu. Not only were they popular with the guests, but the chicken *paprikás* went on to win a number of culinary awards. By 1900, that classic Hungarian dish, *gulyás*, was a hit at the Paris World Fair.

Things were cooking in other ways in nineteenth-century Hungary, too. After centuries of falling behind the rest of the world in terms of scientific and cultural advances, Hungary caught up almost overnight. Modern technologies were imported or developed for cultivating, harvesting, and preserving foods. The Hungarian Academy of Sciences and the Academy of Agriculture were founded, and so were western-style banks. Steamships began to ply the Danube to take Hungary's products to international markets.

In addition, engineers learned how to build modern roads and bridges, including the Lánchid (Chain Bridge), the first bridge across the Danube in Budapest. They had also finally determined how to dam the banks of the Tisza River. Since time began, the Tisza had flooded each spring, spreading across the Great Plain. When the waters receded, they left behind a fine silt that dried up and blew away in the hot summer winds. For centuries, especially under the neglect of the Turkish occupation, the Great Plain was little more than a desert, the Puszta, where nothing could grow and the sandstorms were as bad as those in Central Asia. But once the Tisza was controlled with dikes and walls and dams, spring flooding was minimal (except for the terrible one in 1879 that destroyed most of Szeged). However, controlling the water still didn't solve the problem of soil erosion – until some bright person hit on the idea of planting apricot trees, which have a complex network of roots that could have been designed to hold fine soil close to the earth.

But as the country grew culturally and scientifically, its people became dissatisfied and yearned to regain their independence. In 1848, Europe's year of revolutions, centuries-old resentment of the Austrians boiled over in Hungary. On March 15, there was a rebellion in Pest. By September, the revolutionary leader Lajos Kossuth had led the country into a war of independence that lasted almost a year. In April, the Emperor Ferdinand abdicated, leaving the empire in the hands of his nephew, Franz Joseph I, who would rule until the First World War, when the empire was dismantled. Before he stepped down, Ferdinand abolished serfdom in Hungary and transformed the constitution. The victorious Hungarians moved the national assembly to Debrecen and made Kossuth the president-governor.

Franz Joseph, however, wasn't happy with this state of affairs. He called in the Russian army, which soundly defeated the Hungarians in August 1849. The leaders of the revolution went into hiding and were eventually hunted down and killed.

Over the next twenty years, the Hungarians lived in a state of repression and resistance, while the Austrians had to endure constant skirmishes with the Hungarians. Eventually, a sort of reconciliation was reached and Hungarian politicians began to seek the return of the country's constitutional rights. In 1867, Austria agreed to enter into what has become known as the Great Compromise – the dual monarchy of the Austro-Hungarian Empire.

For fifty-one years, the two countries ruled together over an enormous area of Eastern and Central Europe. With financial help from Austria, Hungary began building and rebuilding its cities, its buildings, its culture, its entire national identity. The arts – music, painting, literature, and architecture – thrived during this period. In 1873, Pest, Buda, and Óbuda were united to form the city of Budapest, which finally and forever became the seat of a government that had been housed in cities all over the country, from Debrecen to Bratislava. In 1896, Hungary celebrated its millennium, and the Parliament Buildings, St. Stephen's basilica, two great railway stations, a system of five grand market halls, and the subway, the first in continental Europe, were all built for the millennial party in Budapest. The city was redesigned as a series of ring roads, much as Baron Haussmann had designed Paris. The country's railways were designed in a similar way.

So many buildings were raised, roads laid down, and institutions established that a visitor to Hungary today might think the entire country was created between 1867 and 1918, and in many ways, it was.

As the nineteenth century ticked over into the twentieth, Hungary was filled with hope and possibility. And right about then, with the country on a fine knife-edge between possibility and disaster, that's when József Wintermantel and Aranka Matula came on the scene.

CHAPTER 4
Flowers in the Chimney

"Why do you have to think about the past? I always say you should look ahead," my Aunt Frances says. "What we have today is a present, and the gift is the future."

"I just don't want to talk about what happened," my cousin Maju says firmly.

"Mother always said, 'Don't look back, look forward.' And that's what she did," says my own mother.

The women love to share the family anecdotes, laughing and reminiscing over a glass of wine or perhaps something a bit stronger. But when it comes to the actual history they lived through, well, they'd rather skip over that. It's more fun to talk about the pranks they played at the DP (displaced persons) camp in Ireland rather than why they ended up there, or how Luizi fell into a latrine rather than why she was running away from the German – or was it Russian? – soldiers. That's how they survived the decades of war and poverty and occupation, of repression and revolution, of being jailed and being dislocated, and of making their way in a strange new world.

Don't dwell on the past. Think about the future.

Besides, they have so much past to remember that at times it's much easier to forget. Just in the ten years from when my grandparents first met to when they finally married, they lived through a world war, two revolutions, two attempted royal coups, a general strike, countless changes in government, and a peace treaty that reduced the size of their country by two-thirds. And that was before their troubles *really* started.

Aranka Matula and József Wintermantel first met in 1914. She was twelve years old and visiting her Aunt Terka in Siófok, a resort town on the south side of Lake Balaton. He was fourteen and staying at the resort with his family. The rich boy and the pretty girl were part of a gang of kids who played together each summer. Then, when the poppies faded and the leaves began to fall, they went back to their schools in cities and towns all over Hungary. All summer long, they swam and they sailed and they rowed boats. They put on skits for the grown-ups and they walked along the strand eating ice cream cones, the boys teasing the girls, the girls tormenting their young admirers.

Siófok was where the bourgeoisie went for their summer vacations, while the aristocracy had their villas on the north shore of Balaton. Here, as elsewhere in Hungary, the different levels of society – the peasants, the aristocrats, the small landowners, the workers, the intelligentsia, and the upwardly mobile urbanites – were strictly segregated. But that didn't matter to the mixed group of children who ran along the sandy beach as the hot summer breeze rustled through the willow trees. They were as oblivious to issues of class and race as they were to the harsher winds of war that were blowing their way.

Aranka and her twin brother Nándi came from a village south of Siófok where the family had been small landowners for centuries. They were poor, and although their mother, Agnes, was still alive, they were considered orphans. Their father had died in an accident while his wife was pregnant with the twins. When they were born, the government placed the brother and sister in an orphanage close enough that Agnes could visit them whenever she wanted. The government held that a poor, single woman couldn't raise two little children on her own, so it stepped in to help, and in so doing, probably offered them a better future than they would have had otherwise.

The twins were well fed, clothed, and cared for at the government's expense; at the same time, they were treated kindly by the nuns and allowed to spend time with their family. They also received an excellent education, a gift that was not readily available to many children of their class. Aranka was especially grateful for this, because even though educational reforms had been underway since the mid-nineteenth century, schooling was still only available to the fortunate few, and rarely to girls at all. She learned to read and write, she learned about history, and literature, and geography; and she learned all the things a young lady should know, how to sew, play the piano, and paint a pretty watercolor.

But she learned her business skills from her aunt. Terka Matula was her father's sister, a spinster and a businesswoman who owned shops and buildings in Budapest, and a successful restaurant in Siófok. She had no children of her own, but every summer, the twins would visit her, helping out where they could and playing with the other children the rest of the time. Nándi was always a reckless little scoundrel and not much use around the restaurant, but Aranka was a serious girl, so Terka taught her how to keep the accounts, balance the books, and make sure the chef didn't drink all the profits. She didn't teach her how to cook, though. That Aranka learned on her own.

Jóska Wintermantel came from a very different world. Although Aranka was an "orphan," she was surrounded by people who loved her. Jóska, who was the oldest son of a wealthy and respectable family, was surrounded by people who didn't.

His family originally came from Germany, Catholic clockmakers who had moved from the Black Forest to Hungary in the nineteenth century. The Magyar population had been decimated by 158 years of Turkish occupation and decades of war with the Hapsburgs, so the government looked to its neighbors to increase the numbers on the census lists. Like many other families, the Wintermantels saw this as an opportunity to start anew, and so they packed their bags and their clock-making tools and headed south. Over the years, they grew wealthier and wealthier, until József, Jóska's father, expanded the family clock-making tradition and began a gold and jewelry business in Budapest. By the time he was in his late thirties, he was a rich, eligible bachelor, a man who could have had his pick among the daughters of the merchant class.

But someone had other plans for him. Her name was Alujzia, a dark-haired, dark-eyed beauty from a once-well-to-do family that had fallen on hard times. She was also one of his employees. Was this a case of a poor girl trying to make her way in the world as best she could? Or was it a rich owner taking advantage of a vulnerable young woman working for him? Or was it, simply, love? In any case, shy glances across the glass cabinets became intensely longing ones; a careless touch on a shoulder became a deliberate caress. It wasn't long before they were entangled in a passionate affair.

Their baby József, who would always be known as Jóska or Józsi, was born a few days after the new century started, on January 4, 1900. Not long after that, at the insistence of the senior Wintermantels, Jóska's parents got married. A second son, Kálmán, was born a year later and two years after that, a little girl named Teréz. Alujzia adored Kálman, and when Teréz contracted polio she thought her heart would break. But from the beginning, Alujzia did not love her oldest son.

As the years went on, she became a rigid snob and a harsh matriarch, the sort of woman whose mouth is always pursed in disapproval. Her granddaughters remember her as beautiful but cold, mean, and unloving; they remember her husband as distant and frightening. As children, when they visited their grandparents, they were never allowed to speak at dinner unless they were asked a direct question, and as soon as the dishes were cleared, they had to get up silently and kiss first Alujzia's hand, then their grandfather's. And then they were expected to vanish.

The Wintermantels' life was one of beautiful homes, sumptuous clothing, and lavish feasts, but it also came with certain expectations. Jóska, especially, was expected to set the standard for his younger siblings by excelling at school, comporting himself manfully at his military training, getting a good degree, marrying well, and eventually joining in his father's business. But from the beginning, he was a disappointment.

He was as softhearted and sensitive as he was mischievous, a prankster who was always getting in trouble and had a habit of getting in with the wrong crowd. He had a wide brow, dreamy green eyes, and movie star good looks. At school, he was too busy having fun to pay attention to his studies, so his grades were never very good. During his military training, he began an affair with his commanding officer's wife. The CO came home early one day and, in a scene straight out of a French farce, Jóska jumped out of the bedroom window to get away from him. He landed on his head, which many would argue was the part of his body least likely to sustain any injury, and permanently lost the hearing in one ear. He also lost any hope of a career in the military, not that it would matter much, since the army was disbanded a few years later, anyway. At university, he joined a political club that was ostensibly dedicated to repatriating the Hungarian lands lost under the Treaty of Versailles. Their highest priorities, though, were drinking, gambling, and womanizing. Eventually, Jóska's irate parents sent him off to Munich to clean up, grow up and, while he was at it, to oversee a branch of the family business there.

While they were upset about Jóska's impressive appetite for debauchery, their deepest cause for concern was something else entirely. During those sultry summers in Siófok, Jóska's teasing fondness for his somber little playmate Aranka had grown into an intense passion for the woman she'd grown into, a charming woman whose sweet face hid a tough, determined character. But to his parents, the relationship was a disgrace, a mésalliance. They thought she was little better than a peasant, a country girl with no pedigree and no fortune, certainly not good enough for their oldest son and heir. As soon as they realized what was going on, Alujzia and József did everything they could to keep the couple apart, even if it meant that the business in Munich was sure to suffer.

During Jóska's years in the wilderness, he wrote long, lovesick letters to Aranka whenever he was sober enough to hold a pen and visited her whenever he could escape the stern eye of his parents. As for Aranka, she calmly got on with her life – she had gone to work with her aunt after she finished school – but never forgot about the handsome boy from Budapest.

In her teens and twenties, Aranka would have been what the Hungarians call *tündéri*, a word that means "fairylike," but isn't as lame as it sounds in English. She was tiny, not even five feet tall, with a soft cloud of loosely gathered brown hair and a rosy complexion. In all her photos, she wears white, and even the straight-as-a-board flapper styles of the 1920s couldn't hide her curvy figure. She was sweet and gentle and kind, but with a spark that set her apart from all the other girls. No wonder lonely, unloved Jóska was smitten.

He wasn't the only one. She had a string of beaux who made weekly trips to Lake Balaton to woo the tiny young dynamo. In the postwar years, unemployment was high and jobs were scarce for the young men who'd survived the war or had been too young to fight. There wasn't even an army they could join, since Hungary's military had been abolished by the Treaty of Versailles in 1919. So they had plenty of time to hang around a restaurant in Siófok, drinking wine and flirting with their pretty young hostess.

When Terka died, Aranka inherited the restaurant and continued to run it while dealing with all her suitors and her irresponsible twin, who was perfectly happy to be a victim of the era's high unemployment. Times being as tough as they were, in addition to running the business, Aranka finally learned how to cook. Her first attempt in the kitchen was disastrous. She had decided to make *vadás* (vuh-DASH), a creamy game stew with dumplings, for her mother's family to thank them for helping take care of her and Nándi when they were little kids. The meat turned out tough and stringy, the sauce badly curdled, the dumplings at once hard and falling apart but she kept at it until she learned how to make a perfectly clear and golden *tyúkhúsleves* (TYOOK-hoosh-leh-vesh), a flavorful chicken broth, the standard by which every great Hungarian cook is measured. She made roasts and stews and *főzelék* (FUH-zeh-lake), vegetables that are cooked, puréed and thickened with roux until they reach their most intense flavor. She took tender Balaton fish and fried them whole, simmered them in spicy soup, or baked them with sour cream and potatoes. Because potatoes were cheap and readily available, she learned to make them every possible way: roasted, boiled, and fried; buttered and tossed with parsley; baked in layers with eggs, onions, and sour cream; sliced up and mixed with sausages and paprika. And she learned how to make her own preserves, pickles and jams and *meggye* (MED-ye), sour cherries, soaked in brandy.

Then Aranka turned her hand to baking. She made cheese straws and the biscuits called *pogacsa*. (Even when she was in her eighties, she always had a plate of *pogacsa* in her cupboard waiting for her granddaughters.) She baked walnut torte, poppy seed strudel and yeast cake studded with cherries. She made plum dumplings and the creamy chocolate cake called Rigo Jancsi (REE-goYAN-chee). She had a sure but light hand as a pastry cook, and found a sort of peace in front of the oven.

One day – it must have been in 1923 – Jóska came to visit Aranka. When he walked into the living room, the first thing his eyes fell on was a big bouquet of flowers.

"Who are those from?" he demanded.

"It's none of your business," she replied pertly. He knew it had to be from one of the other hopeful young men who were hanging around. He glared at the flowers for a moment, then broke into a big smile.

"You know, I would really like a glass of wine, and I'm sure you have some excellent wine in the cellar. Would you get something special for me?" he asked with all the charm he could muster.

"Of course," Aranka said, picking up the keys. When she returned from the cellar with a dusty bottle of Tokaji in her hand, Jóska was gone. So were the flowers. Puzzled, and a bit annoyed as well, she walked outside to look for her beau, only to find him standing in the garden, hands on his hips, gazing at the roof of the house with a satisfied grin on his face. She followed his gaze and almost dropped the bottle of wine. Stuffed into the chimney pot was the big bouquet of flowers.

"They'll go up in smoke," he said gleefully, "just like all your boyfriends should."

She couldn't help but laugh.

"Well," she said, "if you want me to stop seeing other people, then you should marry me. In fact, you either marry me or you don't come here any more."

And so he did.

They married in 1924 and his parents immediately cut off all ties with the young couple. That's OK, they thought, we have the restaurant, and we have each other. But Aranka hadn't counted on the devastation that her brother and her new husband could wreak on a successful business.

Nándi was a gambler. He loved the horses, but the horses he backed never seemed to win. And each time a horse fell down, or broke a leg, or came over all skittish at the finish line, he turned to Aranka's wine cellar for comfort. Jóska, on the other hand, was bored and restless, with nothing to do all day but drink and swap stories with Nándi. Between the two of them, they drank the business into bankruptcy within five years.

It didn't help that during that time, Aranka had other things on her mind. She wasn't just a businesswoman, she was also a new mother. In 1925, she gave birth to a little girl, Eva. A second daughter, Luizi, was born in 1927. Motherhood, she discovered, wasn't easy, especially when you had a business to run and two irresponsible young men to keep an eye on as well. But life was still an amusing adventure for the young family – until the two little girls got sick.

With all the chaos in their personal lives, Aranka and Jóska hadn't been paying much attention to what was happening in the world around them. But Hungary had just been through the most devastating upheaval in its history, and the aftershocks weren't over yet. In fact, they were soon to get much worse.

In 1914, at the time they met, the country was 282,000 square kilometers in area, with a population of 18.2 million people. It extended from Krakow in the north to Sarajevo in the south, from Lvov in the east to the port of Fiume on the Adriatic coast in the west. Hungary was enjoying the benefits of the dual monarchy with Austria. Half a century of relatively enlightened government had improved life for most people, and Hungary had become one of the most advanced countries in Central Europe. Cities were electrified and all their buildings had running water. Schools and universities opened and expanded the opportunities for young people. Art and literature flourished.

There were problems, too, of course, and serious ones at that. Serfdom had only been abolished in 1848, and the situation for peasants was still dire. "There are few countries so much in need of a revolution," British Prime Minister David Lloyd George said of Hungary during the peace talks in 1919. The countryside and the country's lower classes had largely been left behind in the march to progress. Their simmering resentment led to a general strike in 1912 and contributed to the rise of communism among intellectuals and the considerable Jewish population, as well as the working class. In addition, many minorities within Hungary's borders – especially the Roma – were badly discriminated against.

But for the most part, as the new century dawned, things were looking up. Then, on June 28, 1914, a Serbian nationalist named Gavrilo Princip shot and killed the heir to the Austro-Hungarian throne, Archduke Francis Ferdinand, and his consort Sophie as they drove through the streets of Sarajevo. Within months, the world was at war, and not only was Hungary right in the middle of the action, it was on the wrong side.

When the war ended, the winners gathered at Versailles to decide on the reparations to be paid by the losers. No one, not even Germany, paid as big a price as Hungary. The Grand Trianon, where the treaty with Hungary was signed in 1920, was a pleasure palace built at Versailles by Louis XIV, the Sun King, for "partaking of collations," but to anxious Hungarians it seemed that the only thing the victors hungered for was every little crumb of their homeland.

According to Margaret MacMillan's book, *Paris 1919*, Hungary was penalized for a number of reasons. It had been one of the last countries to surrender, so it was considered especially stubborn and dangerous. At the same time, its strategic location had the Allies more than a little worried, especially with the gunfire of the Russian Revolution still echoing in their ears and the resulting westward creep of communism causing concern throughout the West. It didn't help that Hungary, as so often in its history, was in political turmoil, going through leaders like a cook goes through clean aprons. When the talks started in 1918, Hungary was led by the liberal Count Michael Károlyi. Then a radical, intellectual, Jewish communist named Béla Kun returned from Moscow and seized power. (Apparently, the grateful Kun sent his Russian mentors a case of Tokaji wine in thanks for their guidance.) His socialist government was overthrown when Romania invaded in 1919, to be replaced by a series of weak leaders. By the time the talks were over in 1920, Hungary's delegation to Paris was led by the courtly, gracious Count Albert Apponyi – but the damage had been done in the opinions of the treaty's architects.

They were also swayed by clever politicking on behalf of Hungary's neighbors, especially the persuasive and charming Queen of Romania. Each of them wanted – and got – their slice of the land of the Magyars. And, finally, by the time the politicians got around to dealing with Hungary, which was one of the last countries on the agenda, they were worn out, distracted and not inclined to go the extra mile. "What ultimately weighed against Hungary was sheer inertia," as MacMillan puts it.

Hungary lost two-thirds of its land, which was reduced to 93,000 square kilometers, and nearly two-thirds of its population, which was reduced to 7.6 million. Millions of native Magyars were stranded in the new countries formed from the old. Not surprisingly, they were badly treated by their new landlords, who promptly set about removing all traces of Hungary from the language and public records.

Hungary lost its emotional, nostalgic heartland, Transylvania, which became part of Romania. Slovakia and Ruthenia became part of Czechoslovakia. Croatia, Slavonia, Vojvodina, and Bosnia formed a new country, Yugoslavia (and we all know how well *that* turned out). Galicia joined Poland, while the Burgenland went to Austria. Hungary barely hung on to the wine region of Tokaj to the north and the wine region of Villány to the south, and it almost lost the paprika-growing capital of Szeged, which would have been an unthinkable blow.

When Croatia became part of Yugoslavia, Hungary was deprived of its access to the sea. It also lost two-thirds of its roads and railroads. Its shipping system for goods was dismantled and so was much of its banking industry; at the same time, nearly two-thirds of arable land, 90 per cent of timber, and more than half of industrial plants became part of other countries.

For Hungary, the only bright spot in the whole scenario was that so much land had been given away that its new and newly expanded neighbors had to pick up a large part of the actual financial reparations that had been levied on the Magyars.

To this day in Hungary, "Trianon" is a word pronounced as if the speaker had just bitten into something at once rotten and rancid. One can only imagine what it was like in the 1920s, as Hungary tried to rebuild out of the devastation of its economic systems. Politically, the country swung hard to the left, then even harder to the right, trying to find someone, anyone, who could make sense of the mess. Meanwhile, there was poverty and food shortages, and not surprisingly, that deadly companion of conflict, disease.

Typhoid had been working its way throughout war-damaged Eastern and Central Europe, from revolutionary Russia through the much-invaded Ukraine, and on to Hungary and the Balkans. In 1928, it infected two little girls in a resort town in Hungary. One survived. The other did not.

For weeks, day and night, Aranka tended to her suffering babies, bathing their flushed little faces with cool water in a desperate attempt to bring their fevers down. Finally, Luizi's fever broke and she could smile again, and take a little food. Thank God, Aranka thought, and waited for Evike to recover. But Eva just lay there, shivering and sweating and in terrible pain, until her wasted body couldn't fight the disease any longer. The day Aranka buried her oldest daughter, she buried a part of her heart, too. Even though she had another baby, Magdolna, a year later, something in her had become hard and cold.

In that terrible year of 1929, she not only lost her beloved daughter but also lost her business and the last ties to her adored Aunt Terka. While she'd been tending to the two sick girls, she'd left the restaurant with her husband and brother. Jóska and Nándi had had a grand old time, inviting their friends over for meals on the house, raiding the wine cellar, using what little money they earned to play the ponies. When a heartsick Aranka returned to work, there was hardly anything left.

In October, the world's stock markets crashed. By the time Magdolna, who would always be known as the little finch Pintyi, was born a month later, the family had hit bottom. Jóska was drinking, Aranka was distracted, the babies were crying, and the business was failing. Aranka's mother, Agnes, had moved in with them, too, and while she could help Aranka around the house, she was another drain on finances. Jóska and Aranka knew they would have to do what they'd always vowed they would not. Jóska abandoned his pride, straightened his spine, and went begging to his parents.

It was five years since he'd last seen them, though he had kept in touch with his sister, Teréz, and brother, Kálmán. He knew that his sister was hopelessly in love with an officer in the newly rebuilt army and Kálmán was fulfilling the role Jóska was supposed to have played as the loyal heir, practical businessman and responsible big brother. He also knew that, through shrewd investments or simple good luck, József and Alujzia's fortune was more or less intact. They'd lost a bit on the stock market, but the business had remained largely unscathed throughout the war, the reparations, and the troubled times that followed.

In fact, they were doing so well that they'd built a summer home on the outskirts of Budapest, in a leafy enclave called Rákosszentmihály. Each June, when the mercury climbed into the 30s, bringing with it the pollution, humidity, and stink of a big city in summertime, they'd leave their apartment in the *belváros* and escape to the shady gardens of their summerhouse. They would return only when the opera season started up again in the fall.

But this was December, cold and gloomy, and his parents were ensconced in their city apartment. So it was to Budapest that Jóska traveled to tell his parents his sorry tale. When he arrived, they didn't offer him a drink but sat stolidly in their heavy armchairs, their faces cast into shadow by the wan winter light. Alujzia was still beautiful, he noticed, but had grown even harder, with severe lines etched beside her mouth, her posture so straight it looked as if you could snap her in two. József was even more distant than he'd been in Jóska's youth, gazing at a spot just over his son's shoulder as he began his petition. He stood before them, his hands clasped behind his back, struggling not to fidget or to shift his weight from side to side like a desperate little boy who has to pee. In fact, he did have to pee. And he really would have liked a drink. But he got through the story of the recent years, then took a deep breath.

"You know I wouldn't ask it for myself," he said, hating the way his voice squeaked just a little bit, hating to have to beg at all. "But Christmas is coming. We have no food for the babies and no money for the heat. I spent the last of our money on the doctor for Aranka, and she's not getting better as fast as she should. I know it's a lot to ask, but could you help us? A loan, or a job, or something? I will do anything you want, anything, if you just help us out."

Silence.

"It's not for me," he said softly, fighting tears. "Don't do it for me. Do it for your grandchildren. You wouldn't let a Wintermantel starve to death, would you?"

More silence, then his parents looked at each other. Finally, József spoke.

"Very well," he said. "Your family can stay in Rákosszentmihály."

"Tha—"

"But that's not all. You will come and work with me, and learn the business. On my terms. You will follow my rules, and you will behave the way a Wintermantel should behave, not like a spoiled, drunken child. Or you – and your children – will be on your own again."

"I will make you proud, Papa," Jóska said. What he wanted to say was "I will make you love me," but even he knew what a miracle that would be.

So Jóska and Aranka moved into the summerhouse, along with Aranka's mother, Agnes. They had to sneak Agnes in at first, since Alujzia, who could barely tolerate her daughter-in-law, absolutely refused to acknowledge the peasant who was her mother. But Aranka put her tiny foot down with Jóska and insisted Agnes come with them. Aranka knew that she would need her mother's help – and she knew that her mother needed her, too. As she grew older, sweet, kind Agnes had become frail, and bewildered by her changing world. She was afraid to live on her own and she relied heavily on her daughter and son-in-law to take care of her. Still, as much as she loved and needed her mother, Aranka couldn't help but be frustrated by the added responsibility for a poor country woman with little education, failing health, and no ambition but to be warm, safe, and well fed.

It was around this time that Aranka's own sweetness began to turn bitter. She was angry with God for taking her daughter's life. She was angry with her husband and brother for ruining her business. She was angry with the politicians for plunging her country into poverty. And she was angry with her parents-in-law, or maybe just with fate, for turning the carefree lover she'd married into a worried businessman who could find solace only in the bottom of a wineglass.

There wasn't much she could do about any of it, though, so she never complained, but grimly set her jaw, and got on with the task at hand. Day by day, she laughed less and was more impatient with the family, pulling roughly on the girls' sashes when she dressed them, speaking sharply to her mother when she asked a question, banging the pot lids around, ordering Jóska about with a new, hard note in her voice.

Jóska, on the other hand, surprised everyone by doing well at his new job. After a couple of years, he opened his own refinery, where he developed a smelting process that he published in a small book. He began to make a little money, but his business wasn't thriving the way Aranka thought it should. So she stepped in, reorganized the books, and eventually took over the business end of things. If she could make a restaurant a success during the dark postwar years, she could do wonders with a refinery during the years of rebuilding.

Soon, the money was pouring in as fast as if they'd created it at their own factory. The girls went to the best school in town. Jóska had a new Mercedes-Benz. Aranka had a new fur coat each year. And the larder was always full of the best food, the wine cellar filled with the finest wine.

Then Jóska decided it was time to share the wealth with the rest of his family. Like so many children rejected by their parents, he was desperate to prove his worth to them and maybe to buy a little bit of love. Of course, you can't buy love, or even respect, and in his heart he must have known that, but it didn't stop him from trying.

He built a new house at Rákosszentmihály for his mother and his newly retired father. He built another house next door for his sister. Teréz had finally married her soldier, who had gone on to get his medical degree and was still trying to establish his practice. (When they married, the Wintermantels had to pay his annual officer's commission, which turned out to be a rather extravagant sum and might explain why Pintyi says the only advice Aranka ever gave her was "Don't marry an officer – and never run a restaurant.") Jóska's cousin Hanzi built a house nearby, too, and so did his friend Nori, and soon he was surrounded by all the family he could ever have wished for.

Now that his father was retired, Jóska took over the apartment on Rákóczi Út, with the family business downstairs. And although they already had the summerhouse in Rákosszentmihály, he wanted a vacation property, too, a place by the lake where the girls could run around and play the way he did as a little boy. So he looked around Lake Balaton until he found the perfect property, a piece of land on the north shore, across the lake from Siófok in a small town called Balatonalmádi. And that's where he built his dream home.

Balaton is a big lake, the biggest in Europe, but it's also a shallow one. It is 600 square kilometers in area, 77 kilometers long, and 14 kilometers at its widest point, but it is only about 12 meters deep at its deepest. Still, when the storms blow in, as they often do in the summer months, the winds howl through the trees, the thunder crashes as if it's trying to get right down the chimney, and the waves rear up huge and angry.

Jóska's house was a huge stone villa right on the shore. From the terrace in front, you could stroll a few meters to the lake's edge and jump right in. Or, if you were a more cautious type, you could walk sedately into the lake down a flight of stone steps. There was always a boat tied up there, too, and you could take it out for a paddle along the shore and look at all the other houses, knowing all along that the Wintermantel villa was the most beautiful, with willow trees along the shore, and flowers in pots all over the verandah.

Because Jóska and his family shared the Lake Balaton house with his sister and her family (Kálman built his own place not far away), he had it designed as a duplex, with his family on the left if you looked at it from the lake, and hers on the right. From the street outside, Neptun Útca, Jóska would drive his Mercedes Benz down an alley lined on both sides with poplar trees that rustled in the breeze like debutantes sharing secrets at a party. The house was square and covered in ochre stucco softened by wisteria vines. It was more formal than one would expect of a beach cottage today, but still more casual than their family homes in Budapest. The furniture was lighter and more whimsical, Biedermier rather than Victorian in style. Instead of gloomy portraits, colorful tapestries and watercolor landscapes hung on the walls. The china was Herend, but in a jaunty forget-me-not pattern instead of the more ornate style of their formal dishes.

On the lake side, a beautiful verandah swept across both halves of the house. On warm summer nights, the two families would meet on the verandah for dinner, usually something simple and hearty that Aranka cooked up while the children – her own two were soon joined by Teréz's son, Jóska, and daughter, Maju – played all day. Sometimes, Luizi and Pintyi would help in the kitchen as Aranka made *palacsinta* (puh-la-CHEEN-ta), crêpes stuffed with plum or apricot jam, or maybe a big bowl of noodles. Friends and other family members would join them on weekends, including a famous illustrator who would make little watercolor sketches of Luizi and Pintyi at work and at play. They would sip the local crisp white wine as the sun set and the children chased each other through the trees, happy in the knowledge that for once everything in their world was good and at peace.

Or so they thought. Soon, however, Hungary's place at the crossroads of Europe put it into a precarious position once again. From the east, it was threatened by Stalin and communism, brought by Russia's brutal Red Army and its attendant Soviet advisors. From the west, it was beset by Hitler and fascism, courtesy of Germany's racist, anti-Semitic Nazis and their quest for world domination.

Hungary hadn't even finished rebuilding after the First World War. It had no allies and was surrounded by enemies. And now it was between two super powers aching to flex their military muscles and expand their philosophies.

Throughout the 1930s, Hungary had been led by the right-wing "regent" Admiral Miklós Horthy. (Hungary hadn't given up on the monarchy, exactly, it just couldn't find a new king.) Horthy's aim was to establish law and order, to rebuild the economy weakened by the First World War, and to restore the lands taken away from Hungary by Trianon. For a while, it had all worked out fine. The economy was improving, crime was down, the government was democratically elected, relatively rational discussions were being held in the parliament, and some of the lands – most notably, part of Transylvania – were returned.

Then in 1939, Germany invaded Poland and the world was at war again. In Hungary, the government worked furiously to stay out of the conflict, but its own people were already choosing sides. Many of them had leaned to the right after the First World War, blaming the country's ill-timed flirtation with socialism for the disaster of Trianon. All the little right-wing parties that had played at politics throughout the twenties and thirties merged in 1938 to form the Hungarian Nationalist Socialist Party, better known as the Arrow Cross for its symbol of crossed arrows. Just as in the early days of Nazi Germany, small bands of right-wing thugs emerged, brutal youth who used any political excuse to terrorize the citizenry. Many of them later switched sides and used their violent skills on behalf of the communists instead. Communism, too, continued to grow during the leadup to the Second World War, helped by Soviet advance parties intent on ensuring a warm – or at least compliant – welcome when the Red Army finally invaded.

The family patriarch, József, died in 1941. His oldest son, grief-stricken and adrift, looked for a new father figure to replace the one he never really had. He found it in the political movement that was taking over the country. The club he'd belonged to in university had joined the Arrow Cross, and he thought the party stood for all the things he believed in – a stable economy, well-regulated governance, the return of the Hungarian homeland. He didn't really believe all those things they were saying about what the Arrow Cross's German cousins were doing up in Poland, but he also didn't really care. Everything was such a mess – his family, his country, his world – that he was grateful to anyone who could impose a bit of order on things. So he went to meetings, he gave them money, and he wore the Arrow Cross insignia. Still, he must have felt that something was not quite right about his new friends, for he refused to run for office under the Arrow Cross banner, even though he was asked repeatedly, and he never fired a gun in its name. Nevertheless, he would one day pay the price for his ill-considered membership. He would pay with his health, his fortune, his family's pride, and almost with his life.

Maybe he joined the Arrow Cross because, as Pintyi remembers, he simply liked walking around in a uniform. Or maybe it was because, as Luizi remembers, he wanted to save his business and protect his family, and they were both situated right on the edge of the Jewish city. And that was, increasingly, a dangerous place to be.

Hungary had long been a safe haven for Jews in Europe, though not always a comfortable one. There were so many different ethnic groups in the mix – Huns and Magyars and Serbs and Croats and Swabians and Moldavians and Galicians and so many others – that people had mostly learned to co-exist. That doesn't mean they were always gracious and polite to each other. Among the groups that were regularly discriminated against were the Roma, Jews, Romanians, and Swabians. All were considered "foreigners," even though they had lived in Hungary for centuries.

It was the country's Jewish population that became most vulnerable, especially after 1933, when Germany declared the Jews *untermenschen*, "sub-human," and passed a series of cruel and restrictive laws prohibiting them from most arenas of life. At first, Hungary resisted doing the same. Even though the right-wing leader Horthy was no fan of the Jewish people, he knew what an important role they played in the country's financial and intellectual life. Besides, like any true Hungarian, he hated being told what to do. Yet, isolated from the west by geography and politics, and threatened by the Red Army from the east, the country's options appeared to be few and frightening.

By 1938, Hungary knuckled under to the constant pressure from Germany and its own ultra-right-wing nationalists who blamed the Jews for the disaster of Trianon. (Specifically, they blamed the communist leader Béla Kun, who was a non-practising Jew, but his people got to share in the Hungarian anger.) That year, Hungary enacted its first law against the Jews, designed to curtail their presence in the banks, the stock market, the universities, and the professions. A second law was passed in 1939, a third in 1941, each restricting their activities more and more. But if the government leaders hoped that by appeasing Germany with these grudging changes they could keep Hitler's goons outside Hungary's borders, they were sorely mistaken.

On March 19, 1944, Germany invaded Hungary. On August 27, so did the Soviets.

By then, it was clear that Germany was losing the war, even though it didn't officially surrender for another year. Still, defeat came too late for half a million Jewish Hungarians. Shortly after Germany invaded and established its puppet government, the order came to round up and begin deporting the country's Jewish citizens. The first trains began to roll toward the Auschwitz-Birkenau "labor camps" on May 15. Even though the government was alerted soon afterward that the Germans were killing people en masse at Auschwitz, the trains didn't stop until July 10. In less than two months, more than 400,000 people had been shipped out. Few, if any, survived.

Even though anti-Semitism was rife in Hungary, as it was throughout so much of Europe, some small sense of compassion remained. Many Hungarians quietly rebelled against the orders and helped smuggle a number of the country's Jewish citizens to neutral countries such as Sweden and Switzerland, which arranged safe passage to America and other Nazi-free havens.

Even Jóska, outwardly an Arrow Cross loyalist, refused to simply play along. When we were kids our dad used to tell us this story about our grandfather and how he became a reluctant – well, not a hero, perhaps, but a decent man in a time of unspeakable indecency.

In addition to his shop and apartment on Dohany Útca, Jóska had a successful metal works factory right in the middle of the Jewish district called Erzsébet Town. He'd received the contract to make dog tags for the army, and business was doing so well that he'd increased his staff to more than thirty people. The rest of the district, though, was not doing well, for under one of the anti-Jewish laws it had been transformed into the city's ghetto, a place of fear and poverty. During the day, people went about their business quickly and silently, with faces averted. At night, the streets were empty and apartments were darkened as bands of thugs prowled the streets looking for Jews to beat up.

Each day, shortly after dawn, Jóska walked to the factory from his nearby apartment, past boarded-up shops and frightened faces. One morning, as he opened the doors, he saw a flicker of movement out of the corner of his eye and sensed a sort of vibration in the air. Or was he just imagining things? Then he heard it again: a rustle of fabric, an indrawn breath, a shimmer of fear in a dark corner. Jóska walked over to one of the metal presses that would be stamping out hundreds of dog tags in just a few hours. In the shadow behind it stood a man, a woman, and a child, each holding a small bundle, their terrified eyes shining in the dim morning light. Jóska recognized one of his employees and, without thinking, nodded his head. Without breaking eye contact, the man nodded back.

Jóska gazed back at him for a moment, then deliberately turned around and walked out of the factory. He treated himself to a long, leisurely breakfast at a nearby coffee shop, and when he went back, the man was at work on the press. There was no sign of his wife and daughter. But after that, Jóska started coming in later and later, just in case someone else had decided to take refuge overnight.

According to family lore, two of the people who took advantage of this fortuitous circumstance were the family doctor and his wife. Until the day they left Hungary, they often spent the night there, safe from the vicious fists of the Arrow Cross hooligans and the political machine that was sending people off to the death camps with brutal efficiency. After all, what could have been more secure than a metal works factory that was not only in the middle of the ghetto, but was owned by a man who may have been a fascist, but was also the most soft-hearted guy in the neighborhood?

By the fall of 1945, Hungary was dragged into the war for real. Since Germany was already occupying the country, Hungary joined its traditional ally to fight an even greater terror – the Red Army. Soon the country's cities and plains became a bloody battleground for Germany, the Allies, and the Soviet Union. Urban centers that had been painstakingly rebuilt after the First World War were reduced, once again, to heaps of rubble. The chaos was so great that when the grand Hotel Gellért in Buda was bombed, no one knew who did it; the hotel was Germany's headquarters in Budapest, so it could have been the Allies, the Russians, Hungarian rebels, or even the Germans themselves, destroying things as they retreated. Overnight, bridges vanished, buildings were destroyed, and trains derailed.

All through the fall, Aranka and the girls had been traveling from Budapest to Lake Balaton, gradually moving their belongings over so that, when the time was right, they'd be able to escape from the Russians. Teréz and her children, Maju and Jóska, had already moved in on their side of the villa. One day, Pintyi and her mother, escorted by cousin Hanzi and Jóska's handyman, Meszaros, were bringing some Persian carpets and sterling silver to the lake house. The slow-moving train was packed with hundreds of other frightened people, each with his or her own bundle of valuables. All around them was the activity of a nation at war – troop movements, tanks, military jeeps and, above, warplanes. The train chugged westward, approaching the important junction at Székesfehérvár. About five kilometers from the town, a squadron of Allied bombers flew low overhead. There was a soft whoosh, a whistling sound, and a loud bang, followed by darkness and the patter of debris falling from the sky like rain. Then another bang. And another. There was screaming – from the brakes as the train screeched to a halt, from metal buckling under the strain, from terrified people.

Panic-stricken passengers fled from the train, running in all directions. Aranka, Pintyi, Hanzi, and Meszaros managed to stay together as they fled across the fields. They found a peasant hut and scrambled into the cellar, where they listened to the bombs falling outside. After what seemed like hours, the airplanes left, the drone of their engines fading in the distance. They waited a while longer, in case the planes decided to come back and unleash more devastation. When they finally emerged from the cellar, blinking in the sudden light, it was to a world transformed.

The train was a twisted heap of metal, so they began the long and grisly walk toward the station at Székesfehérvár. Pintyi remembers that the leaves of the trees were slick with blood. Body parts were strewn everywhere; some were caught up in the trees and the electrical wires overhead. At one point, a severed arm fell from a branch above them and landed right at their feet. There were so many bodies strewn everywhere that in later years Pintyi said it reminded her of the scene in *Gone With the Wind* when Scarlett looks out across the station yard filled with dying soldiers. These weren't soldiers, though, but women and children, old men and young boys.

In the midst of this horror, the Allied planes returned, swooping down so low that Pintyi could see the goggles the pilots wore. The airmen just looked back and opened fire, machine-gunning the dazed survivors, killing dozens more of them as they ran for shelter in the nearby trees.

Hours later, Pintyi and the others reached Székesfehérvár, and hours after that they finally stumbled into Balatonalmádi, where Agnes, Luizi, and the cousins had heard about the attack and were waiting in terror. No one ever explained why the "liberators" they'd been awaiting for so long had tried to kill a trainload of women and children. Yet, through some miracle, they'd all survived without a scratch. And here they were, in their favorite house, their refuge, their sanctuary, where the lake was shimmering in the evening sun and there was plenty of love and food and good wine. And here they'd stay until the war was over and peace would come again. Or so they thought.

CHAPTER 5

What to Eat When You're in Jail

As in the days of the Huns and the Magyars, terror once again swept in from the east. Like a malevolent advance party preparing the people for the horror to come, rumors swept the country about the invading Russian army. Many of the Red Army soldiers were poor, uneducated boys from farms in the country's remotest regions. As they moved westward, they unleashed savage brutality, looting homes and businesses, and when they were done, burning them down. They killed and maimed anyone who got in their way. They raped young women, little children, old ladies. They took them by force, often in gangs, often for hours, leaving them bruised and broken, leaving them nearly dead and wishing they were.

The Russians marched into Hungary in August 1944, laying waste to villages and small towns as they headed west into the capital. By Christmas, they were in Buda. By spring, the Germans were in flight, and the Hungarians were left to defend themselves.

The first Russians arrived in Balatonalmádi in February 1945 and moved into the Wintermantel villa. They drank all Jóska's liquor, broke Aranka's beautiful furniture, crushed all the flowers in the garden, and tore up the tapestries that covered the walls. They helped themselves to whatever valuables took their fancy; everything else they destroyed. They'd never seen indoor plumbing before and were frightened by the rushing sound of the water closet, so they used the bathtub as a toilet. Soon the house was filled not only with shattered pieces of wood and china, but the stink of sewage.

At least Jóska and Aranka didn't have to watch their beloved home being destroyed. Even though they'd expected to stay there for the duration of the war and maybe forever, the family was long gone by the time the Russians arrived. Like thousands of others, they had decided it was time to leave Hungary.

All the previous summer and fall, the girls had been living in Balatonalmádi with their grandmother Agnes, while Aranka and Jóska remained in the city until the last possible moment. Jóska stayed in the *belváros*, running his business and keeping up appearances. Aranka lived in the family compound at Rákosszentmihály, secretly preparing for departure. She sewed money into her clothes and packed up the smallest, most valuable pieces of jewelry. Then she buried the silver and hid the liquor, hoping that there would be something for them to come back to when everything was over. She might just as well not have bothered. Alujzia, her mother-in-law, was watching her from behind a pair of lace curtains and when the Russians did arrive, Alujzia handed the hoard over immediately, hoping that they'd give her preferential treatment over the neighbors.

Finally, early in the new year of 1945, the day of departure arrived. In downtown Budapest, Jóska visited his now-closed factory one last time. He looked fondly at the machinery gleaming in the empty rooms. There were no frightened faces hiding in the shadows, no smells of hot oil and hot metal, no thumping and clanking from the presses, no crowds of employees gossiping and smoking and working hard. It would be the last time he'd see the business he'd built. By the time he returned, the building had been demolished and the machines were gone. The new government had appropriated them and taken them to the mint, where they pumped out pengös and forints for decades to come.

Jóska got in his cream-colored 1939 Mercedes Benz and drove to Rákosszentmihály to pick up Aranka and have one last terrible fight with his mother about his plans. Then the couple drove through the night to Balatonalmádi to get the girls and Agnes. There, Aranka wrapped silver and jewelry in Persian rugs, as much as they could carry. Then, just as she had in Rákosszentmihály, she and Jóska buried the rest of the silver near a willow tree by the lake. If only they'd thought to make a map showing where, exactly, they'd buried it, they might actually have found it again one day.

Finally, with one last backward glance at the home they'd loved so much, the family left, wheels crunching over the gravel of the drive as the bare poplar trees whispered above. They drove to Szombathely near the Austrian border, where they hoped they could sit out the rest of the war in safety. They had a place to stay, an apartment belonging to a friend who had already escaped to France.

Because of its strategic location, Szombathely was filled with all sorts of interesting people: German politicians, Italian consuls, Hungarian military officers, family friends old and new, and a handful of cute teenage boys. Luizi and Pintyi, who were seventeen and fifteen respectively, had so much fun flirting with them that they almost forgot there was a war on. They were like a couple of Jane Austen's heroines when the garrison was stationed at Bath, with dinners and parties and kisses on snowy evenings. It wasn't such a bad way to spend the war.

Until the Americans bombed them again, and then things didn't seem like so much fun any more.

It was a cloudless morning and the planes arrived seemingly from nowhere, their distant hum quickly becoming a deafening roar. The first bomb exploded in an enormous blast that rattled glasses and sent chunks of dirt and debris flying through the air. Soon, the bombs were falling in a steady and deadly patter. Aranka and the girls hid in the basement, knowing they wouldn't survive if the building took a direct hit. Again, they were lucky, and survived unhurt. Many people died or were terribly injured, their houses and businesses left in ruins.

After the bombing, more and more people began leaving. The girls would be gossiping with a friend one afternoon and by the next morning, she and her family would be gone. Where? Who knows? Everyone knew there was going to be an almighty battle between the Americans, the Russians, and the Germans, and no one wanted to be caught in the middle of it. So they fled, farther west, farther north, hoping and praying they'd find refuge somewhere.

Then Easter rolled around, and for the first time, the two girls wouldn't be able to partake in one of their favorite traditions. Every Easter Monday for centuries, boys would chase the maidens they liked best and douse them with a bucket of water. As they did so, the boys would sing a little rhyme:

Through the greenwood going
I saw a blue violet growing.
I saw it start to wither.
Can I water this flower?

The girls would shriek and run away, but they'd secretly be delighted and would always offer the boys some home-baked goods and a glass of wine. As time went on, the bucket of water was replaced by a spritz of cologne, and the tradition moved from country to city, from peasant class to upper class, from callow youth to men and women of all ages. The tradition is still practised today. But at Easter 1945, Luizi and Pintyi would not be getting splashed by any of their boyfriends.

A few days earlier, the news had come that the Russians were west of Budapest. Jóska had lingered as long as he could – he loved his country too much to want to leave it – but finally decided that no corner of Hungary was now safe. The army had taken his car, so instead of hunting for chocolate eggs, the family was suddenly, desperately, hunting for transportation. By then, there was little available because so many people had already fled and the Hungarian army – or what was left of it – was using the few trucks and carts and cars they'd left behind. Eventually, though, Jóska found a truck driver who was traveling north. He bought him several rounds of palinka, played a few rounds of cards with him, and the driver agreed to take the family as far as the border town of Kőszeg.

The night before they left, Jóska decided he had to see his lover, Emmi, one last time. Back then, before the years of jail and torture and humiliation, before the communists took everything from him, Jóska was a charmer and a bit of a rake. He was such a determined flirt that he even flirted with the nuns at his daughters' school, bringing them trays of sweets and bottles of champagne – to make sure, he said with a wink, that they would treat his girls especially well. And even though he loved his family, he always had a girlfriend on the side – Emmi was just the most recent. It wasn't unusual for a European man in his position to have a mistress, but it still made Aranka bitter and resentful.

Back at the apartment, Aranka, Agnes, and the girls were packing the few possessions they had left. The girls were thinking about leaving another set of friends and about the dangers of the journey ahead. They went to bed early to be well rested for the next day, but sleep proved to be elusive. Midnight came and went and Pintyi still couldn't fall asleep. Then the clock chimed 1 a.m. and she suddenly realized that she hadn't heard her father come in. Worse, she knew where he had to be.

Quietly, so as not to wake her mother and start the inevitable shouting and screaming, she grabbed her coat and ran outside into the cold night to the apartment where Emmi lived with her husband and teenage son, Imre. Pintyi rang for the elevator, hoping she'd be able to get her father quickly and leave without any fuss. But when the elevator arrived at the ground level, it was full – with Emmi, her husband, Imre and Jóska. Jóska was drunk. In fact, he was so drunk he could barely stand up. He slumped against the elevator wall, unfocused eyes gazing off into the distance, humming a little tune. Emmi and her family were crowded around him in a breathless silence, as if Pintyi had just interrupted an argument that had been going on all evening. Pintyi never did learn where they had all been going when she came across them. When Jóska saw his daughter, he stared at her in confusion, unsure for a moment who she was.

Pintyi grabbed him by the hands and started pulling him out of the elevator. "Father, you must come," she said. "Everyone's waiting for us and the truck is coming. We must go."

"No!" Emmi screamed. She clutched him around the neck fiercely and wrapped her body around his. "Józsi, Józsi, you can't leave me."

Pintyi pulled harder on her father's hands. Emmi held on even tighter. Her son and husband just stood there, mutely watching the two women struggling over the man who had disrupted their family life. One can only imagine what must have been going through their minds. Finally Jóska lurched toward Pintyi, and Emmi fell back sobbing into the waiting arms of her son and husband.

On the street, Jóska took a few halting steps, then sank to the ground. Pintyi shouted at him to keep moving. She begged, she threatened, she cried a little bit. She even slapped his face, trying to bring him around. Jóska just sat there, too drunk to speak, too drunk to move. Maybe he thought that if he just stayed still, he wouldn't have to leave the next morning; maybe he was just too drunk to think at all.

Finally, Pintyi managed to get him to his feet. She put his arm over her shoulders and took his weight on her small frame, and they began their slow, staggering journey back to the apartment. When he stumbled and fell, she'd drag him along until he could get to his feet again. Finally, they reached the apartment. No one came to greet them as Pintyi dumped her father onto the sofa and took off his shoes. The rooms were dark and silent, yet it seemed to Pintyi that the air was filled with the tension of people who are angry and frightened. Jóska may have been the only one who slept at all that night, although his sleep was merely the loud, restless stupor of the drunkard. It was a long, wakeful night for the rest of the family.

With the first cold, gray light, their truck arrived. Carrying their clothes and valuables, they climbed aboard in silence – Jóska too hung over to speak, Aranka too angry, Agnes and the girls too afraid of Aranka's anger to risk provoking it by saying the wrong thing. It wasn't an auspicious beginning to the journey, and from there things would only get worse.

After several hours of driving over bumpy, rutted roads, with the sound of machine-gun fire always off in the distance, the driver pulled to a stop in the border town of Kőszeg. "Sorry, this is as far as I go," he said, helping them out of the back. They grabbed their parcels and began walking, but they hadn't gotten very far when they realized they wouldn't be able to carry the heavy rugs filled with silver any further. So they chose a house they liked and dropped the parcels off on a stranger's doorstep.

They walked and walked, and as they walked, they encountered more and more people, all of them heading west. They joined a queue of thousands of other refugees walking into the unknown, young and old, men and women, some carrying babies, others carrying small packs with all they had left in the world. Eventually, they met up with a Hungarian army convoy of horse-drawn wagons heading west. The soldiers, too, knew the war was lost and the Russians were coming, so they were escaping to Austria in hopes of somehow surviving the war. Jóska asked if his family could join them, for safety and companionship. The tattered band of soldiers agreed to let the family walk along beside them.

It was cold and miserable and everyone was hungry, for there was no food to be had and no money to buy it in any case. They walked in a despondent, fearful silence that was broken only whenever a warplane flew overhead and began machine-gunning the convoy. Then everyone would drop whatever they were carrying and run off the road and into a nearby field. They would hit the ground, cowering, burying their faces in their hands and waiting for the guns to stop. One moment they would pray that the bullets wouldn't hit them; the next moment they'd pray a bullet would reach its target and put them out of their misery.

Each step that took them farther and farther away from their life in Hungary was painful, but for Agnes it was excruciating. Aranka's mother was by now seventy-two years old and had fallen arches and bunions so bad that she had to cut slits in the sides of her shoes to accommodate them. Her feet were swollen and tender and aching even when she had nothing more strenuous to do than stand in the kitchen stirring a pot of dumplings. It took only a few kilometers of rough road for her to realize that there was no way she would be able to walk all the way into Austria. She plodded ahead, tears in her eyes, walking more and more slowly. "Hurry, hurry," her impatient daughter kept urging her, until Jóska realized what was happening and took pity. He asked one of the drivers if Agnes could ride in the back of his wagon. Of course, he said. So they bundled up their last few possessions and gave them to Agnes to carry. They helped her climb aboard, and watched as the carriage drove off ahead of them.

"And that's how we lost her," Pintyi says.

An eternity later they'd made it across the border and struck camp just as the sun began to set. Aranka began preparing a little food and Jóska walked around getting to know his new neighbors and hoping to find a little brandy to take the edge off. Meanwhile, Pintyi and Luizi searched among all the thousands of people for their grandmother. They looked in each wagon and peeked in each tent. They asked everyone they could, but no one had seen her, no one knew where she was.

Finally someone said that he thought there might have been two convoys, and that the other one had gone in a different direction. Deeply frightened by now, the girls returned to their own campsite and told their parents. Aranka, feeling guilty and angry in equal measures, told the girls to keep looking. Pintyi and Luizi decided the only thing to do was to retrace their steps in the hope that the wagon had stopped for a rest or had broken down. They found some bicycles somewhere and started pedaling furiously back the way they came.

It was almost dark along the rutted, tree-lined road when they heard a voice shouting, *"Halt! Halt!"* The girls slammed on their brakes, skidding in the gravel, as a man on horseback appeared out of the gloom. He was a German army officer and his face was puckered in concern. "Quickly, quickly go back the way you came," he said. "There are Russian soldiers all around us and it won't be safe a minute longer." Suddenly the girls realized that the whispers they'd been hearing for the past few kilometers weren't the trees rustling in the breeze, but Russian speakers hiding behind the bushes at the side of the road. Terrified, they turned around and rode even faster back to the camp. If they'd had the fear of God in their hearts on their way out, on the return trip they knew they had the devil at their back.

They never did find their grandmother. Although the family searched for Agnes for years, they never found any sign of her, never found anyone who knew what had happened to her, never found a single clue to her disappearance. She'd just vanished and left a hole in their lives that would never heal.

It was a miserable little group that clustered around the fire that night, stomachs churning with hunger and fear and worry. Although they were exhausted, they found it difficult to sleep. Pintyi dozed fitfully, waking several times with a gasp and a flash of terror. Come the morning, the convoy kept moving inexorably west. There was no time to take pity on a sweet old lady who'd gotten lost; she was just one more casualty of the war. Although they didn't have the energy to weep or mourn, they walked with heavy hearts, especially Aranka, who was sick with guilt. She'd been impatient and angry with her mother so often as she struggled with raising the two girls, running the business, and watching her husband drink and cheat and make terrible political decisions.

At night, the group would stop and scrounge in the fields for food, but all they could find were a few half-rotted potatoes that had survived the winter. They'd cook them over the embers of the soldiers' fires. In this way, tired, cold, hungry, and heartbroken, the family trudged across Austria until they crossed the border into Germany. "I can't remember where we left the convoy, but from there we went to Passau, Germany, and in Passau there was a huge, huge air raid and there were bodies all over," Pintyi says. "Then we found a nice Hungarian gentleman sitting in a 1920s car that belonged to Grand Duchess Augusta. Mind you, she wasn't there, but her chauffeur was. He was just sitting there."

The car had run out of gas and so, apparently, had the chauffeur. He sat there looking at the destruction around him with the listlessness of someone who's had one shock too many. Now that his car was useless, he had no idea what to do next. Jóska asked whether the chauffeur would be willing to give them the car if Jóska could find some gas for it. Sure, said the chauffeur, and Jóska, who had become quite an expert at finding all sorts of useful things, did indeed scrounge some fuel. He dropped the chauffeur off at the duchess's apartment and pointed the car in the direction of Munich, where he had family and friends he hoped would help.

They got as far as the picturesque village of Rosenheim. Late that night, they rolled into the main square, where the car gave a sad little cough and ran out of gas. As they sat there trying to decide what to do next, Aranka dropped one of her diamond earrings. She lit her lighter to find it. "Don't," Jóska implored, but Aranka, who was still angry with him about the fiasco with Emmi, ignored him and kept searching.

"We were sitting in the center of Rosenheim. The Americans were coming and the Germans were occupying, and we were in the middle," Pintyi remembers. "One minute we were the only people sitting in the only car in a dark plaza. The next minute, everyone was shooting at us.

"Father was shot through the lung. There was so much blood. He had a cold, and whenever he coughed the blood was just spurting up into the air. It was the first of May and it was snowing on top of everything."

While the Germans and the Americans continued shooting at each other, Aranka and the girls dragged Jóska to a darkened doorway.

Aranka tried to stanch the flow of blood while Luizi and Pintyi desperately searched for help and shelter.

They knocked on every door, tried every doorknob, and banged on every window, but no one was answering and nothing was open. Finally, Luizi grabbed one handle that worked. "Here's something," she called to Pintyi. She stepped inside — and disappeared, right into a neck-deep pile of foul-smelling muck. It was an old outhouse, but the floor must have rotted through or the boards been removed for some reason, and she'd plunged right into the stinking mess below. By the time Pintyi managed to pull her out, they were both covered in excrement, sobbing and wretched and terribly frightened.

When they got back to Aranka, Jóska was gone. Despite Aranka's pleas, the Americans had picked him up and, thinking he was either dead or dying, simply tossed his body on a wagon filled with corpses. It took ages for him to get medical attention, and by then infection had set in. He was in the hospital for months; when he recovered, he was sent to a prisoner of war camp to await some decision about his fate.

Meanwhile, his family was stuck in Rosenheim, waiting for news. They started with no money, no food, and nowhere to live, but Aranka held to her creed of "Don't look back, look forward," and carved a new life for them.

In a suburb called Westerndorf, Luizi and Pintyi found they could work the fields for accommodation. At first they shared the other workers' food, a sort of yogurt they all ate from a communal bucket. Later, the Americans gave the refugees meal tickets so they could eat in a local restaurant. Pintyi remembers her first proper meal after so long: "It was potato soup with potato and potato, three kinds of potato."

While the girls toiled outdoors, Aranka learned to make shoes and started to take in sewing. She made shirts and coats and pants, and when the Americans learned how handy she was with a needle and thread, they began bringing her all their uniforms to alter. "They were very vain," Pintyi recalls, "and they wanted them to fit right to their bodies."

Months later, they finally learned what would be happening to Jóska. The Americans had already handed him over to the Germans.

The Germans would hand him to the Hungarians, the Hungarians to the Soviets. Like thousands of others, he would be going back to Budapest to face charges on war crimes. So Aranka and the girls returned to Budapest and waited some more.

That's how Jóska ended up at the "House of Horrors" at 60 Andrássy Út. In 1939, the Arrow Cross party had made the old villa its headquarters – the "House of Loyalty," they'd called it. By the end of the war, when the communists had taken over the country and were building their new Soviet state, it had been taken over by the State Security Department, better known as the ÁVO. The ÁVO's job was interrogation, torture, and imprisonment; it infiltrated schools and churches, got neighbors to spy on each other, abolished free speech, and eradicated democratic political parties. A few years later, a new force emerged called the State Security Authority, or ÁVH, which was an even higher power than the police and took over the House of Horrors until the 1980s. Today the building houses the Terror Háza, a remarkable museum that explores the two terrors of the mid- and late twentieth century, fascist and communist both.

Jóska was the guy they wanted, of course, but for a while they brought in Aranka and Kálmán and Teréz, too, for a little encouragement. Perhaps the ÁVO thought that if Jóska saw the people he loved locked up in the cold, damp cells with him, he'd tell them all he knew. Unfortunately, he didn't know that much, so the family waited and waited for his release.

Some of the cells were so small you could only stand in them. Some had room to lie down, but no beds, so prisoners had to sleep on the cold concrete floor. Others always had an inch or two of freezing water on the floor so you could never get warm, and after a while your feet began to rot. According to records at the Terror Háza, prisoners weren't allowed to bathe or, at times, go to the toilet. They weren't allowed to change their clothes or underwear, weren't allowed to have toilet paper, soap, towels, toothbrushes, or toothpaste. They were fed once a day, a ration of 490 calories, and they were beaten frequently.

At night, the interrogations would be held. The prisoners would be sleep-, food- and water-deprived to prepare them for the ordeal. Then the questioning would begin, with the help of electric shocks, burning cigarettes, pliers, beatings, and all manner of psychological torture. It would go on for hours, for days, for weeks, for months.

Alujzia was terrified for her favorite son and furious with her oldest for letting his shenanigans, political and otherwise, embroil the whole family. Jóska, who had once been the life of the party and everybody's best buddy, was suddenly the least popular guy in town. His family was angry with him, the Americans didn't want him, the Germans turned their backs on him, and even his own government only wanted to punish him.

The problem was, it didn't appear that Jóska had really done anything they could punish him for. When he came up for trial, there was no evidence against him, no proof of any crime he may have committed other than being in the wrong place – and the wrong political party – at the wrong time.

Not that it mattered to a court that was looking not only to punish war criminals, but to remove the wealthy and powerful from public life, and to silence anyone who could provide a real opposition. It was well known that kulaks (the Soviet's dismissive name for rural property owners), the bourgeois, and aristocrats received much harsher sentences for the same crimes than poor peasants or workers. It didn't do Jóska any good that he had been so rich, nor that he had tried to escape the Russians when they arrived. He was branded a troublemaker and enemy of the new state, and for years his entire family paid the price.

"We don't judge you for what we know you've done, we judge you for what we don't know," the judge said to Jóska, and sentenced him to five years in prison for being a class enemy. Jóska appealed the sentence and it was eventually reduced to three-and-a-half years.

"It took the life out of him," Pintyi says now. "He was never the same after that." In later years, Jóska and Aranka never, ever talked about what had happened. "They went through so much humiliation that they didn't want to share it with anyone."

During those long years, Pintyi and Luizi had to bring food to the prison for Jóska. The prison offered only the most meager of diets for its inmates, but some of the better-connected and less dangerous prisoners were allowed the benefit of having food brought in. Every second day the girls would walk from the school on Váci Utca to their home on Rákoczi and over to the prison on Andrássy Út, where they'd stand in line for hours with hundreds of other families.

"We had to leave early from school, but the master understood," Pintyi says. After all, theirs was not the only well-to-do family in this situation.

"We would run home, pick up the food, and go to the jail," Luizi adds. "He would get some bread, some milk and some daily food."

"It was usually soup, *főzelék* (cooked and pureed vegetables) and some meat." Pintyy recalls.

"Some days it was pasta."

"Wine we couldn't bring," Pintyi remembers. "We always brought a bottle of milk, though, and half of it was vodka. It wasn't even vodka, it was pure alcohol."

"And sometimes it went bad."

"It curdled."

"And when the guards checked the basket, they'd go, 'Yuck.'" The sisters laugh, remembering the looks on the guards' faces when they opened the bottle and saw the disgusting goop it contained.

By now, the family's fortune was gone. At her brother's urging, Aranka had used the last of Jóska's gold to open a hat store. But in the years after the war, no one was very interested in fashion, and the store quickly went out of business. She was reduced to working in a bakery, where she rolled out bread dough and made cakes and cookies that only the Soviet brass could afford and that only they had any appetite for.

It was a bleak time. Hungary's cities were overrun with rats and cockroaches and there was little food in the stores. Food production had dropped dramatically as the peasants were driven from their land. Meanwhile, the state farms were a bad joke, and there were no imports except from other Soviet states, which were all dealing with similar problems. It was the beginning of the long lineups for food, something almost unfathomable in a country as rich and abundant as Hungary has always been.

"For bread you sometimes had to line up for an hour. For milk, sugar, meat you also had to line up. If you went to the market you could sometimes get a chicken, but you had to kill the chicken yourself. You had to line up for meat; you had to line up for butter," Luizi recalls.

"And the meat was horrible. It was full of gristle and fat," Pintyi adds. "But you had to take what they gave you."

"And you had to be grateful for anything," Luizi says. "It was like a favor they were doing for you."

"People relied on family members and friends to let them know: 'There's meat today.' "

"At the end everyone had some sugar and some flour and some margarine. You could get some food, but you had to be creative with what you had," Luizi says.

Institutions such as schools and factories developed their own state-run cafeterias called *menza* where workers could get hearty, inexpensive food. When ingredients were scarce, as they so often were, people would go to a local *menza* and eat there instead. An entire generation grew up losing the skills to cook.

But food shortages were the least of their worries. The new government was intent on establishing a true socialist state as fast as possible. To do that, they had to get rid of all potential troublemakers. These people were conveniently branded "enemies of the working class" and were either sentenced to forced labor camps or were *kimenekült*, forced into exile in the poorer parts of the country where they could help take care of the land. To help identify these "enemies," people were encourage to spy on each other and report on the doings of strangers, neighbors, and even friends and family. Small children were praised for tattling and held up as socialist heroes. People learned to talk in whispers, to keep their opinions to themselves, to think twice before sharing a joke with a friend or co-worker.

According to research done by the archivists at the Terror Háza, some 35,000 Hungarians were imprisoned right after the Second World War, with just as many awaiting sentencing when the war crime trials ended in 1953. Another 15,000 people were "evacuated" from the cities to brutal work camps within Hungary. Some 40,000 were *kimenekült*, exiled to "social camps" mostly on the Great Plain. Entire families could stay together at the social camps, a name that makes them sound like their inmates should have been making macramé picture frames rather than breaking rocks with sledgehammers or digging up potatoes with trowels. Thousands more Hungarians were "abducted" and sent to forced labor gulags in Siberia where the conditions were so terrible that fully half of them died. And between 1945 and 1956, nearly 400 people were executed for political reasons.

While the aristocrats, bourgeoisie, and young men of military age were considered particular threats to society and were dealt with especially harshly, the new Soviet government dealt cruelly with others, too: 200,000 German-Catholic Swabians were "resettled" and 300,000 peasants driven from their land. Eventually, the Soviet system of terror extended so far that it affected one in three Hungarian families.

One of those families was the Sasváris, formerly known as the Stocks, who lived in a suburb of Budapest called Újpalota. Miraculously, Marton Sasvári had managed to avoid the worst of the war and its aftermath. He hadn't joined the Communist Party, but he was a good worker, the foreman of the Danuvia factory, which made guns during the war, electronics afterward, and today produces motorcycles. Marton was well liked and respected among his staff, so it came as a shock one day when a truck pulled up in front of their house and Soviet soldiers jumped out. Marton wasn't home, but his wife, Agnes, and the two children, Frances and Joe, were. They came outside to see what the soldiers wanted.

The uniformed young men demanded to know where Marton was. When they heard he was still at the factory, they ordered his wife and children, "Get in the truck. *Now*."

Agnes began weeping and wailing, wringing her hands and crying out to God to save her. Her hysterics may have rescued the family, for the stunned soldiers just stood there helplessly while Joe ran off to get his father. A small crowd had gathered by the time they returned, and Marton demanded to know what was going on. They were being resettled, he was told, because they were Swabians, Germans, and a threat to the Hungarian Soviet state.

"I am a good Hungarian," Marton said furiously. "My name is Hungarian. My family has lived here for 500 years. We are good workers, and no threat to anyone. Who said we were?"

It turned out that a neighbor, jealous of the Sasváris' slightly better standard of living, had reported their German-ness to the authorities. Luckily, they had more friends among their neighbors than enemies, and their friends joined in, convincing the soldiers that sending Marton away would be much worse for the workers than if he stayed. The Sasváris avoided resettlement, but only by a hair's breadth. They never felt completely secure after that.

The Wintermantels were less lucky. Jóska was released from jail in 1949 to a world all gray and hopeless, filled with poverty and hunger. Less than two years later, his family was sent into exile. By then, Jóska was no longer considered a serious threat to the Soviets, just a mild nuisance. The years of shame and torture had ruined him for anything more than sitting in a chair and drinking all day long. He thus avoided the notorious hard labor camps at places like Kistarcsa or Recsk, which was where Norbert Tesch, an old family friend, was sent. These were essentially concentration camps whose inmates were forced to work with primitive tools in mines and quarries, under such brutal conditions that many of them died. Instead, Jóska, Aranka and the two girls were sent like thousands and thousands of others to the Hortobágy, the Great Plain region where the new Soviet government was having so much trouble running its state farms or *kolhozes*. They were among 100 or so people sent to a village called Tiszabö, on the shores of the lazy, dreamy Tisza River.

Meanwhile, Jóska's brother Kálmán and his family were sent to a camp in another part of the country. while Teréz's family escaped the internment camps because her husband was a desperately needed doctor. They were allowed to stay in Budapest and to keep the summerhouse in Balatonalmádi.

In Tiszabö, Jóska, Aranka, and the girls were billeted with a peasant family – "kulaks," as the Soviets disparagingly called them. Before 1945, this family had been the most affluent in the village, and although they had no electricity or indoor plumbing, their house had several decent-sized rooms, as well as a kitchen and a foyer.

"They forced the kulaks into one room, and they put a family into each of the other rooms," Pintyi recalls. "And in the foyer, where we all had to go through to get to the outhouse, there were four of them there, too, a baron and a baroness and her mother and father."

For the next three years, Aranka, Jóska, Pintyi, and Luizi lived in that one room. By now the girls were in their twenties, but there were no pretty clothes and Saturday night dates at the movies for them. Instead, Pintyi and Luizi worked the fields with the other families of former military officers, former factory owners, and former nobility. They were sent to work not even for money, but for a meager portion of food and a roof over their heads.

"We were day workers. We had to work for the *kolhoz* when they were in trouble. And they were in deep trouble because winter was coming and the potatoes were rotting away in the fields. We were trying to save the cotton fields, too, but the cotton was all wet and black and rotten. Also there were rice fields and that was horrible work," Pintyi says.

Soon their clothes were little more than rags, and there was nothing to protect them from the pitiless sun – no sunscreen was being handed out on the kolhoz. Their skin burned and blistered until it came off in long strips and burned again. Their hands bled, their nails splintered, and they were covered in cuts, scrapes and bruises. Their feet were blistered and bleeding from the 10 kilometer walk back and forth each day to the state farm.

"There were times when there was no forced labor, and Luli and I signed up to work as laborers, not for money, because there wasn't any, but for food. When we worked with wheat, we got some flour at the end of the season, and when we worked with corn, we got some of that, too."

In winter, when there was no work in the fields, they were sent to work on the Tisza. Most of the time, the Tisza is a placid and mellow river. Each spring, though, it becomes a wild, unpredictable thing known for leaping over its banks and flooding thousands of hectares of farmland. For centuries, the Hungarian plains were made barren by the constant flooding that left them covered in sand and silt. It was only when engineers figured out how to control the waters in the nineteenth century that it became the fertile farmland it is today. Still, the system of barriers and dikes was in constant need of repair, so Luizi and Pintyi were put to work cutting wood and carrying rocks. For that they got just enough money to buy food and heat their house during the severe winters.

"We never had any money in Tiszabö. No money whatsoever, but we didn't starve," Pintyi says.

For one thing, when they went to work on the local farms – not the state farm, but the few farms that were still owned by peasants – the owners would bring them lunch every day. "That was good, fattening food. Bacon, lots of bacon, and sausages and green peppers. And their wives would make lots and lots of pastry."

For another, they were learning to live the way the peasants did. They got a pig – a sickly creature that Aranka nursed back to health with some leftover penicillin she'd managed to bring from Budapest – and some ducks and some chickens for eggs. Aranka learned to make cheese and beer. ("You know she could make anything." Pinty says.) They slaughtered the pig and made sausages and bacon.

The funny thing is that even though the work was brutal, the culture nonexistent, and the living accommodations primitive, the social life was not so bad. The girls had friends and boyfriends, all from what had once been the cream of Hungarian society. They remember, for instance, working the fields beside Countess Almásy, a relative of the Laszlo Almásy made famous in Michael Ondaatje's book, *The English Patient*. As Pintyi recalls, "The company was excellent. And we learned how to play bridge. Apart from the hard labor, it was fun. But not everyone would agree with me. It's probably in my nature to look on the bright side."

For a while it seemed as if they'd be sentenced to carry rocks and dig potatoes and sleep four to a room for the rest of their lives. Then, in the spring of 1953, Stalin died, and with him died the will to keep all those thousands and thousands of people imprisoned indefinitely. The Kremlin was now too busy dealing with its own internal power struggles to care much about what a bunch of old counts and factory owners were up to on the Hungarian plain.

Almost immediately, the Hungarian government announced that it was closing the work camps. First to close were the hard labor camps like Recsk, where Nori Tesch had been sent. When he was set free, he traveled to Tiszabö to visit the girls and their parents. The camp had killed the dapper young man-about-town they remembered. In his place was a gaunt and hardened man with scarred hands covered in calluses from years spent breaking rocks in the quarry. But his sense of humor was intact, and he soon had the Wintermantels laughing about his adventures as they drank and ate and played cards by candlelight in the crowded kulak's house.

It was Christmas before the exiles were permitted to leave the social camp at Tiszabö. Late that fall, as the cold crept across the plain and the first snows swirled from the skies, the inmates received their release papers describing the conditions under which they could re-establish themselves. They could live anywhere they wanted, they were told, except Budapest. They could do any kind of work they wanted, except office work, professional work, or indeed, white-collar work of any sort. They certainly couldn't own anything, or run anything, or be in any position of authority. In other words, none of them could return to any semblance of the lives they'd had before internment.

With no money and no options, the Wintermantels went back to Balatonalmádi. It was years since they'd seen the place. Of everywhere they'd ever lived, the old villa on the lakeshore was their favorite house. It was where they had loved, and laughed; it was where they had escaped to when life was terrible and it was where they had escaped from when life got even worse. It was home.

They arrived at the Balatonalmádi train station on a chilly December day, just in time for Christmas, even though there could be no real Christmas this year. For one thing, the Soviets had outlawed religion, so celebrations would be few and furtive; for another, they had no money for gifts or the roast goose or the traditional candies called *szalonczukor* (SA-lon-tsoo-kor) to hang from the tree. Still, they felt that just coming home would be the best Christmas gift they could have been given.

They walked slowly home from the train station. The girls carried the few things they still owned. Aranka carried a bag of the sausages she'd made from the pig they'd killed back in October. Jóska hobbled along, leaning heavily on the cane he'd had to use since his time in the House of Horrors. They went along Neptun Utca, the street they knew so well. They passed familiar houses with gardens that were lush in summer with roses and lavender, but now were barren and gray. Through the leafless trees, they caught glimpses of the great lake, sullen and dull under cloudy skies. Dead leaves rattled in an icy wind spiked with shards of snow that stung the eyes.

As they rounded a bend in the road, the soft yellow walls of Number 19 Neptun Utca beckoned from the alley of bare trees. Even Jóska quickened his pace as they came nearer to the house that was so solid, so true, so comfortable in its place, so wonderfully, thankfully permanent. There was even a light on inside, welcoming them home – how nice, they thought, Jóska's sister Teréz must have come over from next door to get the place ready for them.

Eagerly, they climbed the stone stairs to the door. As Aranka searched for the keys, one of the girls impatiently tried the handle. It turned in her hand and the door swung open. Their hearts gave a little skip and they glanced at each other, suddenly worried. They stepped inside gingerly, calling out, "Hello, who's there?" And there in the living room, frozen on Aranka's plushy green furniture, were a man, a woman, and two boys, staring at them with eyes big and round and their mouths hanging open. For a moment, they just stared at each other. Then Jóska found his voice. "Who the hell are you?" he demanded.

As it turned out, these strangers were the Wintermantels' new roommates. While they had been gone, the Soviets had housed a good communist family in their side of the house. (Next door, Teréz's family hadn't suffered the same indignity because they were still using the place — and besides, she was married to a doctor.) The family – a mother, father and two young boys – had settled in and made themselves comfortable with Aranka's cozy furniture and fine linens.

Each family felt their space invaded by the other, but there was nothing either could do about the situation, so they agreed to split the house. For the next three years, the communists lived in one part of the villa, the enemies of the working class in another. They spoke in whispers and walked softly, each family avoiding the other and trying to maintain a semblance of privacy. Still, they found common ground in the kitchen, where they had to put aside their philosophic differences to somehow create enough food to feed themselves from the few, poor ingredients they could find.

They ate noodles with cabbage and noodles with cheese, noodles with peppers, and noodles with nuts. They ate soup made with turnips, parsnips, carrots, or whatever herbs were growing in the garden. They ate potatoes boiled and baked and fried, sometimes livened up with a few slices of bacon or sausage. They sprinkled paprika on everything to add flavor, nutrients, and the illusion that they were actually eating more.

Finding food was one difficulty; paying for it another. They'd made no money in Tiszabö, their savings were long gone, and no one was working so no money was coming in. Jóska had retreated into a dream world where he sat all day by the window, staring at the lake and drinking wine. Aranka and Luizi rarely ventured outside the house, frightened by a new world where neighbors had become strangers eager to turn in an "enemy" to score points with the secret police. Pintyi, though, took to heart Aranka's maxim of "Don't look back. Look forward." She went out and got a job.

Work around Lake Balaton was scarce, especially in winter, so one day Pintyi hopped on the train and went to the forbidden city of Budapest in search of work. She knew she risked a trip to the House of Horrors if the police caught her, but she didn't care. Someone had to make some money. Besides, she found it unbearable to spend her days in that divided house with those whispering, frightened people.

Budapest under socialism wasn't the vibrant place Pintyi remembered from before the war. Back then, there were parties and balls, beautiful shops, and wonderful restaurants. Now it was bleak and quiet and dull, but it was still a big city with plenty of jobs and good-looking men to flirt with. Besides, Pintyi had many friends in town who were willing to let her stay with them. She made sure never to say too long, though, for if a neighbor figured out what was going on and reported them, they'd all be spending some time in the cruel hands of the ÁVO. For the next year, she bounced from apartment to apartment, spending a few weeks on one friend's sofa, then a few weeks on another's.

Luckily, Pintyi got a job right away. It was a terrible job, but she was lucky to get work at all. The Quint spirits factory hired her to come in overnight and oil the machinery when no one was there. Fine, she thought, it's a start, and set to with gusto. She worked so hard that soon she was promoted, then promoted again. The factory manager put her on day shifts despite the risks, and she quickly moved through the ranks until she reached the group of elite workers who were allowed to work with the alcohol itself. She made enough money to support the family, and the job had another benefit, too: "I didn't have any food, so I filled myself up with alcohol."

Then a friend of her father's found her what sounded like a dream job. The way it was described to her, she'd be working on one of the cruise ships that plied Lake Balaton. There would be travel, adventure, good-looking male passengers, and huge tips. So she quit the spirits factory and took the train to Balaton. But when she showed up for work in Siófok, it turned out that the friend had somehow got it all wrong. The job was nothing more than selling ice cream in a railway station, a low-class job that paid poorly and offered no tips, either.

Heartbroken, she went to her sister Eva's grave and cried and cried. "I cried for two days," Pintyi remembers. "To me it was worse than working in the fields – until I found out that I could make a fortune there."

Once she accepted her fate, she charmed her suppliers, and she flirted with her customers. She made improvements to the decor and the stock. Like her mother thirty years earlier, she developed a loyal following, and she made good money. Then she got a better job at a bigger train station. At first she sent all her money home, then found jobs for her mother and sister, too.

"The last job at that company was on the outskirts of Budapest," she says. She'd graduated to serving espresso and conducting wine tastings. Whenever she wanted, she could slip into the city and visit her friends and family. It was still illegal for her to do so, but it was easier and less dangerous when the journey was so short.

Life settled into a groove that was quiet and comfortable. They weren't rich, but at least they were no longer desperately poor. They weren't happy, exactly, but at least they weren't miserable and frightened all the time. They tried not to think about the past, yet they couldn't bear to dwell on a future with no hope for change. They grew to accept that this is what their life would be from now on. They were, of course, dead wrong.

CHAPTER 6

"Help! Help! Help!"

One moment, everything was peaceful, even hopeful. The next moment, bullets were flying and nothing would ever be the same again.

Of all the dates in 1,100 years of Hungarian history, none stands out like October 23, 1956, the day the Uprising began. That day, in cities across the country, thousands of students had gathered peacefully to protest years of Stalinist rule in Hungary and to demand the kind of reforms that were going on in neighboring Poland. In Budapest, they gathered at Petőfi Square, in City Park, and outside the Broadcasting House. They were unexpectedly joined by thousands of other citizens — housewives left their soup pots, workers put down their tools, even Hungarian police and soldiers dropped their pretence of obeying the Soviets.

Although things started off calmly enough, events quickly escalated, for a great anger had been building. People were angry over so many things. They were angry at the way the Soviets had "expropriated" their homes and banished their families from cities where they had lived for centuries. They were angry that they had to work the fields to produce more and more and always more for the workers' paradise – yet there was never enough food to eat. They were angry that they could no longer travel freely within their own country. They were angry that even their own children were encouraged to spy on them, which meant they could no longer tell jokes, or gossip, or pray, or talk politics for fear of being arrested. They were angry that only a year earlier, Hungary had signed the Warsaw Pact, which gave the Soviet Union the legal right to occupy their country. And they were angry, too, over what the USSR's new general secretary, Nikita Kruschev, had recently revealed about the true extent of Josef Stalin's crimes — the mass killings, the torture, the death camps, the persecution of minorities, the 30 to 40 million dead.

Their anger grew and grew. And then that Tuesday afternoon, much to the Soviets' surprise, the Hungarians rose up and attacked the giant bear sleeping within their borders.

Pintyi was in Budapest that day, and she joined the hundreds of people who had gathered at City Park. She remembers how the protesters, silent and deadly serious, tore down the massive bronze statue of Josef Stalin that loomed over the park. "I was standing there with the crowd and the crowd was so quiet, just the bang, bang, bang of the hammers on the statue," she says. "Finally the statue came down. It was such a wonderful sight."

Meanwhile at the Broadcasting House, the protesters clamored to air their demands on national radio. "No," they were told. "We're not leaving until we can have our say," they responded. "No," they were told again. Up on the roof, ÁVH officers had kept their rifles trained on the crowd throughout the protests and demands. Suddenly, and no one knows why, one of the ÁVH men opened fire on the people below. Police and soldiers began shooting back at the ÁVH and the crowd surged into the Broadcasting House. The Uprising had begun.

The fighting escalated overnight and spread throughout the *belváros*. By morning, much of the city had been reduced to smoldering ruins. Shortly after dawn, the telephone rang at the apartment belonging to the Wintermantels' friends, Kati and Deszö Miklos, who were letting Pintyi stay with them awhile. Pintyi answered the phone to find a friend of her father on the line. "Don't go anywhere," he implored her. "There's a revolution going on." She immediately called her cousin Jóska over at the family apartment on Rákóczi Út. Then she got dressed and went out.

"Jóska and I just wandered the streets," she recalls. "There was blood all over the place, buildings were smoking, it was terrible."

Most people were more sensible and chose to hide in their basements or cower in their apartments. Bullets and grenades were flying everywhere, even through apartment doors and windows. More than one person was shot while making dinner or dusting the credenza. Outdoors, though, it was even more dangerous. Soviet tanks rolled through the streets in search of freedom fighters, their gunners aiming at anyone who looked suspicious and even at some people who didn't. Even more deadly were the bands of angry young Hungarian men who hunted down Soviet sympathizers and members of the ÁVH. The lucky ones they shot on sight. The not so lucky they strung up by their feet and hanged from the lampposts, beating them until they died. They left the bodies there to rot and send a message to others who would betray their homeland.

Along with the rumble of the tank treads and the sound of bullets clattering through the narrow streets, the soundtrack to all the carnage was Radio Free Europe, which played incessantly in every darkened home. The anti-communist broadcasts encouraged the freedom fighters with pep talks and promises that help would be coming from the West. It was all a big lie.

On October 28, reformer Imre Nagy was reinstated as prime minister. He immediately ordered a truce and dismantled the dreaded ÁVH. The occupying Soviet forces began to roll out of Budapest and negotiations began for their complete withdrawal from Hungary. Two days later, Nagy abolished the one-party political system and promised that free elections would be held as soon as possible. In what seemed like a promising sign, the USSR announced that it wanted to mend its relationship with "fraternal socialist countries," clearly meaning Hungary. That was all a big lie, too.

Within twenty-four hours, the USSR gave the order to crush the Hungarian freedom fight. Soviet troops flooded back across the border. The next day, November 1, Hungary withdrew from the Warsaw Pact and asked the United Nations for help. However, desperately hoped-for help from the West failed to appear. The West was too busy with other things – the Suez Canal crisis, for instance – and Hungary wasn't on top of anyone's list of priorities. At dawn on November 4, only twelve days after the Uprising had begun, a thousand Soviet tanks rolled in to Budapest. By 8 a.m., the Hungarian army was crushed and Hungarian Radio was captured. Its final broadcast was simply: "Help! Help! Help!"

The army may have been destroyed and communication shut down, but the fighting continued. Small bands of resistance fighters kept up attacks on the invading Soviets. Even children picked up machine guns and learned how to shoot them. Freedom fighters set up traps in the narrow streets. They spread oil under the tanks to send them spinning off the cobblestone roads. They tossed grenades and shot at the Soviet soldiers until they ran out of bullets. Even when they knew help wouldn't be coming, that they had no hope of winning, that they were horribly outnumbered, they kept on fighting.

By the middle of the month, the armed resistance had been hunted down and systematically destroyed. Moscow appointed its own puppet government in Hungary, the Revolutionary Worker-Peasant Party, and placed János Kádár in the parliament. Mass arrests, torture, and executions followed.

Hungary was once again in ruins. In Budapest, any buildings that hadn't been destroyed were riddled with bullet holes and stained with the soot from fires and bombs. Rubble filled the wide boulevards where the Soviet tanks rolled day and night, the thunder of the treads echoing ominously through the tall, leafless trees. There was no contact with the outside world. Radio, telegraph, telephone, and mail service were all cut off. Roads were blocked, borders closed, airplanes grounded. Lawlessness and chaos gripped the city.

As many as 4,000 Hungarians were dead and 20,000 wounded. Thousands were arrested and hundreds carried off by the KGB to the Soviet Union as prisoners of war. Nearly 300 people were executed, including the hapless Imre Nagy. And 200,000 people fled the country to any nation that would welcome them. Countries such as Canada, the United States, and Australia opened their doors to the refugees who were forced to abandon their beloved homeland.

Those who departed were among the best, the brightest, and the bravest. Many of those left behind were too old or too young or too sick or too frightened to travel. Often they had no money, no education, and no contacts in the West; they were people who'd never left their villages and neighborhoods, terrified of starting anew in a place they'd never heard of, where they didn't speak the language.

"Help! Help! Help!"

The Uprising split the Wintermantel clan into two. Teréz and Kálmán stayed behind with their families; Jóska and his family left. It was not that Jóska wanted to go – far from it. He was quite happy to sit in his armchair at Balatonalmádi, gazing day after day at the blue, blue lake, sipping his wine, and waiting for death to come. He didn't care if he ever had money again, and he no longer believed in the idea of "freedom." He felt too tired, too broken to start again. But Pintyi and Aranka had had it with their circumstances. They'd had more than a decade of poverty and humiliation, of hard work with no reward. The West beckoned, bright and full of hope.

One day, Pintyi and her friends Deszö and Kati Miklos arrived at Balatonalmádi. They were in high spirits, for they'd decided to leave, and wanted Jóska, Aranka, and Luizi to come with them. They'd already talked Dezsö's cousins into joining them and they even had a little bit of money for the journey, having sold the Miklos's apartment in Budapest along with the few valuables they had left. It didn't take long to convince Aranka to come along, but Jóska and Luizi didn't even want to hear about their plans. The family argued for hours, for days, for weeks. The nights grew shorter and the days grew darker. As November turned to December, the first few snowflakes began to fall. If they were going to leave, they couldn't delay any longer.

Reports were coming back of people who had left and others who'd been caught at the border. Some had been arrested. Others had been shot or had drowned while trying to swim across icy rivers. The holes at the notoriously porous border were quickly being filled with additional patrols. Pintyi was convinced that it wouldn't be long before the Iron Curtain would be closed forever.

Finally, they wore Jóska down. He agreed to join them on their great escape, not because he was swayed by their arguments, but because he began to fear that they'd go without him. And left alone, he would surely die of loneliness.

Pintyi, Aranka, and a reluctant Jóska, along with Deszö, Kati, their kids, and their cousins, left Hungary with nothing except what they could carry – their clothes, a few pieces of jewelry, a fur coat, a treasured painting. After a decade of Soviet occupation, they didn't have much left. Every last forint of their personal fortunes was long gone and their valuables had either been sold or stolen or smashed or buried and lost in a garden somewhere.

They went knowing they might never see their friends and family again. Jóska and Aranka left behind their brothers, sisters, cousins, and one of their daughters, for Luizi had decided to stay home. They couldn't tell people they were leaving, just in case a careless word reached the ears of the authorities. They didn't want to put their friends and family at risk; they also didn't want to jeopardize their escape because they knew they'd have only have one chance to make it. So they never had a chance to say a proper goodbye, to kiss their loved ones and hold them one last time. Nor would they ever sit on the verandah at Lake Balaton again, sipping wine and watching the sailboats drift by. They would never eat *Dobos torta* at Café Gerbeaud again or walk along the corso by the Danube River. They would never again see the fields filled with poppies or watch the snow fall in the soft glow of the streetlights outside their apartment on Rákóczi Út.

All told, there were ten of them. In the hours before they left, they sewed money and jewelry into their clothes, then dressed with care, pulling one layer on top of the other. They couldn't carry any luggage, of course, for that would attract suspicion from the police and soldiers posted along the way. They walked to the little Balatonalmádi station and waited for the train, trying to look as if they were just popping over to visit an old friend in a nearby village. A cruel wind whistled down the platform. It was so cold they didn't look out of place all bundled up in their layers of woolens and furs.

From Balatonalmádi they traveled to a small town on the Austrian border. On the train, they tried to maintain the fiction of a cheerful family outing for the benefit of the other passengers and the soldiers on board. They told jokes and shared gossip, and Aranka pulled out some sausages and pogacsa for a quick picnic lunch, just as if they were in a Hungarian fairy tale. Every once in a while, a train would pass them on its way back to the city. It would be crowded with soldiers and the people they'd caught trying to escape. The train would pass so closely that they could see the guns and the handcuffs, and the looks of despair on the passengers' faces. Then even Pintyi couldn't keep up the cheerful fiction. They'd fall silent for a while, icy fear gripping their hearts.

By late afternoon they reached their destination, a sleepy village just a few kilometers from the border. They'd heard about a man who was helping people escape – for a fee, of course. It didn't take long to find him. In those last few days before the Iron Curtain slammed shut, he was always open for business. He told them to come to his house and to bring all their money. What other option did they have? They followed him across the frozen fields and entered a shabby old peasant's hut. It was already crowded with about twenty other people who just stared silently at the newcomers.

"Now this is how it's going to be," their guide said, as he counted the money they'd given him. "You're not going to make a sound. No lights, no fire, no cigarettes, no nothing. At midnight we leave. I go first, then you follow me two by two, as quiet as the grave. I don't want to hear the smallest noise from you – even a whisper and we're dead.

"You –" he pointed at Jóska and Aranka, who were the oldest and frailest in the group – "you go first. The rest follow. And remember what I said: Not a sound, or we're all dead."

Then he left them, heading back to the village to meet the next train, searching for more customers. As a clock ticked inexorably in another room, the refugees sat in shadows on the floor, silent and scared. Darkness fell and gunfire rattled in the distance. Hours later, the guide returned and said, "It's time."

They rose in the darkness and, like obedient children, they shuffled into a long crocodile, barely daring even to draw a breath. When their guide saw that they were ready, he waved his arm, opened the door and stepped out into the night. Reluctantly, Jóska and Aranka followed him.

"That was the most hilarious point," Pintyi recalls. "We were a big group. We were all shaking and scared. And we didn't even get out of the house when father fell in the ditch and mother started screaming at him."

With a thunderous crash, Jóska had tripped on his way out the door and stumbled into a ditch outside, cursing loudly as he went down amid the weeds and refuse. "You idiot!" Aranka hissed. "What's wrong with you? You could have got us all killed."

"Shut up, shut up," their leader whispered anxiously, while the rest of the escapees stood frozen with terror. But Aranka wasn't finished yet, for her temper, reined in for too long, was fully off its leash. She called Jóska every name she could think of – he was a drunken fool, a philandering bastard, and much worse. When finally Aranka stopped berating her husband, he gathered his breath and smiled sheepishly. Pintyi took his hand and they began their slow march to the border.

"I had to drag him across the four kilometers in the mud," Pintyi recalls. It was eerily like another night when they had been trying to escape the Russians, the night Pintyi had dragged her father home from his lover, Emmi.

As the refugees stumbled silently through the darkness, they couldn't help but notice that the gunfire they'd been listening to all night seemed to have moved from the south to the west. In fact, it seemed to be directly in front of them. They figured, though, that this probably wasn't the best time to start questioning their guide.

They approached the no man's land between the two countries. For the first time, they could actually see the warm lights of Austria ahead of them. Every single one of the refugees felt their pulses quicken as hope flooded their hearts. The sound of the guns stilled for a brief moment. Silence hung in the air. Then a burst of gunfire rattled all around them and a storm of bullets spattered into the muddy patch where they were standing. "Stop!" came a voice out of the darkness. "You're under arrest!"

The line of escapees came to a halt. Someone cried out, someone else collapsed onto the ground, sobbing. Not Pintyi. She dropped her father's hands and bolted for the bright lights across the border. She had only made it a few meters when strong arms grabbed her from behind and lifted her off the ground. She couldn't tell how many there were; it seemed as if there were dozens of them, reeking of body odor and drink. She kicked and swore and struggled wildly. They just laughed. As they grabbed her wrists and clicked the handcuffs closed, hope flickered and died.

For what seemed like hours, the refugees just stood there, only a few meters away from freedom. Their bodies were shaking, flooded with adrenaline. They felt sick and cold with shock as they waited to hear what would be done with them. Would they be beaten or shot?

Would they be sent straightaway to the House of Horrors in Budapest? If only someone would tell them, no matter what it was.

But the border guards seemed in no hurry to do anything at all. "Got a smoke?" they asked the group's guide. "Sure," he said, handing over a packet. They all lit up, their gunpowder-streaked faces ghastly in the sudden flicker of light. For the next few moments, they stood and smoked and swapped jokes, pointedly ignoring their captives until they figured they were just terrified enough to do whatever they wanted. Finally they turned back to them. "We'll let you go," they offered, "if you give us all you've got."

It was a scam, the refugees realized, relief flooding their bodies. The guards and their guide were in cahoots with each other in an extortion scheme. They would willingly have given the guards every last forint they had if they hadn't already given everything to the guide. Only one couple had managed to keep anything at all from his greed, a Jewish couple who had had managed to save some of their fortune from the communists. They were reluctant to hand it over at first: after all, how could they trust the guides' new promises when they clearly couldn't trust the old ones? However, the rest of the group persuaded them that their lives depended on it. The biggest of the guards, clearly their leader, nodded in agreement, smiling with a wicked leer beneath his big, black Magyar moustache.

Once they'd been picked clean, the refugees were free to move into the no man's land between Hungary and Austria. Their sudden release brought with it a burst of energy. Even though they were exhausted, they ran across the muddy strip of land. Even Jóska found some speed. By the first gray light of dawn, they had stumbled into the safety of Austria.

A handful of men and women appeared out of the morning mist, locals who were waiting for them with food and coffee. They were horrified when they heard about the extortion scheme on the other side of the border, but there wasn't much they could do about it. Although a couple of the Austrian men went after the Hungarian scammers and engaged in a satisfying beating, they couldn't recover any of the valuables or money. This time, the Wintermantels really, truly had nothing left except hope.

The refugees were taken to a nearby camp set up by the Red Cross, a cluster of big white tents that already held hundreds of other Hungarians. When they finally found their beds, they sank gratefully onto the clean white sheets and rough woolen blankets. The mattresses were only straw, but they couldn't have slept better if they were made of the softest goose down and covered in the finest silks. The camp was clean and safe, and it was also well supplied with food and hot drinks.

Although the West hadn't come to the Hungarians' aid when the tanks were rolling, it did so now. The United States, Canada, the United Kingdom, France, Germany, Switzerland, Australia, and New Zealand made room for the Hungarian refugees by quickly adjusting their existing immigration policies. At first, almost all the refugees wanted to go to the United States, but the U.S. understandably couldn't accommodate all 200,000 people. It eventually took in 80,000. Canada welcomed the second greatest number, about 37,000, while the rest were split among the other countries.

The Austrian camp was only an emergency shelter. Within a few weeks, they were on a plane to a sorting camp in England. There they were housed in the military barracks at Aldershot. (The army wasn't there, of course; it was off fighting in the Suez.) England was still recovering from the Second World War; rationing had only recently ended; and the citizens were still living a very frugal existence. They were generous hosts, but had little to offer. The Hungarians were surprised by the bland, stodgy food. They couldn't help but remember Baroness Orczy's famous comment: "The difference between an Englishman and a Hungarian," said the author of *The Scarlet Pimpernel*, "is that an Englishman lives like a king but eats like a pig, while a Hungarian may live like a pig, but my God, he eats like a king." And they were dismayed when the British had only tea to offer them instead of wine or coffee. Tea is what they drank when they were sick, usually spiked with a bit of rum or brandy, which were also in short supply. In turn, the English were horrified by the vast amounts of hot water the Hungarians used each day to bathe. When you have 1,300 thermal springs, hot water isn't a luxury; in postwar England, though, where many houses still didn't have modern indoor plumbing, it was.

Before the hosts and their unexpected guests had adjusted to each other's whims and while the world powers were still dithering over numbers and protocol, the Hungarians were sent from England to Scotland. By then, Pintyi had decided she wanted to go to the United States, the land of hope and freedom. But on the fast train heading north, she met someone who changed her mind.

The train was so crowded that many of the refugees had to stand the whole way, holding onto leather straps, swaying as the train sped up and slowed down and rounded the gentle curves of the English countryside. In Aldershot, Pintyi had learned to speak a little English because someone needed to communicate with their hosts and nobody else in their group knew even a single word of the strange new language. She'd studied it in school so she could read it a little bit, but she'd had a hard time understanding the speech of their hosts. "By the time I got used to the English accent, they sent us to Scotland, and by the time I got used to the Scottish accent, they sent us to Ireland and then to Canada, which was different, too," she says now with a laugh.

On the train, she ended up standing beside a tall, thin young man with a wave of light brown hair and clear blue eyes. When she heard him say something in English, she was delighted: "He was the only person whose English I could understand!"

His name was Joe Sasvári and he was traveling with his sister Frances and her husband Frank. Frank was a lot older than Frances and both had been working at the Danuvia factory that her dad had once managed. Joe, though, had studied languages at university with the plan of going into the foreign service, maybe even becoming an ambassador. But things hadn't worked out the way he hoped. He'd done his military service and paid his dues, but somehow had never been given the sorts of opportunities he'd dreamed of. He'd joined in the crowds at Petőfi Square. He'd celebrated with his family when the tanks left – and mourned with them when the tanks returned. He was certain that the Soviets knew who had taken part in the protests and that his own participation would be noted. He would never be able to hold any position of significance in the new Hungary and, frankly, he didn't want to. So he and his sister decided to leave. He was twenty-eight years old, and he knew this would be his only chance for a better life.

He told Pintyi about his escape. He still had his old army uniform, he told her, so he put it on, hoping to blend in with the thousands of soldiers stationed all over the country's transportation routes. He boarded a train heading west, where he settled into a seat and closed his eyes, hoping to avoid notice. After a while, though, a heavy boot nudged his leg. He awoke to find a young, pimply soldier staring into his face and shouting, "Wake up! And show me your papers!"

Joe stared back at him for a moment, then jumped to his feet. "Look at yourself, soldier. You're a disgrace!" he shouted in Russian, spittle flying from his lips. He leaned forward, shaking his finger in the youth's face, crowding him so closely that the poor kid was almost leaning backward. It was a perfect caricature of a Soviet military bigwig exercising his power. He grabbed the lapels of the soldier's uniform. "Your boots are filthy. Your buttons haven't been shined in weeks. And when did you last press your trousers?"

Joe shoved him away, his face twisting in disgust. "How dare you disturb a senior officer this way. You're lucky I don't report you to the general. Now leave me alone, and go harass someone who deserves it." Both of them were shaking by the time Joe was done. And a few hours later, he had slipped over the border, where he met up with his sister and her husband.

Pintyi was impressed by Joe's story. In return, she told him all about leaving Balatonalmádi and the scam artists at the border and Jóska falling into the ditch. They laughed a lot. Then Joe asked her where she was planning to go. "America," she said happily. "We're going to Canada," he told her. Canada, he explained, didn't have a draft while the United States did. And he never wanted to fight in another war again. Pintyi had never considered Canada, but suddenly, the wide, empty northern country began to look a lot more interesting.

By the time they arrived in Scotland, Pintyi had fallen in love.

In Scotland, the Wintermantels and Sasváris were housed with nearly three hundred other Hungarians at the Belmont Summer School Camp near Dundee. There they were given jobs. Both Joe and Pintyi became translators for the Red Cross. Aranka went to work in the kitchen. And Jóska was assigned to the boiler room, to maintain the heating equipment. When they weren't working, they made new friends and met up with old ones. The Wintermantels, the Sasváris, the Mikloses, Norbert Tesch and his fiancée Mara were all in Scotland and "we all became a big family," Pintyi recalls.

One of the old friends they discovered was Luizi and Pintyi's old tennis instructor, Ístvan Csiszlinszky, better known as "Cheese," who, it turned out, was also Joe's brother-in-law Frank's brother-in-law. Back when the girls were kids, Cheese had been funny and charming and always down on his luck. The girls had kept begging their father to help him out in one scheme or another. Every once in a while, Jóska would give him a bit of money, but back then, before he lost everything, the businessman was too much of a snob to spend much time with his daughters' instructor, a glorified servant. It was different now that they were both poor, though. The former factory owner and the former tennis pro became good friends. In fact, they found in each other a kind of kindred spirit.

Cheese was assigned to help Jóska in the boiler room. This, it turned out, may not have been such a good idea. Jóska was feeling a bit parched in Scotland: the soups and stews provided by the Red Cross may have fed a man's body, but they didn't do much for his thirst. As he tended to the furnace, he couldn't help but notice that the steam room was the perfect environment to create something that would warm them up in a completely different way. So he convinced Aranka to gather up some potato peels and other scraps from the kitchen, and he and his new friend set to work building a still. It was a primitive operation – buckets to ferment the fruit, a few leftover pipes, an enameled tub to distill the drink, and the steam from the boiler – but Jóska was convinced it would work.

In the 1950s, Scotland was still strictly Presbyterian, especially in the countryside. On Sundays, people weren't allowed to play or to work. They made sure to finish their chores the night before, then spent the day in quiet prayer and contemplation. This was all a bit puzzling to the Hungarians. Aside from the fact that they were far too hedonistic to live in such a restrained way, religion of any sort had been largely removed from their lives. The communists, whose doctrine considered religion the opiate of the masses, had banned religious worship more than a decade before. And earlier, the Nazis had discouraged religion, too, because they didn't want any God competing with their own gods of nationalism and racial purity. Some habits died hard, so there were still traces of the old ways. The state-run cafeterias, the *menzas*, still served pasta or fish on Fridays, the traditional day of fasting in the Catholic tradition, when it is forbidden to eat meat. And people still quietly held Christmas celebrations. But this thing with a whole country shutting down on Sunday – well, that was a bit strange.

Naturally, it was on a Sunday that disaster struck.

A couple of weeks earlier, Jóska and Cheese had started fermenting a nice, strong vodka. Soon it was bubbling nicely, giving off a powerful aroma of alcohol. Jóska had already decided he would distill the stuff on a Sunday, when everyone would be at church and he'd have plenty of privacy. He told Cheese to take the day off. Just in case something went wrong, he planned to take the blame on himself. Besides, this way, he might get the first taste all to himself.

Outside, it was a frosty late winter morning. Inside the boiler room, though, as Jóska poured the fermented scraps from the buckets into the still, things were getting hotter . . . and hotter . . . and hotter . . . until suddenly, with a ferocious noise and a big ball of heat, the whole still exploded.

There was a loud bang, the clatter of pipes and bits of brick falling to the ground, then a silence that rang throughout the camp. From all the corners of the property, the Hungarians gathered around the boiler room, standing, watching in dismay as the door creaked open and a cloud of smoke rolled out. It was followed by Jóska, who staggered into the sunshine, covered in soot, his clothes in tatters, his eyebrows completely missing, a huge grin on his face.

"Oh, Jóska," was all Aranka said. Shortly afterward, the Hungarians were shipped off to Northern Ireland.

By the time they reached Ireland, Pintyi and Joe were very much in love with each other and they soon fell in love with their latest temporary home, too. In later years, when they looked back on those days, they always said that the Irish were like the Hungarians, only with ocean around them instead of mountains and hostile countries. They, too, were poets, drinkers, and fierce warriors when they had to be; they, too, were often invaded and occupied, a country with deadly politics, a country often misunderstood and easily dismissed on the world stage. The country was so beautiful, Pintyi and Joe told their daughters years later, that it was like a fairyland. They loved the green hills and the narrow gray roads that wound through them. They loved the pub culture and developed a fondness for the local stout. And they loved the people, with their dry sense of humor and fatalistic acceptance of the whims of fate.

By this time, the homeless Hungarians had become something of a cause célèbre for religious and charitable organizations in the British Isles. Every few days some dignitary would pop by on a round of the four or five Hungarian DP camps located in Northern Ireland. Then it was up to Joe and Pintyi to translate for their countrymen, most of whom still hadn't learned much English beyond "thank you," "goodbye," and "another beer, please." They got paid about a pound a week for this work. Because Joe's English was so much better, he usually did most of the actual translating. Unfortunately, though, he'd come down with the flu the day a Jehovah's Witness was scheduled to make a presentation, so Pintyi had to take over. That afternoon became the stuff of legends.

Pintyi looked out at the crowd nervously as they shuffled into the hall and took their seats. The Jehovah's Witness cleared his throat and launched into a long, droning speech. Pintyi began haltingly translating. She got about as far as "Good afternoon, ladies and gentlemen –" when she realized she couldn't understand what the speaker was saying at all. "Uhhhh," she said, as he droned on. The Hungarians looked up at her expectantly. Then she suddenly realized there was an advantage to speaking a language no one else in the world could understand.

"Look, here's the problem," she said brightly in Hungarian. "I can't understand a word this guy is saying. So I'm just going to talk to you as if I'm translating him and then at the end we'll all clap loudly and no one will know the difference. OK?" The crowd clapped its approval, and the speaker looked pleased. Then Pintyi launched into her monologue. She recited poetry, she made up stories and she told jokes. The crowd loved her, and when the speech ran its course, they gave the performance a rousing round of applause.

Pintyi was quite pleased with her clever trick, though Joe, who was always much more of a stickler for proper behavior, was horrified to hear what she'd done. And that would have been that, except that someone had had the bright idea of taping the presentation and replaying it at the other camps they were visiting that afternoon. "The lazy bums," Pintyi says. It didn't take long for them to realize that something was amiss, and the next day the camp's director, a Major Brewar, called Pintyi into his office and, as she puts it, "I got the biggest blast in my life." He scolded her for her irreverent attitude and told her that religion – any religion – was to be taken seriously here. "This is not a communist country where religion is not respected," he snapped. Somehow, though, she managed to keep her job.

By April, the various governments had finished sorting out the issues involved in settling the Hungarians into their new homes. It would take months before all the refugee claims were settled, but the Sasváris, the Wintermantels, and their friends were lucky – they were on their way to Canada. One fine spring day, they clambered aboard a BOAC (forerunner of British Airways) plane that would take them from Belfast to Iceland to Goose Bay, Labrador, and finally to Toronto.

CHAPTER 7
Oh—oh Canada

Aranka and Jóska, Pintyi and Joe, Frances, Frank, Dezsö, Kati and all their friends arrived in Toronto at 6 a.m. on a crisp, cool April day in 1957. That same year, the Yonge Street subway line opened, a sixteen-year-old Marilyn Bell swam across the freezing waters of Lake Ontario, and Hurricane Hazel made landfall in Toronto. One wonders which hit the city with a bigger impact – the hurricane or all those planeloads of Hungarians?

They weren't Canada's first Magyar immigrants. The first wave had arrived after the First World War, when the old country was in economic ruin. The second wave, many of them Jewish or members of other persecuted groups, had arrived after the Second World War. The third wave, the Fifty-sixers, made Toronto the biggest Hungarian community outside their homeland, a highly skilled community of doctors, lawyers, engineers, inventors, scientists, intellectuals, artists, restaurateurs, and businessmen.

All that promise was still in the future, though, when the planeload of tired, disoriented Hungarians touched down. Members of the local Hungarian community came out to the airport to meet their compatriots and take them to their newest temporary home, the Westlodge refugee camp on Queen Street West. There the refugees were offered a safe place to stay, as well as help with translation, local contacts, apartment-hunting, and job-searching. With that and $5 each from the government, they were sent off to conquer their new country.

Joe was put to work right away as an interpreter at the refugee center, and the rest of the family soon found work, too. Frances eventually went to work at an insurance company and her husband Frank got a job at a library. Aranka ended up making sandwiches in the Sears cafeteria, where her lack of English didn't matter. In fact, the only member of the group who did not find work was Jóska, who was frail and despondent and spoke not a word of English – and never did learn, even though he lived in Canada for more than twenty-five years. Pintyi got her first job in Canada the day she arrived. And she was fired from it the very next day.

Pintyi remembers walking along Queen Street on that first day, the air filled with the merry clang of the streetcar and the rockin' sounds of Elvis Presley and Buddy Holly, decadent music banned back home. She noticed that the people she passed were dressed in crisp, clean clothes and realized that she couldn't even remember the last time she'd had a new dress. She inhaled the aromas of coffee and fried onions as she passed diners bustling with people reading newspapers that were full of news, not propaganda.

At the first Help Wanted sign, Pintyi walked into a diner and calmly got herself a job. It seems, however, that she wasn't destined to be a waitress, for after getting pretty well every single order wrong, she was fired a day later. "They only hired me for my looks, not my skills," she says now, defensively.

But no matter. Within two weeks, Pintyi had another job, a better one, sorting files in the same insurance office where Frances worked. Besides, back then, she had other things on her mind.

"We arrived April twenty-first. I got fired April twenty-second. I was working again on April thirtieth, and I got married May twenty-first," Pintyi recalls.

It was as simple a wedding as could possibly be. Pintyi and Joe walked to City Hall through the early morning sunshine. "Are you sure you want to do this?" each asked the other as they walked along streets where the trees were covered in the faint green mist of young buds. "Yes, of course. And you?" "Absolutely."

Pintyi didn't have a wedding gown or a veil or flowers. Her father was the best man, and Frank and Cheese were witnesses. Pintyi wore a secondhand wool skirt and a blouse that some kind ladies had given her in Northern Ireland. Joe wore a hand-me-down suit, too big for his skinny frame. They couldn't afford rings, so they borrowed Jóska and Aranka's wedding bands, which were just about their only possessions that hadn't been lost or stolen or bartered for their safety. The vows were spoken in the unromantic language of bureaucracy. That didn't make them any less meaningful. In the end, their marriage lasted nearly forty years, until Joe died of cancer at the age of sixty-two.

Aranka missed the ceremony itself, because she'd stayed home to prepare the wedding lunch, the family's first feast in their new homeland. The first course was the traditional Hungarian wedding soup, the *tjúkhúsleves* (TYOOK-hoosh-leh-vesh), a rich chicken broth with snail-shaped noodles. Back home, the friends of the bride make the noodles, spending hours chatting about their own love lives while rolling out the *csiga tészta* (CHEE-guh-TAY-stuh), the pasta snails, on wire screens. Here, it was up to Aranka to do it all on her own. She started by simmering chicken pieces with salt and peppercorns to make the broth, adding carrots, celery root, and parsnips for flavor. When the broth was done, she let it sit for a bit, then carefully strained it to make sure that it would be clear and golden. She didn't have time to make her own pasta, so she bought some prepared noodles instead. The morning of the wedding, she reheated the broth and cooked the pasta separately, mixing the two together just before serving.

Meanwhile, Aranka was busy with the rest of the feast. She boiled and sliced potatoes for gratin, layering the potatoes with slices of hard-cooked eggs and onions, then covering it in sour cream before baking it. She'd bought a couple of nice, plump chickens and quickly cut them into pieces. She sprinkled them with salt and pepper, then rolled each piece in flour, swept it through some beaten egg, and patted bread crumbs all over it before frying it to a golden brown. She mixed together vinegar, sugar, and water for a simple salad dressing and tossed it with cucumbers sliced paper-thin.

The guests arrived hungry and happy to be greeted by bowls of golden soup, platters heaped with hot, crispy fried chicken, a huge dish of creamy potatoes, and tangy cucumber salad. Pintyi doesn't remember if there was cake. Surely, though, Aranka would have made one of her favorites, the cherry cake or the poppy seed roll called *beigli*. But Pintyi does remember that there was lots of wine to drink.

The party went late into the night, the guests toasting not only the young couple but also themselves and their future. Hungary, tired, gray, hopeless and war-battered, seemed very far away from this bright, cheerful place.

There was no money for a honeymoon, no romantic escape to Niagara Falls or Florida. In fact, "escape" was the last thing on their minds – nothing could be more romantic, they decided, than to stay in one place, to create a home, a real home, with family and friends all around them. So, after the wedding, Joe and Pintyi moved into an apartment and got started on the business of living. And one of the first things Pintyi decided she had to do was to learn how to cook.

During all the escapes and internments and years of living on other people's sofas, Pintyi had never learned to cook so much as an egg. There was always someone else to do it – more often than not, Aranka, who was such a good cook that no one else ever wanted to compete, and why should they? But now Pintyi was on her own, with a hungry husband and a shiny new Canadian kitchen to experiment in. She quickly discovered that learning to cook would not be quite as simple as, say, building dikes on the Tisza River or outsmarting Soviet soldiers, even though she had her mother coaching her from the other end of the phone every day.

The first thing Pintyi remembers trying to cook was fried chicken. She'd brought home a whole chicken and tried cutting it into pieces with a blunt, serrated knife that sent the slippery pieces sliding all over the counter, knobby bits of bone sticking rudely out from the jagged flaps of skin. When Joe saw the mutilated carcass, he simply refused to eat it. "He saw how I was chopping it up and said it was the most disgusting thing he'd ever seen in his life," Pintyi recalls. Instead, for that first meal, she made the pasta dish called *túros csusza* – noodles with cottage cheese and bacon – and that, at least, was palatable.

Thank goodness there was soup, or else the couple would surely have starved to death.

Soup is one of the most important elements in a Hungarian meal. Newcomers to the cuisine may at first be puzzled by the lack of appetizer dishes – after all, how many times do you want to order the cream cheese spread called *körözött* (KUR-uh-zut)? – until they realize that the usual first course in a Hungarian meal is soup. There are so many soups in the culture that the soup pages in a Hungarian cookbook take up almost as much room as the desserts do.

There are cold soups for hot summer days, made from sour cherry, cucumber, apple, quince or strawberry. There are hearty soups for cold winter days, like the smoky Jokai bean soup that is loaded with kidney beans, bacon, sausages, and sour cream. There are the main-course soups, *gulyás* and *halászlé*. There are special occasion soups like the wedding soup Aranka made for Pintyi or the delicious white wine soup called *borleves* (BOR-leh-vesh) that she made each Christmas. There are soups to serve when someone isn't feeling well, like the cumin soup for tummy aches or "night owl" soup for *más napos*, or hangovers. (It's certainly a much safer treatment for a hangover than that other traditional, what-won't-kill-you-will-make-you-stronger cure, the powerful herbal bitters called Unicum.) And there are everyday soups made from everything from asparagus to kohlrabi to lentils to venison. "I always make soup," my aunt Luizi says. "It's very good for you, very healthy, very tasty. It's good for healthy people and good for sick people, too."

Pintyi learned to make soups such as meat broth with liver dumplings and sour-cream-rich cauliflower soup. And, over the years, she became quite adept at pasta dishes and vegetable dishes like *lecso* (LECH-oh) (stewed peppers), lentils and *főzelék*, creamy vegetables puréed and cooked with a roux base. Hungarian cuisine is often criticized for being meat heavy, but the truth is that home cooks have always relied on noodles, broths, and hearty vegetables such as onions, potatoes, cabbage, and peppers, all the ingredients of a cuisine that is poor in cost but not in flavor or nutrition. Meat, for many decades, was a luxury, available to only the elite. That's why good Hungarian hosts will always have meat on their table, and why they will be hurt if you refuse it, even if you are a vegetarian. It's also why Pintyi claims she never really learned to cook meat – she lived for so long without it that she never understood how it works, exactly.

Aranka, though, reveled in the pork and chicken and beef that were so easily available in Canada, even though they wasn't as flavorful as the corn-fed versions she'd once enjoyed at home. In fact, when she arrived in Canada, Aranka vowed that she would have meat every day for the rest of her life to make up for all the meatless years. And so she did.

Aranka was delighted by the bounty of the new country. It was the first time in more than a decade that she'd had plenty of ingredients to cook with. She didn't have to raise her own pigs or make her own cheese; she could just go to Loblaws and get everything she wanted. There were no lineups, except at the cash register. And everything was big and fresh and shiny. She could buy meat that wasn't all gristle and milk that was sweet and rich. She could get fruit and vegetables all year round. She could even get salad in January. She missed the sour cherries and Hungarian peppers from home, but everything else more than made up for that loss.

"I remember they were so proud," Luizi says. "Father wrote us a letter that said, 'For ten dollars we went to the store and we got so much food that it covered the whole table.'"

For the new arrivals, the strangest thing was Ontario's bizarre attitude to drink. The Hungarians loved their wine, their beer, and their spirits, but they wouldn't get much chance to enjoy them in 1950s Toronto. For one thing, wartime rationing of liquor was only just ending; for another, Ontario, like most of Canada, was still affected by the years of Prohibition.

Between 1916 and 1927, Ontarians could only get liquor legally for medicinal reasons, that is, with a prescription. Even when the Fifty-sixers arrived, they still had to fill out a request for whatever drink they wanted and take it to a dreary liquor store as if they were going to a pharmacist. They would hand the form to a clerk, who would find what they wanted and wrap it (or something like it; you could never be entirely sure what you'd be getting) in brown paper. The purchaser then had to take it immediately, unwrapped and unopened, to the place where it would be drunk. Bars still had "ladies and escorts" rooms. Patrons were not allowed to stand up with a drink in their hands. Drinking was not allowed outside, not even in one's own backyard. Nor was it allowed on a Sunday, which meant that last call on a Saturday was at midnight.

Since this terrible state of affairs lasted well into the 1970s, the Hungarians set about finding ways to skirt the laws. Aranka bought red wine by the jugful. She made her own beer. And every summer, she'd buy bushels of cherries, soak them in over proof rum, and let them sit in a dark cool place until Christmas, when she'd serve them over ice cream. Luckily though, Jóska had given up his vodka-making experiments, so there were no exploding stills.

It should have been a happy time, and for the most part, it was. The women realized their good fortune and were making the best of it, making a bit of money, setting up their houses, cooking delicious meals, having a drink and a laugh with their friends. The men, on the other hand, weren't adjusting as well.

When Jóska's eyes gazed at Lake Ontario, he saw only the view of Balaton from his verandah. When he walked down Toronto streets filled with blaring automobiles, he heard instead the rhythmic clicking of the old Budapest trams. When the vicious winds howled from the north, he felt a much gentler breeze brush his face, the breeze that whispered through the poplar trees around the Wintermantel compound at Rákosszentmiháy. He knew he had much to be grateful for – he was warm and safe and had good food to eat and his family all around him – but he never felt at home in this brash new country.

Joe, too, was finding things difficult. When the refugee center on Queen Street closed down, so did Joe's interpreting job. He had hoped to become somebody important and influential, a civil servant or a diplomat or an interpreter. But in WASP-y, 1950s Toronto, where everyone who mattered had gone to school with everyone else who mattered, this was simply not going to happen. For one thing, he didn't have the connections that would ease him into the plum job he craved. For another, the power structure regarded a man with an accent with the deepest suspicion.

Instead, Joe got work as stock boy, a common laborer, lifting and stacking boxes, first at Sears and later at Chrysler. The men he worked with were less educated than he was, but they still felt they had the right to call him names like "the DP" and "the Hun" and to mock his accent. The latter was especially upsetting since he didn't think he had one.

It was a deeply humiliating experience. So night after night, Joe would go over to his sister's place to complain about his work. "Should

I go back to Hungary?" he asked Frances, again and again. "Would it be better to go back?"

The answer, of course, was no. Even though Hungary was the most western of the Eastern Bloc countries, with much greater freedoms and opportunities than most, the Iron Curtain had closed firmly against those who'd left its socialist embrace. Anyone involved with the Uprising – or, indeed, anyone even suspected of being involved – could expect to be severely punished if he returned. And when it came to a choice between manual labor in a warm, Canadian warehouse or manual labor in a chilly, Soviet jail, Joe wisely decided to stick with his current employer.

Back home, things were better in some ways than they were before 1956, while in others they were worse. Although the state took care of people's basic needs, making sure everyone had access to education, food, and health care, it also limited their freedoms.

"In the communist era, if you crossed the road improperly, they checked your ID," my Uncle Frank recalls with some bitterness. In fact, he says, the government controlled every part of life with its dogmatic rule: "You work eight hours, you rest eight hours, you entertain yourself for eight hours."

Throughout the sixties and seventies, people kept slipping over the borders. Those who were caught were sentenced to long prison terms – that is, if they weren't shot while trying to escape, or electrocuted or drowned or crushed by a train, or any other of a myriad ways people died while seeking a better life.

Aranka and Pintyi had an idea of what was going on back home from the letters Luizi wrote. She couldn't say too much, for the mail was heavily censored, but she did let them know that she was fine, that she missed them, and that she'd become the manager of a *menza*, the state-run cafeteria for the national beef producer in Veszprém, not far from their old place in Balatonalmádi. "She worked mainly for the beef," her husband, Frank, says now with a laugh.

At that time, the communists were replacing the Hungary's traditional lean gray cattle with high-production breeds, especially dairy cows. They were also raising almost all of that cattle for export, so while Hungary continued to be a major beef-producing country, its own citizens rarely got to savor any of the roasts, stews, or burgers – except at Luizi's *menza*.

"Our cafeteria was the best in the city," Luizi remembers. "Even the legal community from the other side of the city would come to us for lunch." Although Luizi didn't cook at the *menza* – she didn't really learn how until years later, when she moved to Canada and got married – she planned the menus and oversaw the staff and the organization.

"If we had a holiday or special occasion, we had wiener schnitzel with soup, a *húsleves* or consommé. Pork, not veal, because of course the cows had to grow up," Luizi recalls. "Sometimes we had mushrooms, *paprikás* mushrooms, because in that area we had a very nice mushroom, *vargánya*, that grows wild. It looks like a portabello, but it tastes much, much juicier. *Paprikás vargánya* – that was excellent food with dumplings."

Still, even though she worked at a national food production facility, Luizi still had difficulty getting some essential ingredients. Sour cream, for instance, was often thickened with flour or other mysterious substances. And one thing definitely off the menu was game, even though Veszprém was right near prime hunting territory and even though venison and rabbit and other wild beasts had traditionally been a major part of Hungarian cuisine. No one was allowed to have guns except the Soviet elite – just in case the citizenry should decide to take up arms against their leaders. For a while, ingredients were so scarce that the *menzas* probably saved many people from starving.

In fact, the *menzas* were probably the best aspect of the new communist culture. (If the Hungarians are going to get just one thing right, it'll be the food.) From Monday to Friday, every day at noon, a bell would ring and the factory or school or whatever institution the *menza* was located in would shut down for lunch. All the workers would head there, joined by families from the neighborhood. At 12:30 p.m., lunch would be over and they'd head back to work.

But not everyone had access to a *menza*. For one thing, only some institutions in bigger centers had them. For another, the food they served was cheap, not free, and inexpensive though it was, some families just couldn't afford it. Frank remembers what it was like as a kid living in a small Hungarian town in the late fifties. "When we took lunch to school, all we had year after year was two slices of bread with *lekvar* [jam] in between. Real poor kids took the proletariat sandwich. That's a joke," he adds. "It's one slice of bread between the other two."

Working at the *menza* was a good job for Luizi, and she wasn't unhappy, but she couldn't help wondering what life was like on the other side of the curtain. Her family never stopped asking her to come and join them – in very careful wording, so the censors wouldn't catch on to what was happening. At first, she wasn't ready to make the move, but sometime in the 1960s, it became clear that her family needed her more than ever.

Aranka was nearing mandatory retirement age and worried about what she would do all day long with just her and Jóska rattling about the house. Pintyi was pregnant with her first daughter – me – and worried about how she would balance her responsibilities. Joe had started taking university classes in addition to his full-time job and was worried about the future, about becoming a father, about the Bomb, about everything. He began suffering from terrible migraines and Pintyi worried that he was headed for a nervous breakdown. Pintyi needed her big sister, and Aranka wanted her family together again.

Luizi refuses to say much about how she left Hungary. As she tells it, her escape was surprisingly easy: One day, she went to visit friends in Austria and from there she took a train to Italy, where she got on a boat bound for North America. Simple as it sounds, though, she must have organized a clever ruse to be allowed to leave Hungary when thousands couldn't. And she must have had some help finding money for the transatlantic passage at a time when Hungarians couldn't exchange their forints for Western currency. Somehow, though, she managed it, and when she arrived in Canada, the reunion was joyous. By then the Wintermantels had bought the big house on Appleton and Aranka was letting out rooms on all the floors except the one where they lived. Luizi moved into the attic, and shortly after their baby was born, Joe and Pintyi moved into the second floor suite. It was the first time they'd all been together in seven years.

Luizi's first work experience in Canada was even worse than Pintyi's – and it didn't last much longer. She got a job putting strings into pouches for a yo-yo company. "I was sitting against a wall and I was crying," she recalls. "It was terrible. I hated that job." After that, Pintyi and Frances managed to get her a job at the company where they worked, and soon all three of them were working in the insurance business.

For a while, everyone seemed to be happy and settled. Even Jóska came out of his years-long funk to reveal his mischievous side, especially after Pintyi had a second baby, Franciska, whom everyone would call Fran. While Pintyi and Joe were at work, Jóska would take care of the little girls. He would take them to the park or the zoo, where he would make up stories about the animals and sing silly songs. Back home, he would make snacks and hide money for his granddaughters in a pair of baby shoes that he kept in his writing table. The girls soon learned to check Nagypapa's desk for pennies and dimes every time they came to visit.

Everyone was content, it seemed, except Joe.

He was restless once again, and his headaches and bad moods were getting worse all the time. The university courses hadn't led to jobs, and he couldn't lose the sense that there was a big world out there that he wasn't experiencing.

One day, he and Miska bacsi, Luizi's fiancé, decided to take a road trip. They got in the family Volkswagen and drove from Toronto clear across the country, right to Vancouver and on to Vancouver Island. There, amid the towering mountains and dark rain forests, Joe found peace. The two men were gone for months and when they returned were barely speaking to each other, having gotten thoroughly on each other's nerves with all that time spent cooped up in a tiny car. Still, they regaled us with stories of bears on the highway and whales in the ocean, of an idyllic land where the air was soft and the opportunities were endless.

From that day on, Joe wanted nothing more than to smell the salt breeze each day when he woke up and to listen to the cry of seagulls rather than the roar of traffic and the mocking voices of his co-workers. From that day on, it was inevitable that we would be moving west.

Eventually, both Joe and Pintyi managed to get transfers out west and, once again, Pintyi left her parents, her sister, her friends, and her home, and headed into the unknown. She wept to leave them behind, but as always, decided to look forward, not back, even if looking forward meant gazing in the direction of the setting sun.

British Columbia became home, but it did not make us settled. We eventually moved four times within the province. It was as if the nomadic genes of the original Magyars had been passed down across the centuries, only instead of a tough prairie pony, we had a Volkswagen Beetle, and instead of a soup cauldron, we had a paper bag full of salami sandwiches.

With each new place, we lost a little bit more of our Hungarianness. Joe was eager to shake off the past and encouraged his girls to speak English at home and without the Hungarian community around us, we lost the ability to wrap our tongues around that difficult language. He discouraged us from learning the country's history and traditions. He encouraged Pintyi to cook North American dishes instead of *gulyás* and we lost our taste for the food we'd grown up with, especially after we moved to the Kootenays, where it wasn't so easy to find exotic things like paprika.

Joe and Pintyi had found themselves a pair of jobs in a Rocky Mountain village called New Denver, a place that seemed about as far away from civilization as you could get. They went to work as house parents in a provincial government detention center, a home for juveniles who'd broken the law but weren't old enough or bad enough to go to jail. Joe saw this as the opportunity he'd been looking for, and Pintyi decided to humor him even though she had been perfectly happy with her job in insurance. By that fall, we were headed for the hills.

New Denver was a town of 500 people tucked into the narrow Slocan Valley in the southeastern corner of the province. It was a wilderness village where bears and bobcats would stroll happily across our lawn, so remote that we could only get one TV station, the ABC affiliate out of Spokane. We had to drive two hours each Saturday to Nelson to do our weekly grocery shopping.

Joe loved it because, for once, he wasn't the only outsider in the area — in fact, in the 1970s, it was full of misfits and loners. The Kootenays had become a haven for draft dodgers, hippies, drug dealers, witches, and all sorts of counterculturists. Earlier, during the

Second World War, the newcomers had been the Japanese who'd been interned there by the federal government. Before that, it was the Doukhobors, who'd fled from religious persecution in Tsarist Russia. A radical splinter group called the Sons of Freedom would occasionally launch a series of protests that involved arson and, much more entertainingly for us all, mass nudity.

Us? We were just a family with a taste for paprika.

That didn't stop other people, especially their kids, from laughing at the latest newcomers. The little girls soon learned that to fit in with their neighbors, they'd have to eat like them. So when Pintyi made *gulyás*, her daughters would beg for Campbell's chicken noodle soup. When she made their favorite "grizzly noodles" (*grizes tészta*) (GREE-sesh TAY-stuh) — noodles with fried wheatlets, nicknamed for the local bruins — they'd turn up their noses and ask for Chef Boyardee spaghetti in a can. And when she gave them salami sandwiches for lunch, they'd clamor for Cheez Whiz.

There was no Cheez Whiz or Chef Boyardee on the table that first Christmas in New Denver, though. Missing their daughter and granddaughters, Aranka and Jóska got on a Greyhound bus and traveled all the way from Toronto to see them. After the cramped, five-day trip, they staggered off the bus in Castlegar, pale, wan and horrified to learn they still had a two-hour mountain drive ahead of them, but bravely smiling and smothering their granddaughters with hugs and kisses.

That night in New Denver, they unpacked suitcase after suitcase full of gifts, including a couple of party dresses that Aranka had made out of pink and gold fabric that was as pretty as wrapping paper. On Christmas Eve, Pintyi made her daughters get into their new dresses, accessorized with white tights and black patent leather shoes, so they'd be ready for the festivities later. Then Joe took them for a drive, while Pintyi and Jóska decorated the tree and Aranka prepared a Christmas feast of fried fish and potatoes and salad and chestnut puree.

After Christmas, Aranka went back to Toronto and Jóska stayed in New Denver for a full year. At seventy, he was slowing down, getting achier and more forgetful, but still he cooked and took care of the girls, told them stories, and lavished everyone with love. The following Christmas Joe and Pintyi drove the family back to Toronto. It was a terrible trip.

All five of us were packed in the ancient white Volkswagen Bug Joe had plastered with big fluorescent flower decals so it would be visible against the snowy roads. Jóska was crammed in the back with his granddaughters, and they were sick and cranky the whole way. It was so cold that halfway across Montana, the engine froze solid in the middle of an empty highway. It took hours before anyone showed up to tow it to warmth and safety. There was rain and sleet and snow, and snow, and more snow. Finally, just outside Toronto on the Queen Elizabeth Highway, a drunk driver rear-ended the little Bug and sent it flying over the guardrail. It rolled six times before coming to a stop at the bottom of the embankment. Ambulances rushed us to hospital, but miraculously, the injuries were minor – Jóska with a broken arm, Joe with ringing in his ears, the girls with concussion, and everyone with a sense that Toronto was not exactly welcoming us home.

When we finally arrived at the old house on Appleton Avenue, bloodied and bruised and banged up, it was to discover that our little world had changed while we'd been magicked away in our mountain valley.

Like our family, the other Fifty-sixers had been building new lives for themselves. Perhaps they'd thought, when they arrived all those years ago, that one day they'd be able to go home again. But now it seemed that the communist regime would last forever and that few of us would ever be able to return to the boulevards of Budapest and the beaches of Lake Balaton. So, like Aranka, the other Hungarian refugees looked resolutely to the future, and gradually let the past fade into forgetfulness.

True, some of them opened Hungarian restaurants, started Hungarian clubs, and attended the annual Hungarian debutante balls in Toronto and Calgary. Some of them read the Hungarian papers from back home and made traditional foods each night. But for the most part, they became as Canadian as anyone could be. And even when the older folks clung to their Magyar-ness, they made sure that their sons and daughters were truly Canadian, so that the younger generation could have the sort of unconflicted life that was denied the older. Even if the parents or grandparents had to open a restaurant or deli to make a living, they worked hard to make sure that was the last thing their children would ever have to do.

When Joe and Pintyi returned to Toronto, they found that the Hungarian community, always a fractious one at best, had splintered even further. The delis and restaurants that opened in the fifties and sixties were starting to close one after the other. Neighborhoods where Hungarians had once gathered were being taken over by new waves of immigrants. Their friends had begun to leave, too. Deszö and Kati had moved to Baffin Island, of all places, to open an inn, while Mara and Nori had moved to Vancouver. Some people moved on to the States, others back to Europe, to Germany and France and England. Meanwhile, though, the trickle of new arrivals from Hungary hadn't stopped — and it was among them that Luizi would finally find love.

A few years earlier, a young architect named Frank Ferenczi had found that opportunities were few in Hungary, but restrictions were many. One day in 1967 he got himself a visa to Yugoslavia and traveled to the northern border, where a rushing river separated the communist country from Austria. There he met a Croatian man who helped him swim over. From there, he made it to Vienna, and from Vienna to Winnipeg, where he'd been hoping to find work as an architect. The only job he could find was as a welder's helper, though, so he kept traveling, west to Vancouver Island, south to Ecuador and, shortly after we returned to British Columbia, north to Toronto.

There he renewed his friendship with an old Hungarian pal who had rented a room in a big, old house on Appleton Avenue, one floor down from an elegant woman named Luizi. Frank and Luizi met one evening, and it was love at first sight. She wooed him with pastries; he wooed her with gin and tonics. A couple of years later they were married.

As with Aranka and Pintyi, it wasn't until she married that Luizi began to cook seriously. She soon discovered that, like her mother, she could go to a restaurant, taste a dish once, and recreate it at home. "You can feel the different spices and everything," Luizi says. "Actually, I don't use a lot of spices. Paprika and black pepper is good enough for me. I always say I don't want to use too much spice because I want to taste the vegetable or meat that I'm making. Like asparagus is such a special thing, you want to be able to taste it."

By the time Frank and Luizi got married, though, the rest of the family was gone from Toronto. Aranka and Jóska had sold the house, packed their bags and moved to Vancouver. In part, they wanted to be closer to their grandchildren, but they also disliked the changes their old neighborhood was undergoing. They had begun to feel isolated and unwanted, afraid of the gangs of young toughs who prowled the street.

Aranka and Jóska bought a gorgeous old house just off Spanish Banks beach. For nearly two decades, that house, with its leaded glass windows, big old-fashioned kitchen, and lovely garden filled with rose bushes and monkey puzzle trees, became the family's definition of home. Even as we moved from house to house, from village to town to city, it was the one constant, the place we knew would always be there. It was the place we gathered each year for Christmas, the place we ate and drank and laughed and argued.

A couple of years later, in 1974, Luizi and Frank moved to Vancouver, too. Although they'd gotten married in Toronto, they held another ceremony in Vancouver's Hungarian Catholic Church. Their nieces were bridesmaids, dressed in ugly pink and blue polyester dresses with elasticized ruching across the bodice. They giggled throughout the ceremony.

That same year, Aranka and Jóska celebrated their fiftieth wedding anniversary. They got a letter of congratulations from then-Prime Minister Pierre Trudeau and everyone went out to a Hungarian restaurant and ate Transylvanian platters of delicious fried foods. The tables were all arranged in a big square and everyone sat around the outside so no one had their back to anyone else. The toasts kept coming all night along with the wine, and Aranka and Jóska were given a pair of gold-plated goblets, one inscribed with her name, one with his, and meant never to be parted.

Meanwhile, Joe and Pintyi finally left the valley and moved to Vancouver Island, where Pintyi suddenly seemed to realize that her daughters had been missing out on their Hungarian heritage. We traveled to Hungary to visit the family for the first time, staying with Joe's mother, Agnes, who made us cry, and visited with Gubby and Ke-ke, who made us laugh. We went to the old summerhouse on Lake Balaton, which was always cool and dark no matter how bright and sunny it was outside. It smelled a little sad, haunted by ghosts of the past.

In 1983, Jóska fell ill. One day, it seemed, he was the same old gentle soul we knew, going for his daily walk, amusedly deflecting his wife's criticisms and amusing his granddaughters. The next, he was diagnosed with prostate cancer, and was lying in his room, his life ebbing slowly away.

He refused to have surgery, refused to go into hospital for treatment. Perhaps he didn't want to be surrounded by strangers speaking a language he couldn't understand. Perhaps he knew it was his time to go. Or perhaps he couldn't let go of a decades-old fear; after all, a man who had lived through those terrible years in the torture chambers on Andrássy Út knew better than most what could happen in a big institution.

So he lived out his last days at home, surrounded by the people who loved him the most. Aranka, Luizi and Pintyi cared for him around the clock, bringing him a bowl of soup, a glass of wine, a handful of pills to ease the pain. They comforted him and told him stories, and wept when they were out of his sight.

Jóska died without ever seeing his sister or brother again, or their children, or their children's children. He died without ever again walking through the family's gardens in Rákosszentmihály or gazing out at the waters of Lake Balaton. He died without ever going home again.

If only he could have held on for just a few more years. In 1989, one by one, the communist regimes of Eastern Europe began to fall. And when the Berlin wall came down on November 9, suddenly we all could see our way back home again.

CHAPTER 8
1989

That Christmas, everyone got a chunk of the Berlin Wall. There must have been half-a-dozen identically shaped gifts under the tree at Aranka's place that year. One by one we all – Mom, Dad, Nori, Mara, Fran, and I – opened them to find the same thing: a small drawstring bag filled with a gray and crumbly bit of the wall that symbolized, more than anything else, the separation of Eastern Europe from the rest of the world.

The Wall between East and West Germany had come down only a few short weeks earlier, on November 9, 1989. That day, we had turned on the TV to see crowds of teenagers standing on the wall, waving and cheering. Two weeks before that, Hungary had declared itself a republic. Just like that, on October 23, right on the thirty-third anniversary of the 1956 Uprising, the communist regime ended in Hungary. By Christmas, the communist governments had also fallen in Bulgaria, Romania, and Czechoslovakia. Suddenly, it really and truly seemed possible to go home again.

There was a lot to celebrate that Christmas. But then, there always was.

Christmas was always Aranka's holiday. All year long, she planned for the big day when she would throw open her house to her family and closest friends. But each year, our little group seemed to be getting smaller and smaller. Jóska was gone. Luizi and Frank had moved back to Toronto. Nori and Mara were spending more and more time in Europe and this would be their last Christmas in Canada. Our family friends Muci and Ali, who usually joined us at Christmas, had other plans this year, and Frances and Frank were staying home in Toronto. I was working in another province and Fran was working in another city, so we'd dropped by just for the festivities. It was a small celebration that year; little did we know that it would also be the last one we'd spend together.

We always celebrated Christmas on the Eve, not the morning. I could never understand the appeal of celebrating in pajamas with toast and hot chocolate when you could celebrate in high heels with champagne and caviar. (Actually, we got the best of both worlds – our family feast on the Eve and then our Christmas stockings and turkey dinner on the twenty-fifth.)

Nagymama would collect wrapping paper and gifts all year long. By the beginning of December, she'd be cleaning and baking, making *pogacsa* and *beigli* (BYE-glee) and other tasty morsels. She'd stock up the liquor cupboard and, while Jóska was still alive, make sure to keep the key well hidden from her husband.

The tree wouldn't go up until the twenty-fourth. When we were little, Dad would take me and my sister for a drive in the afternoon while Nagymama, Mom and Luizi would put up the tree in the living room, decorate it, and place all the gifts below it. When it was completely dark, we came home. But we still couldn't see the tree. Instead, we'd have to wait impatiently in the breakfast room where all the adults were drinking cocktails and we'd get a glass of soda water with a splash of wine in it.

Then we'd hear a little silver bell. "Baby Jesus has arrived!" someone would say, and the doors to the living room would swing open on a magical scene. In a corner of the darkened room, where a pair of armchairs and a side table usually stood, a sparkling tree had appeared. It was covered in lights and *szalonczukor* – twinkling foil-wrapped Christmas candies all the way from Hungary. Nagymama would have hung wrapped liqueur-filled chocolates from the tree, too, along with all the battered old decorations she'd carefully wrapped up and put away each year since 1957. Our eyes would open wide in awe, especially when we saw the mountain of gifts glittering beneath the tree, courtesy of the Baby Jesus. He was always very generous, we thought, especially since it was *his* birthday we were supposed to be celebrating.

Someone would put an old, scratched German recording of "Silent Night" on the equally old record player. As the sweet strains filled the air (along with a certain amount of crackling and popping), we'd all walk slowly into the living room, where we'd stand silently before the tree until the song was over. While it played, you could see the different thoughts flicker across the faces aglow in the Christmas tree's light: everything from grief to joy to greed, at least on the faces of two little girls hoping that the big box had the Barbie airplane, not new winter boots like last year. More nobly, and increasingly as we grew older, we'd think about how lucky we were to be alive and healthy and together. We would use the time to reflect on the year past and to wonder about the year ahead. When the last scratchy strains of the violin crackled and sighed to an end, the room lights would go up and we'd all hug and kiss each other, tears in our eyes, before opening the champagne and, of course, the gifts.

"Don't tear the paper!" our frugal Nagymama would call out. "Save the ribbons!"

Each of us would grab a chair that became our gift station. I liked the small blue and gold brocade love seat that made me feel like a princess; it was big enough for tons of gifts but too small to share with anyone else, and it had the added advantage of being close to the tree. Dad would always play Santa Claus – over the years, the once-skinny young guy had developed a physique that made him particularly suitable for the job, not that he appreciated it when people pointed this out.

There were gifts of books and clothes and jewelry and crystal, and in 1989, enough pieces of the Berlin Wall to pave the front walkway. Each time one of us opened a box to find the increasingly familiar drawstring bag, a shout of laughter would go up. To Fran and me, it was just a bit of pop culture kitsch. To the rest of the clan, it was something else, a symbol of how fragile our freedoms were; how quickly they could be lost; how little separated freedom from oppression; how easily families, friends, and lovers could be exiled from each other.

None of us had ever dreamed that the communist regime could collapse so suddenly, without any bloodshed. Yet it had not happened without warning. While the West was indulging itself in the Me Decade, with its yuppies, power suits, and flashy cars, things had been loosening up on the other side of the wall, too. In 1985, Mikhail Gorbachev had become leader of the USSR and introduced his ideals of openness (*glasnost*) and restructuring (*perestroika*). He began by reducing the Soviet Union's control over the countries of the Soviet Bloc. Things got so mellow that by 1988, he told the United Nations that, should rebellion break out in any of the Eastern European countries, he would not send the tanks in to quell the uprising.

In January 1989, the Hungarian Parliament voted to allow freedom of association and assembly, and scheduled elections for a year later. In March, eight opposition groups formed an opposition roundtable to take on the official government. By June, the Hungarian government was discussing how to make the change from totalitarian state to electoral democracy. In Budapest, the martyrs of the 1956 Uprising were exhumed and reburied in a state funeral attended by 200,000 people. In October, the Communist party voted to reject Leninism; soon after that, Hungary officially became a real republic, not a people's republic. And that November the 155 kilometers of concrete and barbed wire built in 1961 to separate East and West came crashing down.

All that political upheaval gave us a lot to talk about that year while we were enjoying Aranka's magnificent Christmas feast.

Dinner always followed the gifts, though even while we were going through the loot under the tree, Nagymama offered us platters of goodies – cheese straws, *pogacsa*, and open-faced sandwiches, as well as a few sweets. Dinner itself would start with *borleves*, wine soup. It was a hot and spicy mixture of white wine simmered with cloves and cinnamon. Nagymama would beat in the eggs just before serving the soup, making it all rich and creamy, then dish it out quickly into pretty little soup cups arranged on a silver tray. Then she'd assign one of the men – ideally, one who hadn't had a lot to drink – to bring the tray into the dining room.

The dining room was actually a sunroom at the back of the house that did triple duty as a guestroom, conservatory, and dining room. For Christmas, she'd add two extra leaves in the table and fit as many chairs around it as she could. We'd all be sitting there, with glasses full of champagne and little angel placecard holders in front of us (everyone wanted the angel with the harp; no one wanted the angel with the broken wing) waiting to hear the first melodic tinkle of the soup cups rattling on the tray as it made its stately procession from the faraway kitchen. When everyone had a cup in front of them, we'd raise our glasses in a toast. "*Boldog karacsony!*" we'd cry. "Merry Christmas!"

Once the soup cups were cleared, the platters would start coming out. In the old Catholic way, the main course was always seafood. Some years, Nagymama would make a traditional roasted carp. She'd make a special trip to Chinatown to buy the carp live from a tub on the sidewalk, getting the shop owner to kill it for her with a quick blow to the head. Then she'd bake it with peppers, tomatoes, sour cream, and just a little bit of paprika on top of a layer of potatoes. Other years, she'd prepare salmon, poaching or roasting a big filet with lemons and dill and cream. The best years, though, were when she made lobster ragout, meaty chunks of fresh lobster simmered in a sauce rich with butter and wine and served over rice.

She'd also have a roast pork loin stuffed with a Debrecen sausage and sliced thin, as well as a sort of meatloaf stuffed with boiled eggs and cut so that each piece had a perfect slice of egg in the middle. Sometimes there would be other roast meats as well, served cold or hot depending on her mood and how much space there was in the oven.

Then there were all the side dishes: a mayonnaise salad of chopped carrots, peas, and corn decorated with deviled eggs; scalloped potatoes layered with sour cream and sliced boiled eggs; *rizsi bizsi* (REESH-ce BEESH-ee) – rice cooked with peas and herbs; red cabbage tossed with caraway seeds; and so much more I can't even begin to remember it at all.

There would be lashings of wine, of course, and even we kids would get a little splash in a glass of soda water. This drink is called a *fröccs* (FRISH) in Hungary, and is a popular hot weather drink as well as a treat for kids and refresher during the day for both men and women. Unlike North American spritzers, which are always made with white wine, the *fröccs* is more often made with red. It is, in fact, such a key part of social drinking that there are several levels to the *fröccs*, depending on the ration of wine to soda water. As kids, we were served the *hosszúlépés*, the "long step" – that is barely a splash of wine in a tumbler of soda; as we grew older we graduated to the *kis fröccs*, the "little spritzer," and then the *nagy fröccs*, the "big spritzer," and finally to a glass of wine on its own. It's a most civilized way to teach youngsters to appreciate wine – and to tolerate it without getting drunk and obnoxious on their first time out.

When the main courses were done, out would come the sweets. The centerpiece was always a Monte Bianco, an enormous mound of pureed chestnuts and sweetened whipped cream. There would always be *beigli*– in fact, it wouldn't be Christmas without the traditional rolled-up pastries filled with poppy seeds or walnuts. There would always be platters of cookies, too, just in case we were still hungry.

Then, finally, we'd indulge in the cheese course. In France, cheese is served before the sweet because its purpose is to give guests something to nibble on while finishing the wine. In Hungary, the conversation is always more important than the wine, so the cheese course is designed to give people something to nibble on while they finish the conversation, which can go well into the night and even the next morning. Often, the conversation would revive the old family stories.

"Do you remember that Christmas at the camp in Tiszabö?" they'd start. "Oh, remember that time in Scotland when Jóska's still blew up? Remember how Luizi fell into the latrine in Rosenheim? Do you remember?"

Sometimes the conversation would be about me and my sister, about work or school or the boys we were dating. But it always turned to current events and politics, and that Christmas was no exception. In fact, that Christmas, everyone was buzzing with the news about the fall of the Wall, hardly daring to believe it, yet suddenly realizing that they could go home again, that they could see their friends and family again, that they could even live there again if they wanted to. Oh, if only the Soviets hadn't taken away the old house on Lake Balaton three years earlier!

As we kissed each other goodnight, tipsy on wine and champagne, weighed down with our bags of gifts, we couldn't know that it would be the last Christmas we'd spend with Aranka, the last time we'd sit around her dining table.

That Christmas, for the first time, she looked fragile. Even though she'd still managed to climb onto the roof to fix a broken shingle the previous summer, we could tell that she was starting to wear out. She was moving more slowly and had made fewer dishes for the feast than she ever had before. We had all worried that after Jóska was gone, Aranka would fade quickly. Every day of their life together, she had scolded him and nagged him and snapped at him, and locked up his booze, and made him eat his vegetables – and she had adored him with every fiber of her being.

On January 20, she turned eighty-eight. I was back at work in Calgary by then and sent her pink roses for her birthday. That night she called me to thank me, and we talked for a little while about this and that. She sounded tired and a bit low, but I wasn't worried – she was my indestructible Nagymama.

A day later, she was found dead, collapsed on the floor by her bed. It seemed that she'd gotten up in the night and had somehow fallen, hitting her head on the bedside table. And just like that, that sudden blow knocked out the center of our little family. With Aranka died any interest I had in my Hungarian heritage.

CHAPTER 9
Roux the Day

It's funny, though, how things you think are in the past will sometimes pop right into the present. I never thought I'd care about my Hungarian heritage. I never thought I'd want to know how to make a *paprikás* or a *pörkölt* or any other Hungarian dish. And even if I did, I certainly never thought I'd call ever my mother for cooking advice. And yet . . .

My mother often said that the cooking genes had skipped a generation and she always said it in a way that suggested she wasn't exactly upset about it. Although she had a few specialties – cheese straws, soup, *főzelék*, and these lovely little meringue cookies – cooking was not her great passion.

I, on the other hand, was what one friend likes to call a "food fascist." My first career goal was to be a "cooking lady," which was not exactly a goal encouraged by parents who thought "doctor," "lawyer" or "prime minister" sounded more impressive. Still, I managed to parlay that early enthusiasm into a career as a food writer, and that's not a bad thing at all.

Over the years, I've worshipped at the shrine of Julia Child, Martha Stewart, Alice Waters et al. I've collected twenty years of *Gourmet* and *Bon Appétit* magazines and developed a bigger collection of cookbooks than most bookstores have. I've taken classes just to learn how to sharpen my knives. I've always had a pantry filled with the best and most authentic (read: expensive) foodstuffs, including, right at this moment, no fewer than seven different bottles of truffle oil. Even though I've always had minuscule kitchens, I've managed to accumulate practically every appliance known to kitchenkind, as well as the best pots and utensils I could afford.

I'm largely a self-taught cook, though, and when I was in my twenties, learning how to chop and braise and roast and bake, Mom's kitchen made me crazy. She didn't have a single really sharp knife, accurate measuring cups, proper mixing bowls, or any of the appliances I had come to consider necessary to making even the simplest of meals. I mean, how did people cook before there were Cuisinarts and Kitchen Aid mixers? I ask you.

Her pots and pans and utensils were old and battered and, often, half-melted. None of them matched, and many of them bore patches of rust. In our Vancouver house, the oven was about fifty years old and had two temperature settings – about a zillion degrees and Off, neither of which was conducive to making delicate cakes or pastries. Though somehow Mom always managed to make her cheese straws turn out right.

We didn't have a pantry and the fridge was always crammed with pots containing an inch or two of a mysterious foodstuff that looked like the leathery remains of some ghastly crime. My dad never quite mastered the concept of food storage, so he was always chucking things into the fridge without wrapping them properly (or at all): opened cans of tomato sauce, unwrapped bricks of cheese, a lone pork chop on a plate. At the back of the fridge the scariest thing of all was the can of bacon fat that Mom would top up regularly. She would scoop out big dollops of fat from the can for frying. We always hoped that she'd never get to the earliest archeological layers – the drops of grease clinging to the bottom of the can were probably as old as we were.

I'm the kind of paranoid cook who dumps out the milk one minute after midnight on the expiry date, while Mom would often scoff at the concept of "best before" labeling. "It's just a marketing ploy to make you spend more money," she'd say, giving the milk the sniff test and ignoring the fact that it came out in gelatinous globs. "See? It's perfectly fine."

This attitude was partly why I hesitated to ask for advice. The other reason was that I'd tried it before, with somewhat dubious results. The first time was when I was eight and wanted to make a cake. Mom gave me a promotional cookbook from Purity, the flour people, and hoped I'd just figure it out by myself, which of course I couldn't do since it turned out to be a lot harder than using my Easy Bake Oven. So, with a sigh, she set me up with a pot and one of those old, metal hand beaters (not being much of a baker herself, she didn't have mixing bowls or an electric mixer) and taught me the basics of cake-making. She explained how to cream butter and what it meant to alternate dry and liquid ingredients and reminded me how lucky we were that we could buy icing in a can so we didn't have to waste time making our own.

The cake turned out all lopsided and lumpy and a bit gooey in the middle, but I was pretty proud of it and took it to school to share with the rest of Grade 3.

"Yum," my teacher said, not all that convincingly. "But what are all the black flecks? Did you use a vanilla bean?"

Vanilla bean, I thought? What the heck was that?

Later I told Mom what Mrs. Bell had said, and we both looked sadly at the pot we'd mixed the cake in. It was a Teflon-coated pot, and it was no longer very Teflon-coated at all.

The last time I asked her for culinary advice, I was in high school and wanted to roast a duck to impress a boy who was a bit of a gourmet. Dinner at his house was always something fancy like made-from-scratch asparagus soup with crème fraîche and rack of lamb from their very own herd of sheep. I figured duck would impress him. And it probably would have, had it been any duck but this one.

"Just put it in the oven, it'll be fine," Mom said.

"Are you sure?" I asked dubiously.

Sure enough, there was no finesse to this duck, no delicate cherry compote or juniper-infused jus or savory stuffing or even, I'm embarrassed to admit, a rudimentary bit of trussing. Nope, it was just a duck, in a pan, roasted at high heat until the bones stuck out of its poor, furnace-blasted legs and the breast was covered in big, blackened blisters.

"Um, I'm not really in the mood for duck," Geoff said, eyeing the sad specimen splayed in the charred yet rusty roasting pan. "How about pizza?"

To her credit, Mom's kitchen was generally a fun place. There was always plenty of wine and the radio was always on and she didn't care too much if dinner didn't turn out exactly right, so things were pretty relaxed unless Dad was having a bad day. In my kitchen, on the other hand, tensions would often run high and tears were not unusual. Still, for the longest time, I couldn't imagine asking Mom for any more cooking tips – if anything, that was *my* area of expertise.

But one bright spring day in 2004, there I was on the phone, trying to learn how to make my childhood favorite, "grizzly noodles." It's a simple noodle dish that Hungarian moms have been making forever. Still, the first time I made it, you'd have thought we were trying to perform neurosurgery by remote control.

"First, you take the wheatlets –"

"Um. OK. What are wheatlets?"

"You know, wheatlets. They come in a bag."

"Uh, no, I don't know. Do you mean wheat germ? Cream of wheat? Something like that?"

"No, just wheatlets."

"Oh. Well, how much do you need?"

Pause. "Half a cup?" Another pause. "Maybe a third of a cup?"

"Well, which is it?"

"Let's say a third of a cup. And then you need some butter."

"How much butter?"

"Oh, I don't know – a bit."

By now I was grinding my teeth. A large part of my day job is editing recipes so that they will make sense for average cooks. I am used to translating complex concoctions by fancypants chefs and I was not willing to be defeated by a simple peasant recipe. Ha! What I didn't know was that my difficulties with the noodles would set the pattern for my entire foray into Hungarian cooking.

I'd started on the project as a bit of a lark, a goofy idea born of boredom. Years earlier, I'd regularly taken on these big cooking projects— one year, I taught myself how to make candy; another I learned how to cook Thai; yet another year it was Italian, or French, or Southwestern. It had been a while since I'd embarked on one of these culinary explorations, but I figured Hungarian cooking would be the same as all the other times.

I was wrong.

For one thing, you know how people are always saying things like "simple isn't easy"? Well, that's especially true with Hungarian cooking. The techniques were all different from anything I'd ever cooked before, and it made my head melt just trying to understand why things were done a certain way.

Take stew. In the familiar western stews — such as Boeuf Bourguignonne or Irish stew — meat is browned and braised in liquid, then a thickening agent is added to create the sauce. Hungarian stews, on the other hand, be they *pörkölt* or *paprikás* or *tokány*, are basically eastern or Asian stews. This means that the meat braises in its own juices and no thickening agent is added; instead the liquids are simmered until they are reduced to a sauce-y consistency.

Another difficulty was that the recipes all seemed to call for tools I didn't own. Suddenly I found myself buying things that I remembered from my grandmother's kitchen, but that most cooks of my generation don't have, such as weight scales (like most Europeans, Hungarians describe pastry recipes in weight, not volume), meat grinders, potato ricers, crêpe pans, and even a spaëtzle maker.

Ah, yes, the spaëtzle maker. The traditional accompaniment to *pörkölt* and *paprikás* is *galuska* (GUH-loosh-kuh), tiny succulent dumplings that are tooth tender and perfectly formed for absorbing the sauce. They are similar to the German spaëtzle, though the Germans tend to fry their little dumplings with onions and herbs while the Hungarians simply toss them with butter.

Mom always make *galuska* by hand, chopping the batter with a knife directly into boiling water. Her *galuska* were slightly bigger and more rustic than most recipes call for, but delicious nonetheless. When I tried her method, though, it was a disaster; producing great big spongy blobs that disintegrated in the pot and had a decidedly watery consistency when served with the veal *paprikás*.

So I bought the spaëtzle maker. "You don't need that," Mom said scornfully. "Oh yes I do," I retorted, and tried the *galuska* again using the spaëtzle maker.

If you've never seen one of these gadgets, it looks kind of like one side of a cheese grater, with a box-like compartment that slides across the holes. You lay it across a pot of boiling, salted water, fill the box with batter, and then slide it back and forth. The batter drops through the holes and into the water to form perfectly shaped little dumplings.

With this special tool, I produced *galuska* that were tiny little spongy blobs with a decidedly watery consistency. I said a lot of bad words, decided to blame the cookbook, and looked up another recipe. This one explained that what we needed to do was form gluten, which means you have to beat the flour and eggs and water together *hard* for quite a bit, then let it sit for a while, until gluten is formed. That's what gives you the firm, as opposed to mushy, texture.

Oh, I thought, it's like pasta, and tried again. This time they were perfect. (Mind you, a third cookbook advises strongly against beating the batter this hard or letting it sit this long, so I guess it's whatever works for you.) But how ridiculous it seemed that I could master something as complicated as Thai spring rolls with a spicy tamarind-chili sauce the very first time I tried to make them, while it took me three attempts to make something as basic as dumplings. And that was before the Hortobagyi *palacsinta* fiasco.

The Hortobagy is a region in eastern Hungary comprising a large chunk of the Alföld, or the Great Plain. Its administrative capital is the baroquely beautiful city Debrecen, which is where this dish was invented about a hundred years ago at the elegant Hotel Arany Bika. *Palacsinta* are crêpes. *Palacsinta* done in the Hortobagy style (let's call them "HP" for short) are crêpes filled with a savory meat filling and topped with a paprika-and-sour-cream sauce.

I looked up a couple of recipes for HP and the method looked pretty simple. Just sauté some onions, add some paprika, stir in some chopped meat, simmer it for a while, then stuff the filling into the crêpes and cover them with a sauce made by stirring some paprika into sour cream.

I decided to make HP for a dinner party, and to make the recipe even easier, used ground chicken instead of chopped meat. One of the difficulties I found with my year of living Hungarianly was how few dishes I could serve to my non-meat-eating friends; this was one I thought would work. But it was a disaster. Oh, everyone was polite, but the texture was horribly nubbly, the crêpe filling had no flavor, and the sauce wasn't a sauce at all, but sour cream with paprika in it.

"Well, at least the crêpes were good," Lionel said consolingly.

Later, when I asked my Aunt Luizi how to make HP, she looked puzzled and said, "Well it's very simple," she began. "You can use chopped ham mixed with sour cream, or a bit of leftover *pörkölt*." And suddenly the light went on. Of course, a Hungarian would automatically assume that you prepare the filling the way you would a *pörkölt*; you wouldn't even have to tell them that, just as you wouldn't have to explain to a western cook what you mean by browning the ground beef for tacos or creaming the butter for a cake.

So I tried it again. This time, I made a *pörkölt* with boneless, skinless chicken thighs. I let it simmer for a couple of hours, then left it to cool overnight and let the sauce drained from the stew. The next morning, I ground the chicken in my shiny new meat grinder (which, please note, had taken weeks to find). Then I stirred some sour cream into the sauce and mixed half of it with the chicken, and set the other half aside. I made a batch of crêpes, stuffed them with the chicken, baked them, poured the set-aside sauce over them and served them for Sunday dinner. They were fantastic. My aunt would have been proud of me.

One down, but many to go. It seemed that each dish went through a similarly frustrating process. Sometimes I couldn't understand the measurements. Other times I didn't understand the techniques, or why you had to do things a certain way, such as why you needed to make a roux for so many dishes. Roux, in case you didn't know, is a mixture of flour and fat used for thickening sauces and stews and vegetable purées; it always seems to me that there must be some better, easier way to reach that perfect consistency. Obviously, in the case of Hungarian cuisine, I'm wrong.

Sometimes the ingredients were foreign and unobtainable: white bacon, a special type of high-gluten flour, cake yeast, palinka, purple onions, sour cherries, or *túro*, a creamy yet slightly grainy, slightly tart ewe's milk pot cheese. (Most recipes suggest using cottage cheese instead. But I've found cottage cheese to be pebbly, watery and bland, so I use ricotta, which is a bit too creamy and mild, but certainly more like *túro* than cottage cheese is.)

And, of course, sometimes things just went wrong for no good reason at all.

But the real reason all of this was so hard was that it wasn't just a case of learning a new cuisine or a new culture. It was *my* culture that I was exploring, *me* I was really getting to know, and that made everything more difficult.

I came to think of it as the Magyar Madness, a sort of insanity born of loneliness and boredom. It was the solution I found when I didn't know I'd asked a question, the purpose I'd discovered when I thought my life was full enough already.

The day I called my mother for help in making "grizzly noodles," Lionel and I were, once again, living in a strange new place, the third city and the fifth home we'd lived in over the past five years. My latest employer was the fourth I'd had in that time; my job the seventh different position I'd held. I was in Calgary, but I'd left my family scattered in Victoria, Vancouver, and Budapest; my in-laws were in Prince George; most of my friends lived in Vancouver and Toronto; my heart, I'd left who knows where.

It seemed that I'd always been on the move. Dad kept us on the go when we were kids, of course, and then after I graduated from university and became a journalist, I moved from Vancouver to Alberta, back to Vancouver, on to Toronto, back to Alberta – back and forth across the country I ricocheted, ostensibly for work, but really always searching for home.

The last five years though, had been particularly peripatetic. I had twice lost all those things you come to rely on – the great gym with that awesome trainer who knows just how hard to push you, the bakery that makes the perfect baguette, the butcher who knows you by name, the hair stylist who will always squeeze you in at the last minute, the rhythms and cadences of the places you love. This time, though, I was finding it much more difficult to rebuild my life. It was harder to find new friends and a cozy local pub and a greengrocer I really liked. Eventually, I realized that a big part of my malaise was that I'd sort of forgotten who I was. I felt as if I'd lost a part of myself during the many moves.

It got so bad that I even lost the ability to order food in restaurants. Now, ordering well is a real skill that combines a knowledge of ingredients, techniques, trends, and seasonality as well as the skills and specialties of the chef. It's also important to note, for instance, whether it's a Monday (traditionally, chef's day off) or Thursday (the day the fresh food arrives for the weekend).

Ordering in restaurants is one of the things that, normally, I'm really, really good at. Suddenly I found myself staring at menus in bewilderment, unable to remember whether I preferred pork or poultry or how I felt about sweet sauces on meat or whether I really liked foie gras or if it was just a trend thing. Lionel thought it was kind of funny, the way he also thinks it's funny that I can remember almost every restaurant meal I've ever had.

I didn't find it quite so amusing; in fact, I found it rather alarming, just as I also found it alarming that I'd stopped doing all sorts of things I used to like to do, like hiking and biking and shopping for clothes and talking for hours on the phone with my friends, and that I seemed to spend all my time either at the office or in front of the TV. It didn't help that Lionel was working nights, which made it difficult to establish a new social life, or that all my new colleagues seemed to be either kids or family types with kids of their own and commitments in suburbia.

My life was badly out of balance. Things hit rock bottom the day I stood in the kitchen, wondering what to make for dinner – spaghetti carbonara or pad thai? pad thai or spaghetti carbonara? – and realized that I'd been making the same half-dozen dishes every week for the past two years. If we hadn't bought a charcoal grill and learned to use it, I wouldn't have made a single new dish in that entire time – and I'm a food writer; I'm *paid* to try new things. I was so shocked by the realization, I dropped a full glass of red wine on the floor.

Shortly after that, I saw a *Gourmet* article on a modern, deconstructed chicken *paprikás*, and began to wonder about Hungary, and what it was really like. Instead of being embarrassed about it, I became curious. Instead of turning up my nose at the history, and the people, and the accomplishments and, above all, the food, I decided to open my mind to it, to all of it. And that's when I realized that what was missing, what I was searching for, was home. I took the first step on the long journey homeward in the summer of 2004 when I visited my mom in Vancouver and made her teach me how to make cheese straws.

Every woman in our family has her own version of *sajtos rúd* (SHY-toesh rood), cheese straws, and the way we make them says a lot about who we are. Mom makes hers the way my grandmother used to, only not quite so professional-looking; my Aunt Luizi uses Emmenthal cheese instead of cheddar because her husband prefers them that way; the ones I make now are extra-fancy things with puff pastry and cumin; my sister, well, she hasn't fully embraced the cult of the cheese straw yet, but she will. As I did.

Mom's cheese straws were the most famous in the family; everyone loved them, and we kept asking her for the recipe. Though Fran and I had both tried to make them ourselves, all we'd ended up with was a big pan of melted cheese goo. It was almost as if Mom had put a spell on the recipe so that only she could make them. However, I now had a plan: I'd get her to make a batch and I'd take notes while she did it, so that I could understand where we were going wrong.

The recipe is a simple one – all you need is a pound of grated cheese, half a pound of butter, a pound of flour, and a little bit of salt, water, and baking powder (and, if you like, caraway seeds to sprinkle on top). You cream the butter and the cheese together, setting aside about a handful of cheese to sprinkle on top later. Mix the flour, salt, and baking powder together separately. My mother likes to do it on a countertop, which explains the lack of mixing bowls in her kitchen. Then dump the butter-cheese mixture on top of the flour mixture and gently but firmly knead it together. You'll need to add a bit of water to help bind it, as much as half a cup, depending on how dry your climate is.

Then you have to let it rest. Form it into two logs and set it aside for at least an hour at room temperature. Then roll out the dough, brush it with a bit of milk, sprinkle it with grated cheese and caraway seeds, and slice it into sticks. Then place it in a cool oven, no more than 310°F (155° C), for 45 minutes or so. "You don't bake it, you dry it out," Mom instructed.

It suddenly dawned on me, as I wrote furiously, that this was the first time I'd really sat in a kitchen and had Mom show me how to cook something. Aside from the cake catastrophe, we'd never really been the sort of family to sit around and bake cookies together or have cake-frosting parties or anything domestic like that. Mom was a busy career woman and a great role model in that sense, but if she'd had to spend her Saturdays with us in the kitchen, she'd probably have torn her own eyes out in boredom and frustration. It was, well, kinda nice.

My appetite for all things Hungarian was now whetted, and I wanted to learn more, and more, and more. Unfortunately, I only had one Hungarian cookbook and was having a hard time finding any others. I'd hoped to use Nagymama's old recipes, but Dad had thrown them out in their last move to the condo downtown. All I had was an old recipe collection that Luizi had put together, and while it was charming, I couldn't understand a thing in it.

No matter, I thought. I'll check out some restaurants and take it from there. That's when I discovered that while I'd been rejecting my culinary heritage, so, it seemed, had everyone else. Even though the city where I lived had a large Hungarian community, it had just one Hungarian restaurant, a casual bistro that offered only a small taste of this far-ranging cuisine. True, there was a Hungarian deli, but it didn't carry much more than bacon and salami – about fifty varieties of each. I slowly came to realize that, where once there had been dozens of Hungarian restaurants and delis across the country, now only a few remained.

I began to look further afield for Hungariana. I found hundreds of TV cooking shows about Italian food, French food, Japanese food, every kind of food – except Hungarian. I found magazines with recipes for every kind of cuisine from Afghan to Zimbabwean – except Hungarian. I found websites with plenty of advice for all sorts of ingredients – except Hungarian.

Hungarian food was once considered classy and exotic, Hungarian restaurants were places for extra-special occasions, Hungarian chefs were among the best in the world. Yet all that wonderful tradition now seemed to have vanished and Hungarian food, it appeared, was desperately out of fashion. Maybe it was too fattening (though that didn't stop southern barbecue from being trendy) or too European (though old-fashioned French was experiencing a resurgence) or too time-consuming (though the Slow Food movement was gaining momentum).

I decided that the real problem with Hungarian food was that it didn't have a champion, a celebrity chef, a passionate writer, a food lover extraordinaire. And then I decided that that person could be me.

But first I'd have to go to Hungary and taste the food at its source, devouring all I could about its past, present, and future. So I booked a flight, let the cousins know I was coming, and planned my gastronomic journey home. In the end I made two trips — the first with Lionel, the second with my mother — and I took a great big bite out of the culture and the cuisine. Of course, I wasn't just hungry for *gulyás* and *Dobos torta*, but for my history, my family, my home. In that, too, I hoped my appetite would be sated.

CHAPTER 10

Lakeside

It might seem like an awfully long way to go for a good meal, especially since we weren't entirely convinced we'd find one. But there we were, Lionel and I, wandering the streets of Budapest in search of what we decided to call "modern Magyar" cuisine. Our goal was to explore Hungary's culinary evolution – or at least, given that we had only a couple of weeks in the country and no idea where to begin, to eat a lot of really great meals. Some people believe you have to tour a lot of monuments and museums to get to know a place. Me, I prefer to do my exploring over a glass of wine and a plate of something savory. And I figured there was no better way to get to know this country of 10 million food-obsessed people than by sitting down and dining with them.

It was October when we arrived in Budapest. The first autumn rains had washed away the lingering heat of summer and with it the hordes of backpackers, who were now replaced by a different sort of tourist entirely, the well-dressed kind that could be found each night in the throngs outside the Opera and Ballet on Andrássy Út. There was a busy-ness to the city, a sense of returning from the cabin or the beach and getting back to work and culture and all the other the important aspects of a proper social life.

For us, fall meant another thing entirely: harvest season. Throughout the country, winemakers were crushing their grapes, hunters were bringing down birds and deer, and farmers were gathering in their produce. On restaurant menus, wild mushrooms, game, and fall vegetables were making an appearance. We were in foodie heaven.

Before we launched fully into our culinary exploration, however, we decided to take a little side trip and check out two of Hungary's other notable traditions — its spa culture and the exquisite porcelain known as Herend. Both, luckily, would take us in the direction of Lake Balaton and a third destination — one we would only attempt if I was feeling brave enough — the old family house in Balatonalmádi. So, after a quick weekend visit with family in Budapest, we rented a car and drove down to the Balaton region, to Lake Héviz, the second biggest thermal lake in the world and the biggest one you can actually swim in.

The lake has a surface of 50,000 square meters, and it's so warm you can swim in it year round; even on the coldest winter day, the water's temperature never drops below 30° C. It's fed by an underwater spring that pumps millions of liters of water into it a day, so much that all the water in the lake is changed every twenty-eight hours. The lake is surrounded by an entire spa village, with a hospital, hotels, restaurants, a park, and other facilities. People have been coming here to take the waters for at least the past century.

Héviz is the country's biggest spa, but it is far from the only one. Spas are as much a part of Hungarian culture as wine, paprika, and gypsy violinists. The country has some 1,200 thermal springs — it is, after all, located in a gigantic volcanic basin — more than a hundred of them in Budapest. The Romans and the Turks both loved their spas, and many of the older ones, such as the Art Nouveau spa at the Hotel Gellért and the Széchenyi Gyógyfürdö in City Park, are gorgeous temples to watery well-being that evoke those old empires. In fact, one suspects that part of the appeal for those invading armies was the thought of a nice, hot, bubbling spring to soak their weary feet in after a long day of marching and marauding.

Héviz is located at the northwestern tip of Lake Balaton, about eight kilometers from the town of Keszthely. We drove out there on a crisp fall day, when the sky was bright with optimistic sunshine, past the shops and restaurants of Buda and onto the toll highway M7, past the IKEAs and the BP stations and the Tesco "hyperstores," past the fields and the trees that were just turning golden, past old, thatch-roofed peasant houses and charming roadside cafés. At the tip of Lake Balaton, we turned right to follow the northern shoreline, happy to avoid the southern road and Siofok, a 24-7 party spot of condos and nightclubs, the Cancun of Central Europe. Although it would have been fascinating to track down the restaurant my grandmother had once owned, I knew it was long gone, destroyed by the Allies when they bombed the city nearly into oblivion at the end of the Second World War.

The road narrowed to a single lane that wove along the edge of the lake, past cottages and villas, each with a patch of vines facing south and a sign saying "panzio," "zimmer frei" or, much more rarely, "vacancy." Tourism is the mainstay of business in the Balaton region, but the infrastructure is still in its infancy – most accommodation is of the bed and breakfast or "panzio" variety. And even though the number of English-speaking visitors has increased in recent years, most of the tourist trade still caters to Germans and Austrians.

Suddenly we caught our first sight of the lake, a flat sheet of celadon glimpsed between scrubby trees. It was so big that we couldn't see the other side, though we could make out a small regatta of sailboats way off in the distance. Then the road took a sharp bend to the left, and with a jolt of surprise, I knew where we were, even before I saw the sign saying "Balatonalmádi."

I remembered a small, sleepy town with the hum of crickets and the sweet scent of strawberries in the air. I remembered a big old yellow house, and a slow-moving train with wooden benches for seats, and the station where we always got an ice cream. I remembered walking along the road by the railway tracks, where there were no cars and the poplar trees rustled in the breeze overhead. I did not remember this place, with its big gas stations and traffic jams and crowds of cottages and its "Thai-Hungarian-fusion" restaurants and the big, splashy amusement park right next to the shabby old ruin of a – wait a minute, was that our house? All I caught was a glimpse of a sad graying villa hidden in the trees, and then it was gone.

"Do you want to stop?" Lionel asked.

"No," I said, feeling a bit shaky. "No, let's come back later."

After Balatonalmádi, the resort clutter faded and the view became more and more beautiful. We passed the lovely Tihány peninsula, with its protected park and historic Benedictine abbey. Later, we reached Szigliget, with its famous thirteenth century fortress that was so strong it had never been taken by the Turks – instead, the Hapsburgs destroyed it to prevent the Hungarians from ever using it to mount an attack against Austria. Signs with clusters of grapes on them began appearing, telling us that we were traveling along the Badacsony wine route. At times we'd be slowed by a farm vehicle we couldn't pass, so we just meandered along, enjoying the way the sun dappled through the trees that lined the road. On we went, past all the villages that had "Balaton" in their name, Balatonfüred, Balatonudvari and so on, until we reached Keszthely and the turnoff to Héviz.

Suddenly, the air became cooler and damper. A light mist wreathed the tall, dark trees. A whiff of sulfur, a small crowd of people walking along the road, strange pointy roofs, and there was the lake, fenced off to our right. A minute later, we climbed a steep hill, and we'd arrived.

We would be staying at the Hotel Danubius Aqua, which was a favorite getaway for the elite during the old Soviet days, with its own thermal spring and medical services. Over the past few years it has been undergoing a massive, four-part renovation to rid it of the last traces of its 1970s utilitarian charmlessness and make it appealing to guests like Lionel and me. I must say I did enjoy the sight of the staff in their crisp white medical clothes mingling with the guests wandering around in white terry cloth robes. I can't think of a better holiday than one where you get to spend all day in your bathrobe.

In North America, spas are luxurious getaway destinations; in Central Europe, a trip to the spa is not considered an indulgence at all, but a crucial part of the health care system. This particular spa had no aromatherapy candles or pan flutes or tip envelopes, but it did have a doctor, nutritionist, and dentist on staff. No only that, but health care plans in Hungary and its neighbors actually cover spa services, which is why many of them are only available with a doctor's prescription.

The water, which springs from the ground at a toasty 36° to 38° C, is one of the two main attractions of Héviz; the other is the mud, a thick, black goop that comes from the bottom of the lake. This mud is mixed with the healing thermal water and then heated to 40° C in a big metal vat. Mud is taken very seriously here. The mineral content of the mud, which also contains minute levels of radioactivity, is believed to penetrate the skin, remineralizing it, regenerating the joints, repairing muscle damage, and helping "balance" the organs.

"It's peat mud. More than 20 per cent of the mud is peat and other organic elements. Also sulfur, minerals, and most important, plant estrogen," said Dr. József Szakonyi, the hotel's specialist in rheumatic disorders. He chuckled slyly. "After two, three days, the ladies are feeling very good."

Unfortunately for the dilettante spa-goer like myself, mud treatments are one of the treatments considered medicinal and only available with a doctor's prescription. If we'd signed up for a "kur" package, it would have started with a physical exam, followed by a list of treatment recommendations that would ideally have included mud. But we weren't interested in that because we wanted to spend time exploring the region and frolicking in the lake, so that meant no fancy treatment packages for me, although I did manage to schedule a massage.

It was just a short stroll down the hill and then through a small park to the lake, which was carefully fenced off. It's in a crater, with no shallow end, which makes it a bit risky for novice swimmers. To access the lake, you enter a rustic building through a set of turnstiles and then follow a long passageway that opens onto a bathhouse in the middle of the lake. The bathhouse has a couple of strange, pointy towers in what is an old peasant design, and several decks with loungers where people can lie out in the sun.

Héviz was once one of the most glamorous destinations for Central Europe's bright young things, but these days it attracts mostly the elderly and infirm, many of them from Germany, Austria, and other nearby countries. When we stepped out on to the deck after changing into our swimsuits, we found that all the loungers were filled, so we climbed down a ladder and into the water, which was as warm as a bath. It had a pleasantly strange feel to it — soft, soapy, almost gelatinous. It smelled faintly of sulfur and other minerals. We struck out past the huge patches of lily pads clustered along the shore, past the lifeguard rowing his boat lazily across the water, past the heads bobbing up and down in the lake, and over to the underwater benches and railings. It was easy to tell where they were, because that's where all the bobbing heads came to a stop and turned their faces to the sun.

Swimmers are discouraged from spending more than three hours in the lake at any time, but after an hour of paddling about, we were pretty much ready to go. We found a couple of loungers on a deck and lay in the sun for a while, letting its rays dry us and feeling all wholesome and re-energized, no doubt from the faintly radioactive water. Afterward, I felt as relaxed as if I'd had a mud wrap after all. At Héviz, there really is something in the water.

That night, we had dinner at a funky, traditional *csarda* (CHAR-duh) about a block from the hotel. *Csardas* used to be inns where travelers could stop for a bite to eat and where people on the wrong side of the law could find refuge from the constabulary. Some *csardas* were cleverly built right on county lines, so that if a man was wanted in one county, all he had to do was walk to the other side of the inn and his pursuers would be powerless to arrest him. Nowadays, the only crimes being committed in most *csardas* seem to be in the kitchen, where the food isn't always of the highest standard.

This *csarda* was a relatively new restaurant, with a big outdoor patio covered in vines, a gypsy band, and a menu featuring all the typical Hungarian specialties from *gulyás* served in a cauldron to wiener schnitzel served with a mountain of fried potatoes. The nights were still warm enough to sit outside, so we joined the customers on the patio, where the violinist was roaming from table to table, gazing deeply into each woman's eyes as he drew his bow across the strings of his fiddle.

We ordered a "mezzo," a half-liter of house wine, and perused the menu, which was in Hungarian, German, and English. The English descriptions were a bit skimpy, so I found myself reading them, then checking the Hungarian name of the dish, then comparing the two to figure out what each dish really was.

"Oh. My. God. " I said to Lionel. "We have so got to order the *liba maj* (LEE-buh my)."

"The what?"

"Goose liver. It'll be in a little pot with goose fat on top, and you spread it on bread and sprinkle it with salt and eat it with sliced purple onion and it's so, so amazingly delicious, you will just die. Besides, just look at how cheap it is."

Back home, we'd had many, many foie gras courses, some good, some not, but all terribly fancy and terribly expensive. In Hungary, goose liver isn't exactly cheap, not for locals anyway, but it's a bargain compared to what we pay in North America. Not only that, but it's such a part of the culinary tradition that it's available everywhere, even in the most rustic of restaurants.

Hungary, I found out later, is the world's biggest producer of goose liver, exporting some 1,800 tonnes of raw livers each year, most of it to France. In fact, most of the foie gras available in France these days actually comes from Hungary. (So, apparently, do the escargots and frogs' legs.) The French then perform their magic on it and turn it into a "French" product, much the same way they transform Canadian mustard seed into "Dijon" mustard.

Unfortunately for the thousands of Hungarian farmers raising pudgy geese, this rich market is seriously threatened under European Union guidelines. The EU has decided that the process for getting those livers so big and fat and delicious – it involves force-feeding the birds as much as 12 kilograms of grain in about two weeks – is cruel to animals. It will be banned by 2019 unless the Hungarians can come up with a kinder, gentler way of fattening their birds. Meanwhile, countries such as France, Canada, and the United States are turning to duck liver instead of goose, which means the days for *liba maj* may be numbered. It is, indeed, a guilty pleasure and one we figured we'd best make the most of while we could.

At first, Lionel just watched skeptically as I prepared the *liba maj*, layering a piece of bread with the goose liver, goose fat and onions, then sprinkling it liberally with salt. I bit into it with a happy little moan – it was all silky and savory, with the crisp bite of onions to cut the fattiness of the liver. "Here, try it," I said, pushing the little pot toward him. He spread a little bit of liver paste on a piece of bread and started to take a bite.

"No, no, no," I said, grabbing it from him and showing him how to do it properly. "You must put some of the fat on it, it's the best part. Then the onions, then the salt." I handed it back to him. "Here."

"Whatever you say," he said, closed his eyes nervously, and bit into it. His eyes sprang open. "Oh my God, this is really good."

"See? What did I tell you?" I sat back smugly.

After the *liba maj*, Lionel had a pot of spicy *gulyás* and I had a crispy duck leg with red cabbage and potatoes. It's not just the goose livers that are so well loved by Hungarians, but all the darkly flavorful birds, the ducks and the geese and the game, whether they're using the fat for cooking, or the skin for cracklings, or the legs and breast for roasting. Hungary may be one of the world's biggest producers of that boring old bird, the turkey, but its biggest attraction for a food lover is its gamier birds.

Once we'd had enough of the *cigany zene*, or gypsy music, we decided to turn in and get an early start for the next day.

After I'd been pummeled into relaxation at my morning massage, we got back in the car and headed for Herend. Back in the days when I hated everything about being Hungarian, the one thing I loved was Herend porcelain. I started collecting it when I was eighteen or so, a pattern known in Canada as "Chinese Bouquet." (In Hungary, it's called Apponyi Fleur, named for the much-admired Count Albert Apponyi, the nobleman and diplomat who tried to save Hungary at Trianon.) It is at once elegant and whimsical, simple and ornate, featuring stylized "fleur des Indes" peonies, rosettes, and leafy garlands on a white background with gold trim. The fleurs on my collection are green but the pattern also comes in blue, pink, or paprika-colored flowers.

The very first piece I ever got was a cake plate, which has two handles that look like rose branches with a couple of rosebuds and trailing vines at either end. Since then, I've collected dinner plates and soup plates, platters, vases, teacups, coffee cups, and a magnificent soup tureen. China was the one gift everyone in the family was happy with, the one gift that they felt was like passing on our heritage and that I felt showed they really understood me. Over the years, I've amassed a gorgeous collection that has skyrocketed in price from about $130 a place setting when I started collecting it to about $500 now.

I'm embarrassed to admit that part of what appealed to me so much about Herend was that I'd heard somewhere the late Princess

Diana collected it. Her pattern was the Rothschild Bird, designed, obviously, for the Rothschild family and featuring pretty painted birds and bugs and all sorts of winged creatures. Herend has been called "the Hermés of porcelain." Like the classic leather and scarf company, Herend never goes out of style; it is always a sign of quality and class and beautiful design.

One of the interesting things about Herend is that the factories kept producing exquisite porcelain even during the Soviet era. It is quite possibly the only industry that did not suffer from the mediocritizing effect of the communist regime. However, I remembered that when Fran and I visited during the bad old days, only a very little Herend was available to Hungarian citizens. Most of it could only be found in "dollar-and-mark" stores for tourists or abroad.

To get to the village of Herend where the "manufactory" and "porcelenarium" are, we would have to head to Veszprém and the eastern end of the lake, then veer northwest toward the Austrian border. Rather than take the lakeshore drive again, we decided to travel through the Bakony, the storied backcountry on the dark side of the mountains. Back in the day, brigands and poachers roamed this region, and many fairy stories are set in its mysterious wilds. Today, it still looks as if time has forgotten it, with tiny old villages that are crumbling picturesquely. It is also the place to go for game hunting and mushroom foraging.

We negotiated the big turnabout outside Veszprém, and got on the highway to Vienna. Suddenly, we were upon the turn to Herend. It wasn't a particularly busy day, but there were still several tour buses in the massive parking lot. The complex itself housed shops, a factory, a museum and other, porcelain-related businesses. Next to the museum was the Apicius restaurant, where they offered delicious-sounding food like Game Gravy with Vegetable Strudel or Chicken Breast Stuffed with Camembert, all served, of course, on Herend porcelain.

We toured the "mini-manufactory," where we learned how the sticky clay was made into porcelain. We watched as talented workers rolled the clay into strips for making basket weave or carved the petals for making the roses, then held our breaths as another one carefully painted on the patterns by hand. Each piece goes through seventeen pairs of hands, hands that are carefully chosen and trained to create these fragile works of art.

Then we traipsed over to the museum, where we learned that Herend dates back to 1826, when it was but a small factory that produced stoneware. A few years later, the factory was sold, and its new owner, Mór Fischer, started making artistic porcelain in 1839. Herend porcelain was a hit at the big exhibitions of the mid-nineteenth century – Vienna in 1845, London in 1851, New York in 1853, and Paris in 1855 – and started earning medal after medal for its beauty and design. Royalty from Queen Victoria to the Mexican emperor had Herend on their tables, and the noble families of Europe followed suit.

By the beginning of the twentieth century, the company had yet another owner, Jeno Farkasházy, who had started introducing novelties and winning a new round of awards and a new roster of clients. Things continued quite happily until 1948, when the factory was nationalized. Although the communist government at first wanted to turn the factory over to plain, proletarian stoneware, somehow they were prevailed upon to keep creating the beautiful porcelain for which it had always been known. I couldn't help but reflect that porcelain, though it seems so fragile and delicate, is actually quite tough and resilient, and that resilience was somehow symbolic of how it had managed to survive those brutish years. After the fall of communism, the factory was privatized in 1993. Today 75 per cent of the operation is owned by its workers, which is a pretty cool thing for something that is so dedicated to beauty, luxury, and tradition.

Once we'd had our little history lesson, we hit the Herend shop, where the pieces may be less expensive than they are in North America, but they're still not cheap. After much dithering, I picked up a little teapot and a gravy boat. At about $400 for the two, this was, I'll have you know, an absolute steal. I cradled them in my lap all the way back to Héviz and kept them tucked away safely for the rest of the trip.

My grandmother collected Herend, too, many years ago, and most of the pieces were still at the old house at Balatonalmádi the last time we were there, back in 1979. It was a simple pattern of blue forget-me-nots on a white background, and we'd managed to bring a couple of pieces out with us – an old teapot, a pitcher, a small dish – that now sit in my china cabinet. I was thinking about this the next day as we drove along the lakeshore, wondering what happened to the rest of it and knowing I'd probably never find out.

Lionel and I had decided to spend that day exploring the sights in Tihány and Szigliget and going as far as Balatonalmádi to look at the old house. Mom had warned us that it was in terrible shape, and we'd caught a disturbing glimpse of its decay on the way down, but I still wasn't prepared for what we saw when we got there.

The house is on Neptun Utca, a one-way street that runs alongside the railroad track to the big "strand" or lakeside playground. The season was over and the park was firmly locked up, but the swings and slides, the stalls with their bright tacky signs were still there. A fence ran all around the park in which the house sat forlornly to one side. The gates were all locked with padlocks, except one that led out to a concrete dock. We walked out there, but we couldn't get close to the house – mud and weeds blocked our path.

We wandered back out onto the street, to the empty little cash booth closest to the house, and peered through the railings at what used to be our family home. The sky had clouded over and a cold wind was blowing off the lake, the dark and miserable day a fitting backdrop for what we saw. Most of the poplar trees that had once lined the driveway were gone. Red tiles were missing from the roof, some windows had no panes, shutters hung open at crazy angles. The stone steps were crumbling and the stucco peeling off in large, leprous patches, its bright ochre paint faded to a murky, muddy brown. My throat tightened, and tears filled my eyes. If there was one place that meant "home" to my family, this was it, and look at it, it was horrible.

Of course, it wasn't really our place any more and hadn't been since 1986, so perhaps I had no right to mourn. The way it worked under the Soviets was that no one was allowed to own property, but if property was already in your family, you had the right use it as long as you continued living in it. However, you had to share. So, even though my grandfather had built the house so his family could live in one half while his sister's family lived in the other, in practice our cousin Maju's family lived part time in their half of the house, while other people lived in ours. Finally, in 1986, the Hungarian government appropriated the house, saying they needed it for a public park.

The government paid my mother and aunt Luizi a fraction of what the house would have been worth on the free market. They paid them in forints, which Mom and Luizi couldn't take out of the country or exchange into dollars. All they could do was leave the money sitting in a Hungarian bank or buy things on the rare occasions they traveled to Hungary. Unfortunately, they couldn't buy very much because, until the nineties, there was a limit to how much a foreigner could spend in forints. Besides, all the good stuff, the Herend porcelain, the antiques, the Tokaj wines, foie gras, and caviar, was only available in "dollar-and-mark" stores. And then, to add insult to injury, after the fall of communism, Mom got one of her cousins to invest what was left of the money – and lost almost every forint of it.

Three years after the communists had appropriated the house, their regime ended. And while other parts of Hungary were quickly privatized, sold off and developed, the agreement my mother and aunt had signed stated that the government was not allowed to sell the house for profit. So imagine the shock I felt what I saw a big sign beside the house reading "Elado" – for sale – with a phone number. Suddenly the grief that had consumed me turned to rage, and for the first time ever, I really understood why everyone in my family hated the communists so much.

It used to make me crazy listening to those old Hungarians going on and on and on about the communists (who were occasionally interchangeable with the Russians and even the Turks) and how evil they were. Every once in a while I even tried to reason with them. "They weren't all bad," I'd say. "They did some good for the poor. At least everyone got health care and an education and, really when you think about it, the philosophy is one of fairness and . . ." At that point, my sputtering, furious mother would cut me off, calling me a "pinky commo" at the dinner table.

But when I saw that sad ruin of our beloved home, I really *got* that helpless rage that people who had to leave Hungary had felt. I really got it because I was suddenly consumed by it. Those bastards! I thought, blinded by tears, my hands shaking so hard they could hardly hold the pen to write down the phone number on the for sale sign. How dare they drive us out of our home, the home my grandfather built, where we would never be able to visit, to bring our own children to laugh and sing and play like my mother and my cousins once did. How dare they let others move into our house, how dare they steal our house, how dare they let it fall into this terrible ruin, and above all, how *dare* they try and sell it for profit.

Lionel just watched with a worried expression as I ranted at him. He couldn't really understand what the big deal was. Maybe he was right and it wasn't such a big deal. But it sure seemed like one. Finally, he said, "Look, there's a phone number on the for sale sign. Why don't you write it down, then get your cousins to look into it when we're back in Budapest?"

"Good idea," I said, and scribbled the number furiously on the back of a receipt.

The anger stayed with me all that day. It stayed with me when we stopped at the Tihány abbey and we ate Hortobagyi *palacsinta* and drank crisp white wine on a sunny patio. It stayed with me as we clambered all over the fort at Szigliget, where I had dark thoughts about how it could have been used to fight off the Soviet tanks if only the Austrians hadn't destroyed it. It stayed with me through our last dinner at the *csarda*. It stayed with me the whole drive back to Budapest.

CHAPTER 11
Modern Magyar

Even after we got back to Budapest, it took a while for that anger to dissipate. It didn't exactly help that almost the first place we visited in Budapest was the Terror Háza, or Terror House, a museum dedicated to those twin totalitarian regimes of the twentieth century, fascism and communism. Everyone in the family said, Don't go, but then they couldn't stop talking about it, which meant there was no way I couldn't go. The Terror Háza has been the most notorious venture in Hungary since the fall of communism, one of the most audacious memorials ever planned, and love it or hate it, no one can ignore it – or its message. It is not, however, the best place to hang out if you're feeling really, really pissed off at history.

We'd started the day with much more innocuous pursuits, ambling first along the river and then along the shop-filled, pedestrian-only Váci Utca, which meanders from the big market to Café Gerbeaud in Vörösmarty Tér. There we hopped on the Millennium Subway, a.k.a. the Little Subway, which was the first subway line in continental Europe. It's called the Little Subway because both the train and the route it travels are so small – it comprises two wood-trimmed cars that have recently been restored to their Belle Époque beauty and it only goes from Vörösmarty Tér underneath Andrássy Út to Hösök Tere (Heroes Square).

We got off at Heroes Square, a massive area designed for big, public gatherings and demonstrations of military might. It's flanked by galleries and museums; in the middle is the Millennium Monument, an enormous, double-colonnaded curved plinth that houses statues of the country's kings. It features a 35-metre-high stone column, topped with a statue of the Archangel Gabriel; below him are seven bronze horsemen led by King Arpád.

During the Soviet era, many military demonstrations were held in this square. The day the regime ended, hundreds of thousands of citizens showed up to cheer on the departing tanks. Since then, it's been used for national celebrations, a mass held by Pope John Paul II, a royal visit by Queen Elizabeth II, and a video by Michael Jackson. It has also appeared in scenes from Madonna's movie Evita, proving that times here have, indeed, changed.

Behind the square lies City Park, a leafy enclave where you can find the zoo, the Széchenyi thermal spa, and the famous Gundel Restaurant. And toward the Danube stretches elegant Andrássy Út, a tree-lined boulevard with graceful old villas, embassies, the opera and ballet, and right in the middle, near Oktagon Square, the Terror Háza museum.

We walked along Andrássy Út, past well-preserved Belle Époque villas now housing foreign embassies that would not have been welcome here twenty years ago. We passed Art Nouveau apartments, some crumbling badly, others with uniformed doormen outside. The farther we got from Heroes Square, the more commercial the street became, with restaurants, shops, cafés, and news kiosks replacing the villas and apartments.

When we reached No. 60, we stopped. The old, neo-Renaissance building was painted dark gray, and a black metal addition jutted from the roof – when we stood below it and looked up, we could see the word "TERROR" had been cut out of it in huge letters. Outside the Terror Háza, big billboards had been set up and young people were taking signatures and donations, many of them in the form of flowers. I couldn't understand what the signs said, so I asked one of the young guys standing beside it with a bunch of wilted carnations in his hand. "It's a campaign against the Nyílos," he said. "The what?" we wondered. "The Nyílos, neo-Nazis," he replied.

Which just goes to show why the Terror House is so important, and so controversial.

The original Nyílos were Hungary's Arrow Cross party, cousins to Germany's Nazis, so nicknamed for their symbol of crossed arrows on their epaulets. (A *nyíl* is an arrow.) Strangely, some people yearn for those pre-Second World War days when an ultra-right-wing government maintained social order across the land, even if, or maybe especially if, some groups had to suffer terribly for it. You'd think that they'd remember how that all turned out, but apparently not. And it's not just cranky senior citizens upset about their lousy pensions and the changing world around them who are looking back to the fascists, but young people, too. It's meant not only a rise in ultra-right wing politics but, just as in Germany and other parts of the world, a wave of young Hungarians turning to neo-Nazism. Terrified of what that could mean for their country and unwilling to lose their fragile, hard-won freedoms, the government and human rights groups have been fighting back with a powerful campaign. How fitting that they should have set things up outside the Terror Háza.

We opened the ominously tall, heavy doors and went inside. A haunting piece of music was playing, measured and melancholy, as we went through the foyer and bought our tickets. Right away we knew not to expect subtlety: as we passed through the turnstile, smack in front of us was an enormous Soviet tank, right in the place where a courtyard had existed before first the Arrow Cross and then the Soviet secret police took this building over and made it their headquarters. The tank was surrounded by hundreds, thousands of black and white photos of victims on the walls.

The exhibits start on the top floor and work their way down, floor by floor, through history. At the very top was a temporary exhibit about the thousands and thousands of Jewish children who died in the Holocaust. Clear glass cases held clothes and toys recovered from the camps. Photos lined the walls. At one end of the room, a film played, footage of the now-elderly survivors reliving their terrible childhood in the camps.

I was not the only one openly weeping as we made our way to the next level and the story of how the Arrow Cross came into being, or the level after that, which described the Soviet take-over and the years under the communist regime. While the events of the Holocaust have been kept alive in popular culture, in books and movies and TV shows, Josef Stalin's atrocities were largely hidden behind an Iron Curtain of secrecy. Yet it is believed that Stalin may have killed five times as many people as Hitler, committing genocide on Muslims (three million), Ukrainians (eight million) and Jews (untold numbers), and imprisoning and torturing millions of others, including my family.

Many of those who survived Stalin and escaped to tell their stories did their best to forget the past. It was exactly that forgetting that the museum was doing its best to overcome. True, it was in part politically motivated, for it had been established by the center-right government elected after the fall of communism. Even so, the message contained in the exhibits, the film footage, radio broadcasts, photographs, and newspaper articles, was clear: This happened only yesterday and could easily happen again.

Certainly, I knew it would be difficult to forget this place, especially the jail cells in the basement. There were young kids down there, running around laughing and playing hide-and-seek. Meanwhile I stood there shaking as I looked into the cell so narrow an inmate could only stand up in it, or the one with no beds and icy water on the floor, or the one with rubber hoses and electric needles laid out so neatly for the interrogator. I couldn't help but see my crippled great-aunt in here, or my feisty grandmother, or my rascally grandfather.

When Lionel and I finally emerged into the late afternoon, we were drained and disoriented and I felt as if I'd been weeping for hours. It was getting dark and a light autumn rain was falling. A welcoming golden light glowed from the cafés and bars around Liszt Ferenc Tér and we realized how hungry we were, and how badly we needed a glass of wine. And then, just when we needed it most, we found Vörös és Fehér.

The name means "Red and White," which is only fitting, since this cozy, modern bistro is owned by the Budapest Wine Society and its wine list is the main attraction. It's not the only attraction, though, for it was here that we got our first taste of modern Magyar cuisine. Like any great cuisine, modern Magyar emphasizes fresh, local, seasonal ingredients prepared in an artisanal way that draws on the both the regional techniques of the past and the international influences of the present. It is fresh and flavorful, each ingredient distinct and proud, not disguised by overly seasoned sauces.

At Vörös és Fehér, we found all the ingredients one would expect on a Hungarian menu: goose liver, duck, venison, even a *paprikás* dish. But it was a million miles away from either the stately formality of the fancy Hapsburgian restaurants or the same-old-same-oldness of the casual *csardas*. On that first visit, I had duck and Lionel had a catfish *paprikás*. But rather than a huge, greasy duck leg with a mountain of red cabbage, my *kacsa* was a tender slice of breast with local morel mushrooms in a delicate red wine sauce. Lionel's *paprikás* was just as deftly prepared: toothsome catfish, which we decided is a much undervalued fish, in a paprika sauce that was a perfect balance of sweet and hot and creamy. For dessert, we had a strudel, a classic Hungarian sweet that combined all three of the best-loved fillings – sour cherry, poppy seed and sweetened, ricotta-like *túró* – in pretty layers.

We were so impressed that we returned a couple of days later. This time I had roast venison with red wine sauce. Medallions of perfectly tender venison were placed atop airy potato croquettes formed into doughnut shapes and accompanied by a savory sauce enlivened with wild mushrooms and huge chunks of goose liver. Every element of the dish was true to its place, and true to a classic recipe, but handled with a light and whimsical hand. That same hand was at work with Lionel's risotto, an updated version of the classic side dish called *rizsi bizsi*, rice and peas. The Vörös és Fehér version had generous pieces of goose liver in it, and a sprinkling of fresh dill.

As impressed as we were by the food, we were simply blown away by the wine, for this was the first time we'd been able to experience the renaissance of the Hungarian wine industry. The wine list carried dozens of exquisite Hungarian wines, none of which I'd even heard of before.

Hungary's climate and volcanic soil are ideal for vinifera grapes and, in fact, the country was growing vines and making wine even before France. If its history hadn't been so fraught with turmoil, Hungary would be among the world's most respected wine producers today, instead of being something of an oenophiliac punchline. Since the Soviets left in 1991, though, the entire industry has bounced back remarkably. In fact, Hungary has become the wine world's best-kept secret, and one of the best ways to get in on the secret is to dine at Vörös és Fehér.

On our first visit, we started with a couple of glasses of Tokaj Szamorodni, an aromatic late harvest wine with a ghost of the aszú's complex flavors. It was the perfect accompaniment to a foie gras pâté we shared. Then we had a bottle of Trio, a deep, plummy cuvée of Cabernet Sauvignon, Merlot and Kékfrankos from the Takler family vineyard in Szekszárd. We finished with a couple of glasses of Tokaj Aszú, Puttonyös 6, that tasted like pears in caramel.

Another great restaurant where we enjoyed modern Magyar cuisine was Janko, up in the Castle district, right across the road from the Budapest Hilton, which was until recently the fanciest hotel in town. At Janko, there are no dark, carved wooden benches and no *cigány* band would dare set foot in its bright, minimalist environs. To one side is a small art gallery; over the long bar is a beautiful mural of red poppies waving in the wind. (Somehow, though, I suspect it isn't exactly a big hit with locals. My cousin Maju checked it out when we told her we were having lunch there, and she just shook her head and said, "I feel sorry for you." And then she went off to a *pörkölt*-and-*paprikás*-style *csarda* down the street.)

At Janko, the walls are white and so are the plates, all the better to highlight the innovative cooking going on in the kitchen. The chef is using local ingredients and local traditions to create dishes that are at the same time very old and very modern. For instance, there was hare ragout with asparagus pastry, cold fruit soup with milk froth, duck breast with fresh fruit, spit-roast calf with snail ragout, and gray beef with forest mushrooms. Janko also offers local cheeses and charcuterie – goose liver sausage, mangalica pig bacon, roasted local vegetables, chicken liver pâté, goose liver sausage, quail's egg, marinated peppers, and caramelized red cabbage with balsamic vinegar. And, of course, an all-Hungarian wine list. It was a remarkable interpretation of the best the country had to offer.

All of this – the wine, the food, the blessed lack of strolling gypsy violinists – was about as far away as possible from what we'd come to expect from Hungarian food. What's been happening in the nation's kitchens, from young home cooks inspired by Paprika TV (the food channel) to the chefs at top restaurants like Alabárdos, Janko, and Vörös és Fehér, is a remarkable transformation that is something of a metaphor for all the changes the country is going through. By opening its doors to the rest of the world, Hungary is reclaiming her own traditions. By experiencing the best of other cultures, she is finally able to appreciate the best of her own. By celebrating the best of her own bounty, her climate, and her terroir, Hungary is ready, once again, to take her place among the world's best producers of food and wine.

No longer is Hungarian cuisine a matter of quantity over quality, as it was during the Soviet era. Back then, cooks had a limited selection of ingredients, all produced in Soviet Bloc countries. While the rest of the world was experimenting with international cuisine, with food from Morocco and India and Asia, Hungarian cooks had access to neither exotic, imported ingredients nor their own unique ingredients. Much of the traditional produce vanished, to be supplanted by higher yield, easier-to-grow, easier-to-sell crops. The small family farms were replaced by big state farms producing huge amounts of potatoes and beets. Uniquely Hungarian livestock like the long-horned gray cattle and the shaggy-coated mangalica pig were replaced by better producing breeds of beef and pork. The wine, once some of the best in the world, became some of the worst in the world and a nation of wine lovers turned to beer and spirits, which they no longer savored but drank in oceanic quantities.

There was no contact with chefs from other lands to explore new fashions and methods of cooking. There no understanding of how international attitudes to food were changing, no sense that the chef was becoming a real celebrity and that cooking had come to be considered a noble pursuit. The restaurant customer didn't know any better either, and wanted nothing more than big, hearty servings. The food was boring, bland, stodgy and greasy, but at least there was a lot of it.

At home, cooks made do with what they could find in the grocery stores. They had no Food TV to inspire them to *Wok with Yan* or flirt with *The Naked Chef*. There were no foreign cookbooks, no Julia Child or Silver Palate to inspire them. They just made the same food their mothers had made, only without the abundance and quality of ingredients that had existed before 1945.

Today, it's a very different story.

"It is very much in fashion to make this healthy food, not what your mother made," explained Eszter Balázs, the restaurant critic for the English-language *Budapest Sun*. We spent an afternoon sipping coffee at the old Astoria Hotel, which was once the secret police hangout and is now just a faded old dining room with ghosts drifting through the chandeliers.

What's fashionable now is fresh, healthy ingredients – chicken and turkey instead of beef and pork, and salad and vegetables instead of starchy dumplings, noodles, and potatoes. While the older generation loves their food battered and fried or prepared with lashings of sour cream, the younger generation is roasting it, steaming it, broiling it, or eating it raw. Home cooks in their twenties and thirties may still make *pörkölt* or *paprikás* occasionally, but it is probably to impress their in-laws.

In Budapest, Asian food is as trendy as Italian, and some of the city's most interesting restaurants offer Thai, Indian, and Japanese, sometimes all in the same place, sometimes prepared in a fusion with Hungarian cuisine, which is actually a surprisingly good mix. (At Tom George in Budapest, for instance, I had a local river fish in a Thai green curry served with creamy Hungarian egg noodles.) Seafood – and not just the local river fish – is more fashionable than it's been in nearly a century. Before 1919, Mediterranean fish and shellfish made their way from the then-Hungarian port of Fiume swiftly up the Danube to the tables of Magyar gourmands. That port was closed to Hungary after Trianon, but once again, the city is swimming with seafood, especially in the many sushi bars.

In a country of meat eaters, another surprising trend is the rise of vegetarianism. I did not see a single menu without vegetarian options. By contrast, when my vegetarian friends Sue and Carol visited Hungary in the eighties, they nearly starved to death. Luckily, they could get by on bread, potatoes, and palinka (lots and lots of palinka), but Sue's relatives were both puzzled and hurt when the Canadians refused to eat the food they'd prepared, especially since meat was considered something of a luxury.

Perhaps the biggest change has been the great ingredients now available in stores and markets. Where people once lined up for hours for milk and bread and margarine, now they only have to go to the corner store for pineapples and fresh organic meat and almost anything they can imagine. Many ingredients are homegrown and seasonal, so fresh and of the moment that the store's stock changes not every few months, but almost every day. Others are imported from lands that only fifteen years ago were almost mythical, so cut off was Hungary from the rest of the world. "There are ingredients I never even heard of. I don't even know the lettuces they have," confessed Eszter, who first learned about fine food during the years she lived in Paris. "There is this big market, an indoor market. In front of it are these old *nénis* (ladies) and I always buy from them because they bring them from their own gardens."

She was talking about the Központi Vásárcsarnok, which everyone calls the Nagy Csarnok, or "big market," for short. It is the biggest of five huge *vásárcsarnok*, or market halls built in Budapest in the 1890s. Like Les Halles in Paris, they were grand buildings of brick, concrete, iron and glass; temples to eating well, and temples, too, to the riches the land could provide. The Budapest markets were designed to gather up the forty small open-air markets around the city and bring them indoors. The idea was to improve the flow of goods and traffic and to reduce the pollution and litter caused by the old markets.

The Nagy Csarnok is in downtown Budapest, only a few meters from the Danube, and when it was built, an underground passage allowed boats to carry supplies into the market. That passage is long closed, but the market is busier than ever. It was designed by an architect named Samu Petz, professor of public architecture at the Technical University of Budapest, in a Hungarianized version of the Eiffel style that was so popular at the time. It has cast iron girders and lots of glass, tiles by the Hungarian art porcelain company, Zsolnay, and elements of Hungarian folklore.

After two world wars, the market was badly damaged. Its glass ceiling was broken and left unrepaired, so water poured in and stained the interiors, which were littered with rubble. Shelves remained bare; stalls remained empty and locked. Like the other markets, it largely fell into disuse during the four decades of communism, when modern stores replaced the old farmers' markets and there was barely enough food available to fill an old *néni*'s shopping cart, let alone an entire cavernous hall. But in 1994 the city renovated the hall, and it is now one of the largest markets in all of Europe — and one of the few that still exist right in the middle of the cities they were built to serve. In fact, all across Hungary, the traditional markets are returning to their former glory, while new farmer's markets and flea markets are popping up.

I've visited markets all over the world, and the Nagy Csarnok is one of the most impressive I've yet seen. It is built on three floors and there you can find all the ingredients of Hungarian cuisine and the bounty of a land lain fallow for too long. On the top floor are the booths of linens, pottery, and souvenirs, as well as the stalls where you can get a savory snack: *langos*, fried fish, a sandwich, a beer, a glass of wine, a bowl of soup, sausages, fried chicken, even a salad bar. The biggest crowd is always outside the *langos* stand, where tourists and well-shod matrons mingle happily at the tall tables with the brawny men who carry in the crates of produce each day.

On the main floor are fruit, vegetables, poultry, meat, prepared meats, baked goods, cheeses, and all the other essential items for your daily meal. There are bins of chicken legs and chicken livers, chicken feet and chicken bones for soup; there are fresh goose livers and goose legs, turkey cutlets and whole turkeys. There are bins of *tepertö*, cracklings made from goose or pork fat. And above the counters where bacon and salami are sold, there are always strings of sausages hanging to dry.

The main floor is also where you will find the sorts of foodstuffs you will want to tuck in your luggage. You will find tins of *liba maj*, bottles of palinka, locally grown saffron, dried mushrooms, and, of course, paprika — bags and bags of paprika. Hot paprika, sweet paprika. Paprika from Szeged and paprika from Kalocsa. Paprika in fancy, decorative bags, paprika in practical no-nonsense bags, paprika in tins, paprika in ceramic jars. Paprika spread in tubes and paprika paste in jars. Even, if you look hard enough, paprika palinka.

Going down to the basement, though, is like entering a whole other world. As you descend the escalator, your nose prickles with the vinegary scent of *savanyuság* — all the pickled vegetables, the cabbage, peppers, beets, and other veggies that are sold from big buckets. Down here is also where you will find game, such as wild boar, venison, rabbit, duck, and pheasant, as well as seafood and fresh river fish. There are tanks of big flat *harcsa*, or catfish. The salesman uses an old-fashioned net to scoop a fish out of the tank, plops it onto a counter or the floor, then gives it two sharp blows – smack, smack – to the head before wrapping it up for a cook to take home and make into fried fillets or *paprikás* or *halaszlé*.

This is also where you will find caviar for about half the price you'll pay in Canada. You have to make sure you know what you're getting, though. Certainly, there is plenty of real Russian sevruga, osetra and beluga, but it's easy to be seduced by the cheap prices of something called *cari*, which is packaged to look like the real stuff but is just some sort of mediocre Russian roe. (It's the stuff you'll find it in many of the *csardas*, where they'll serve it with brown bread and butter.)

Certainly, the Nagy Csarnok proved to be a temple to fine food, but it was far from the only one we discovered. We fell in love with the Four Seasons Hotel in the old Gresham Palace, a perfectly renovated Art Nouveau palace at the foot of the Chain Bridge, that became our "local" while we were in town. It was conveniently close to everything, especially the English-language bookstore on Oktober VI Utca where we'd stop every day to stock up on newspapers and magazines. The hotel bar had a nice list of Hungarian wines, most of them from Villány, and I began to think we'd have to come back and visit the wine regions to taste more of what they had to offer.

A very different bar was the one my cousin Gábor took us to one night. Lionel, Gábor, and I walked for what seemed like miles into a dark, distant residential neighborhood. At one building with no sign and no number, he knocked on a wooden door. After a few moments, it creaked open. "Gabi!" exclaimed the stocky man who answered it. "It's been ages since we've seen you!"

We walked down into an old cellar with arched ceilings and rough wooden benches. Most of Budapest was built in the late nineteenth century, but this cellar seemed a lot older than that. In the air was a blue haze of smoke and the yeasty smell of beer. Dim lights flickered from the ancient stone walls. We met up with Gábor's best friends and I suddenly realized that almost everyone in there was male, except for the woman behind the taps. There were no big-screen TVs, but this was a sports bar — in fact, it was a private club owned by a former soccer star. There was something almost Edwardian about the place, a sense of secret handshakes and male-only camaraderie.

The guys started the evening by ordering us all shots of the herb-based liqueur called Unicum, which many consider the national drink. "It'll prevent a hangover tomorrow," they said. "And if you do get a hangover, you should drink some Unicum, because it will cure it."

We downed the shots. Whoa, nasty, they were.

The guys were drinking beer, big, one-liter bottles of Borsodi. I wanted a glass of wine; I was given a bottle. We'd already had dinner, but the guys ordered some food from the kitchen where the cook prepared authentic Transylvanian dishes. I had a taste of one dish, what looked like a pork stir-fry but was called a *tokány*. It was delicious.

Meanwhile, the soccer star walked around all night, chatting to his guests, every one of whom he knew, many of whom were playing cards and taking bets on how Hungary's sports teams would do the coming weekend. Lionel and I felt honored to be there.

Even though all the guests were young, the whole scene seemed fabulously retro, especially when the guys started talking about these great adventure holidays they'd been on together, without their wives and children, and how their wives were at home, cooking and cleaning and taking care of the little ones. If they'd been wearing officer's uniforms instead of roll-neck sweaters, or flannel blazers instead of polo shirts, we could have been whisked back about eight or nine decades.

The same crowd might have visited Kéhli Vendéglö. If Janko and Vörös és Fehér are where to find the new cuisine, Kéhli is where to find the gloriously old. It's described as a tavern and has been serving up rich, old-fashioned food in the suburban Óbuda for over a century. It was the favorite restaurant of the Falstaffian writer Gyula Krúdy, "the poet of fragrances, tastes, colors and fair ladies," whose passion for the place helped save it from demolition when the old neighborhood was destroyed twenty-five years ago.

It was not only Krúdy's favorite restaurant; it was also the favorite of my Aunt Frances's lover Pál. When I discovered that Pál had an almost obsessive passion for food, he became my new best friend. Pál, it turned out, was the kind of person who had a favorite restaurant in every small town, who knew about the explosion in quality wine in Villány, who could argue for hours about the merits of Szeged versus Kalocsa paprika.

The night he took us to Kéhli, I learned that the best way to get over your anger at someone is to dine with them. I was still feeling raw over the Lake Balaton house and the Terror Háza, and I could easily have blamed him, the token old communist in the group, as some other people in the family did. But all it took was a few spoonfuls of the delicious beef marrow and some red wine from Villány and I was ready to forgive anyone anything.

What's done is done, I thought, and it makes me sad, but not so sad I can't enjoy an excellent venison chop and some lively conversation. And so we talked about food and Hungary, about the past and about the future, and I learned more about the place than I had in three weeks of driving and walking and eating and drinking

"When you come back, I'll take you to Kalocsa for the paprika, and to a wonderful wine cellar I know in Badacsony. We must go to Erdely (Transylvania), too," he said, while Frances nodded happily. "I know some great little restaurants there, and the food is so different from Hungarian. It's cooked with herbs like marjoram instead of paprika. Then you have to go to the Matra and taste these wild berries that grow there – honey berries, they're called. And we must take a trip to Villány. It's such a long time since I was there. Next time you're here, we must go to all these places."

Yes, we agreed, next time we definitely must go.

CHAPTER 12

The Family at Dinner

As it turned out, I was destined never to join Pál on his gourmet tour of Hungary. Even when Lionel and I visited in October 2004, we knew that Pál had been unwell for some time. That was why Frances had recently moved full-time to Budapest after a decade of traveling between Hungary and Canada. She'd decided that even though her social life was in Toronto, her home was with the man she loved. It was a difficult decision, and, as it turned out, a heartbreaking one.

She'd sold the Toronto apartment over the summer and moved all her books and clothes and art to the apartment on Áttila Út. She and Pál settled into life in Budapest. But where there had once been evenings at the opera and dinners in fine restaurant like our meal at Kéhli, visits with friends and trips to Pál's beloved Transylvania, now they stayed in every night. By November, Pál was too ill to go out, but he was well enough to cook, and every night he made his favorite dishes, the savory stews and creamy sauces he'd always enjoyed.

For a while it looked as though he might be getting better. Then, right after Christmas (or Hanukkah, I suppose, since he was Jewish), Pál collapsed with a massive stroke and was rushed to hospital. While snowflakes swirled outside and revelers toasted each other with glasses of sparkling wine, Frances sat day after day by Pál's bedside, joined only by his children. Not wanting to darken the holidays for her friends and family, Frances told no one about her grim vigil and sat there wrapped in loneliness.

On New Year's Day 2005, Pál died.

Frances was inconsolable. Even as she mourned the loss of her lover, she also mourned the decision she'd made to move to Budapest, the loss of her friends, her apartment, her family, her life back in Canada. But she wasn't destined to be alone for long. That February, after forty years in Canada, my aunt Luizi and uncle Frank sold their house in Willowdale, closed up his architecture practice, and moved back to Budapest. It seemed like a sudden move, but in fact it was one they'd been considering for years. And now, finally, the time was right.

I guess I wasn't the only one searching for home and finding it in the land of paprika. Luizi, Frank, and Frances were part of a huge wave of the surviving Fifty-sixers who have been flooding back to Hungary since 1989, buying up apartments in the city and villas along Lake Balaton and patches of vineyard anywhere they can find them. The fall of communism has made Hungary a very attractive place for the people who never stopped calling it home. And since Hungary joined the European Union, their children and grandchildren have been able to get Hungarian passports, which they find are a valuable asset that will let them live and work anywhere in Europe.

Today's Hungary is, however, a very different place from the one the Fifty-sixers left behind, and while many of the changes are good ones, some are not. Young people are rude and brash, complains Frank, and all anyone wants any more is to make money. Old people won't let go of the past and are still bitter about things like Trianon and nostalgic for the social order of the 1930s when they should just look to the future, complains Frances. On the other hand, they've gone ahead and elected a socialist government, Luizi says. What were they thinking? Worst of all, Frank says, people have forgotten how to cook. But at least, all three admit there is a spirit of creativity and innovation and opportunity.

Mom and I got the chance to see those changes for ourselves when we traveled to Hungary in the spring of 2005. It was a very different trip from the one I'd taken with Lionel the previous autumn, a trip down memory lane rather than a journey of discovery. Then again, for me, a trip down memory lane *was* a journey of discovery, so maybe it wasn't so different, after all.

When my mother and I arrived, summer's muggy heat was just creeping up on the city. Although the weather report each day insisted that the temperature was only 21°C or 22°C, the humidity made it feel much hotter. We were staying in Frances's apartment while she was away – her mourning took the form of a desperate need to travel, and already she'd visited China and Quebec and was planning a trip to France later in the year – and at night we had all the fans and the air conditioning going full blast.

With the heat came the tourist hordes. They were there on school trips, family trips, and seniors' trips. Visitors came on bus tours from Germany and cheap weekend flights from Britain. In fact, while we were there, one of the two English-language papers reported that Budapest had become such a popular destination for the Brits that there were now five daily flights from London. Young hipsters stopped in Budapest while on a sort of ironic Grand Tour of the former Soviet capitals. Their middle-aged parents arrived hoping for some sort of meaningful experience (and a bargain on embroidered tablecloths would be pretty good, too). Some visitors came as they always had from Hungary's former Soviet Bloc neighbors; others came from as far away as the United States and Japan.

All along Váci Utca and the Danube Corso, restaurants posted their menu cards in German, French, Italian, English, and Japanese. There were lineups at the Internet cafes. Waiters became more impatient, prices went up, and the crowds at the most famous tourist attractions became unbearable. So Mom and I skipped out on all the tourist frenzy, and spent time with the family instead. And where I'd found one version of modern Magyar in the city's restaurants, shops, and public places, now I found another one, at home.

One night, her cousin Maju hosted a dinner party at her place. Luizi, Frank, Mom, and I were there, along with Maju's boyfriend, Laci; her sons Gábor and Támas; Gábor's wife Timmy and their three kids; and Támas' girlfriend as well as his son from an earlier marriage. It was quite a crowd, and Maju produced for us a feast of classic Hungarian dishes. We dined on soup, salad, roasted vegetables, and three kinds of roast: pork loin stuffed with sausage; *vagdalt hús*, which is a sort of upscale meatloaf; and a roasted beef brisket in a wonderfully tasty sauce. Interestingly, although Maju sticks to the traditional culinary repertoire, like many Hungarian cooks, she doesn't hesitate to take modern shortcuts – using Knorr *pörkölt* sauce mix from a packet to pour over Hortobagyi *palacsinta*, for example, or instant pudding mix for the pastry known as *krémes* (KRAY-mesh). To round out the meal, Mom and I brought wine from Villány, Luizi and Frank brought a magnum of champagne, and one of the boys brought a chocolate torte from the city's best bakery.

We ate in the room where once József and Alujzia presided over their formal meals. They would have had servants to make the meal and dish it out. The linens would have been perfectly starched, the bronze chandelier would have glowed warmly, the furniture would have been polished to perfection. All these years later, the lights flickered dimly and a TV set sat on the sideboard while we perched on mismatched chairs around the old Victorian dining table. My great-grandparents would have had a seizure, I thought, especially if they could have seen what the youngest generation was up to.

I remembered Mom's stories of how she and Luizi were expected to be silent, neatly dressed and perfectly behaved, and how they had had to kiss their grandfather's hand when they left the table after the meal. Clearly, those rules no longer applied. While we sipped our wine, Maju's grandchildren raced happily around the apartment singing, shrieking, and calling loudly to each other. Toys littered the apartment. Shoes were piled up in a tumble by the door. Throw rugs lay bunched up in heaps where careless feet had scattered them. At one point, a horrendous racket broke out in the room next door, as somebody began, quite literally, pounding the ivories. It sounded like someone was dropping buckets of cement onto the piano.

"Who is making that terrible noise?" Maju demanded and poked her head around the corner. "Oh – it's you, Pintyi."

Frank rolled his eyes and, as another piercing cry set the crystal drops in the chandeliers tinkling, muttered something about W.C. Fields preferring his children "well done." I had to laugh. Is it any wonder that, in a country that has had a zero rate of population growth for decades, its youngest citizens are cherished, indulged and, in fact, spoiled rotten? They are the country's great hope for the future, so their elders seemed to be saying, let them live a little, let them have some fun.

Not long after that joyously chaotic meal, we had a much quieter, more thoughtful one with Mom's cousin Kálmán and his wife Edina. For decades, Mom had lost touch with the brothers Kálmán and Ístvan. Then a few years back, they all decided to trace their family's roots and took a road trip, first to the Black Forest and then to the town of Perjámos, which was then in Hungary and is now part of Romania and renamed Periam. The area had suffered badly under the Turkish occupation, and in the eighteenth and nineteenth centuries the Hapsburgs had encouraged German immigrants like the Wintermantels to move to Perjámos and increase the decimated population. Within a few decades, the Wintermantels left Perjámos for Budapest. After Perjámos became part of Romania under the Versailles Treaty, they never visited their old hometown again until the road trip in the 1990s.

When Mom and her cousins visited Periam, they'd hoped to find the missing pieces of their family history. What they found instead was that someone had gone through the church records and destroyed all the papers relating to Hungarian families. They'd also gone through the churchyards and sandblasted all the Hungarian names off the tombstones. Not a trace was left of centuries of Hungarian history, or of the people who had once lived there. The experience had upset and unsettled the cousins. It had also brought them closer.

So when Kálmán and Edina invited us out for lunch a few years later, Mom and I were thrilled. Because they live way out in the suburb of Újpest, Kálmán and his son Zsolt, the young center-right politician, came to get us at Frances's place. We drove out along Váci Út, a long, wide thoroughfare edges with shopping malls, big box stores, sports complexes, abandoned buildings, and empty lots of rubble and weeds. Back in the old days, this was where all the factories were, including the one my dad's father ran. Even the bright primary colors of capitalism couldn't disguise the forlorn nature of the area. When I asked Kálmán about it, he smiled a little sadly.

When they closed the factories down, he told us, many people thought it was a good thing because they could be replaced with businesses that were more competitive. But for many of the people who'd worked in those factories, it was a complete disaster. All their lives, they'd lived in a worker's regime with total security. Each state factory provided medical care, day care, a fitness center and a *menza* where the entire family could eat for very little money. They basically created a state of learned helplessness for an entire generation.

Then, when the communist era ended, the economy changed overnight to a capitalist system. Among the first to go were the old, unprofitable factories making goods that it seemed no one wanted any more. Suddenly, thousands of people who'd always been protected by the state were out of work and looking for jobs they didn't have the skills to perform. Not only that, but many of them didn't know how to find a doctor or childcare, nor how to cook, nor any of a number of skills we take for granted. Add to that all the older people who'd lived through the war and the revolution and the years of communism with the promise of security in their old age. But in many cases their pensions were so small that they were having a hard time surviving in the new capitalist environment. Oddly, though, just as Frances had once complained to me, they didn't look with nostalgia to the socialist period, but to the good old days of fascism in the 1930s. People. Who can ever figure them out?

When Kálmán talked to me on that drive, it was one of the first times I'd heard anyone in our family say anything good about the old Soviet system, and it was a real eye opener, especially coming from someone who'd managed to make both systems work.

Zsolt invited us to his house, which was just a short walk away from Kálmán's, for a cocktail before lunch. Like many of the younger-generation Hungarians we met, he and his wife Adrienne were interested in food and wine in a way their parents had never been. When we arrived, Adrienne was watching Paprika TV and reading through a stack of cookbooks by Judit Stahl, a former newscaster who has become Hungary's version of Nigella Lawson. And Zsolt, who has about a million projects on the go on every level of government, also finds the time to pursue a very modern interest in wine. The previous fall, he'd introduced us to the people at Monarchia, a major wine import-export company doing great things for the national wine industry. This time, when Mom and I told him we were planning a tour of wine country in Villány, he became animated and excited. "You must go to Bock and Gere," he said. Yes, we will, we told him. He gave me a beautiful map of old Hungary and its wine regions and detailed directions to the wineries we absolutely must try.

After a quick drink, we walked over to Kálmán's place, a bright, airy house in the midst of a lush garden filled with big old trees, including a young pine they'd brought home from their trip to the Black Forest. His wife Edina is one of those remarkable women who out-Martha Martha Stewart. She's smart and well informed and impressively good at all the traditional female arts, like the beautiful embroidered tablecloths, runners, and cushion covers, from her own hands, that fill the house.

For lunch, she prepared *tyúkhúsleves,* a golden chicken broth with lovely little shell-shaped noodles. Then, because Kálmán had had a health scare recently, she made a healthy meal of turkey cutlets baked with a light paprika-flavored sauce and served with a salad.

Still, Mom couldn't help but tease Kálmán, who didn't drink, ate healthy food, exercised every day, never gambled, and refused to engage in political discussions of the more hysterical sort. "Are you sure you're really a Wintermantel?" she asked.

He just laughed.

Not long after our lunch with Kálmán, we invited his brother István and his wife Ildikó for a light dinner of local cheeses, cold cuts, and salad at the Gellért Hotel. Istvan would be undergoing eye surgery the next day and was having difficulty seeing, but he wanted a chance to visit with Mom. And I think he also wanted a chance to talk to me, too, for we were both journalists, though we'd had very different experiences. For years, István had been the editor of national news publications, then when the regime change came about, he had joined a polling firm until he retired. As a fellow journalist, I simply can't imagine what it would have been like to be an editor under a government that did not believe in freedom of expression. What István's experiences were, I don't know, for he refused to talk about it.

Certainly, István was in love with information, with the Internet, with the accessibility of news from the West. I was touched and flattered to hear that he'd been reading some of my stories online. And that, I think is the answer to all those people who wonder how Hungarians could elect a socialist government after all those years of communist repression. It's not the same world anymore. It's become so much smaller, and so much more transparent. The Internet and membership in the European Union provide safeguards against the sort of repression that existed in the communist years. And they ensure that people like István can read the news from all over the world.

The highlight of our trip, in many ways, was the *bogracsa* out at our cousin Tommi's place. The afternoon we drove out there, I couldn't help but reflect on how Frank had complained that Hungarians had forgotten how to cook. Surely not, I thought, for I was looking forward to this in a big way. I'd always wanted to go to a real *bogracsa*, and when Lionel and I were in Hungary, Tommi had offered to host one if I ever came back. Well, here we were, heading out to Rákosszentmihály, where Tommi had been stirring a paprika-scented broth for hours and hours.

Tommi is quite possibly my favorite cousin. He's a little older than us, and when Fran and I were at Sárospatak, he looked a lot like the Partridge Family-era David Cassidy, only without the puka shells. He was a terrible flirt, always teasing and joking – he must have inherited my grandfather's genes, for no one else in the family could be as audaciously charming as he was. Now, of course, all these years later, the feathered hair has turned gray and is close-cropped, and the skinny jeans he wore back then probably wouldn't be such a good idea any more. But he still has that naughty look in his eye that makes you wonder what kind of mischief he's getting up to this time. His wife Jolcsi and daughter Szilvi wouldn't let him get into too much trouble, but you can tell the potential is always there.

Tommi inherited what was left of the old family compound at Rákosszentmihály, and he invited all of us – Luizi, Frank, Frances, Mom, and me – out on a sunny afternoon for a real, authentic *bogracsa*. Basically, a *bogracsa* is a party whose main focus is *gulyás* cooked the way the original Magyar tribes cooked it – in a cauldron over an open fire. It's always a casual affair held outdoors: some *gulyás*, some bread, perhaps some dessert and, of course, lots of wine and beer to drink. Even if the women typically do most of the work in the kitchen, a *bogracsa* is always a man's job, possibly because it gives him the excuse to hang around outside all day drinking beer while appearing to do something constructive.

The Family at Dinner

It seemed like an awfully long way to Rákosszentmihály. "Can you believe we went to school downtown from here every day when we were little?" Mom said to Luizi at one point. We passed the church where my great-grandparents were buried in the family vault and then we turned into a leafy suburb. Suddenly, it seemed as if it was only the two sisters in the car, as if the rest of us didn't exist at all.

"Oh, it looks so terrible," Luizi said.

"Look at how much construction is going on!" Mom chimed in.

"There must be a lot of crime, look at all the security gates and barbed wire."

"But there's money, too, look at how big and expensive some of the new places are."

It appeared that this was a neighborhood in the midst of urban renewal. In the 1980s and early 1990s, we were told, squatters took over a lot of the houses and many of them fell into terrible disrepair. But in recent years this has become a desirable address again, and there is a wave of renovation and rebuilding going on.

The buildings of the old family summer home are all there, if somewhat the worse for wear, but only Teréz's house is still in the family. As we walked by, we wondered briefly about the people who lived in the houses that used to belong to Nagypapa and to his parents and we wondered what they'd done to them, how they'd fixed them up (or not), whether they'd made them beautiful again (or not). We reached Terez's old house and knocked on a tall wooden gate that looked as if it had been designed to keep out intruders rather than welcome guests. It was silent beyond the gate, and we waited and wondered for a few minutes if we are in the right place. Then Tommi throws the gate open and he, Jolcsi, Szilvi, and his mother Cica néni greeted us with hugs and kisses.

As we walked into the back yard we could smell the aroma of the *gulyás*. On the patio, a long table had been set with soup bowls and baskets of bread. Tommi and Jolcsi poured glasses of wine for all of us and we sat down, but not before Luizi and Mom wandered around the rose-scented garden, remembering. "That's where Mother buried the silver, remember?" one of the sisters asked. "Yes, and that's the window where Grandmother was watching her." In one of the neighboring houses a small lace-curtained window looked out over the shaded flower bed where Nagymama famously buried the family silver — and where her mother-in-law, "mean grandmother," dug it up and gave it to the Russians, along with the keys to the wine cellar.

Not far from the patio, a blackened cauldron hung from a tripod over the makeshift fire pit, a small metal barrel with a hole cut out of the front so more wood can be easily added. The tang of wood smoke filled the air and saturated the *gulyás* cooking in the pot. Every few minutes, Tommi leaned over and lazily gave it a stir, releasing its rich, peppery aromas. I asked him how he made it, and he was only too happy to describe the process.

"First, I bought a leg of beef, a whole leg, tendons and all, because the tendons are the very best part. Then I had it all cut up," he said, making a chopping motion with his hand. "The pieces have to be very small," he added.

He got the fire going outside in the garden and let it die down a little bit so it wouldn't be too hot. When he thought it was just the right temperature, he hung the *bogracs* over the fire and melted some lard in it. Then he chopped up not one, not two, but seven golden onions and stirred them into the hot lard until they were soft and clear.

By then the fire was dying down, cool enough that he could stir in a couple of handfuls of paprika without fear of the sugars in it burning. Next, he added the meat all at once, stirring it so that every morsel of meat was covered with the paprika-onion mixture. He built the fire back up and let the meat cook until it became tender, about half an hour or so.

Then he filled the cauldron with water and let it simmer, absorbing the flavors of the meat, the paprika and the smoke, for hours and hours. As it cooked down, it became thicker, so he'd occasionally add more water. The onions became so soft they all but vanished in the broth; the meat so tender it fell apart with the touch of a spoon. He let the soup cook all afternoon, then an hour before we were scheduled to arrive, he added some potatoes and carrots, peeled and cut roughly into bite-sized pieces.

"You can also add parsnips if you like, or even turnips, but carrots and potatoes are the best," he said.

Szilvi helped him serve the soup while Jolcsi passed the crusty bread. The *gulyás* was deeply flavorful, slightly smoky from the fire, sweet and spicy, just perfect. We dunked the bread in it, making sure to soak up every last drop of broth.

"Did you get some tendon?" Tommi asked me. "I'm not sure," I said, doubtful that I wanted any tendon at all. Then he scooped some gently into the bowl and I took a hesitant bite. He was right, it was delicious, with a texture between fatty and gelatinous, but much more appetizing than that sounds, especially as it had somehow absorbed even more of the smoky paprika flavor than the rest of the meat.

We all had seconds and some of us had thirds. And then, just when we thought we couldn't eat another bite, Tommi brought out a huge bowl of perfectly ripe strawberries. Now, if you buy your strawberries at the supermarket, you have no idea of what a real strawberry tastes like. What you know is a pale, spongy mouthful of something that has a faint ghost of strawberry flavor. Taking a bite of a real strawberry is like filling your mouth with sweet sunshine. It tastes like you would imagine the color red should taste, strong and syrupy, with a spicy note as if it had absorbed the aromas of an herb garden baking in the June sunshine. These were those strawberries.

We ate them with *fánk*, a deceptively simple fritter made with sour cream and *túró*, then sprinkled with icing sugar. Jolcsi had spent the afternoon making them and they were delicious – the perfect finish to a meal of intense flavors.

As we drove back into the city, I couldn't help but remember Frank's complaint that Hungarians have forgotten how to cook. Obviously *some* people haven't forgotten how to cook. Maybe the problem is that some of us have forgotten how to eat, how to take our time and how to savor every bite. Maybe we've forgotten how to enjoy something as simple as a perfectly ripe strawberry, or maybe we don't even know what a perfectly ripe strawberry is any more. Maybe we've forgotten that a great meal is only made that way by the company we keep and the conversation we share, and that anger and bitterness do not make appetizing condiments.

Maybe.

In any case, all the elements for a perfect meal were in place the night we went to Alabárdos, named for the medieval suit of armor and the large weapon that overlook the place. The restaurant was recommended to us by several winemakers as a place that showcased the best of modern Hungarian cuisine – great service, gorgeous decor, exquisite food, and a fantastic wine cellar. All counts turned to be true.

Frances was our host on a warm starry night up on Castle Hill. We sat out in the 400-year-old courtyard, in between walls as ancient as Hungarian history itself, shaded by a huge tree and a canvas umbrella almost as big. As we walked through the courtyard, we could see that the restaurant itself was a series of small rooms filled with lively chatter. Soft lights twinkled and a classical guitarist strummed gently. Flowers bloomed from big pottery urns and the tables were all covered with tapestry cloths ornate in springlike colors and set with pieces of Zsolnay porcelain.

We started with a bottle of local sparkling wine, and within minutes the conversation was sparkling, too. It's hard to say whether the service, the wine, or the decor was more impressive. But the hands-down winner was the food, the best of which provided a perfect balance between tradition and innovation. True, there were things on the menu like scallops and salmon, neither of which are indigenous to Hungary, and they were only all right. Where the chef Attila Bicsár is a master is with the ingredients of his native land.

I started with a fresh cold pea soup –very traditional, except for the latte-like froth that skimmed the surface. I followed that with a perfectly roasted guinea hen stuffed with foie gras and served with wild mushrooms and the wild berries called honey berries that Pál had so wanted me to try in the Mátra Mountains. Dessert was a green apple sorbet with rosewater, a slight Turkish influence there, I think. It was topped, whimsically, with a candied rose petal. It was one of the best meals I'd ever eaten, and the company only made it more so.

At one point, I looked around, at Luizi with her goose liver, Mom with her wild boar pörkölt, Frances with her scallops, Frank with his multi-course tasting meal and Maju with her salmon, and I thought how Pál would have loved this. And silently, I raised a glass to him, and to all the food lovers like him, the people who make it possible not just to eat good food, but to grow it, sell it, make it and keep on making it better, fresher, and more authentic.

Bon appétit, guys. *Jó étvagyöt.*

CHAPTER 13

Take Me Down to Spicy Town

About thirty seconds after we picked up the rental car in Buda, I learned something new about my mother: She couldn't read a map. Nope, and she couldn't read street signs either, or remember where any exits or landmarks might be, or give directions that a driver could actually follow.

"Didn't you know?" my uncle Frank said later. "I think it's genetic. None of the Wintermantel women have any sense of direction."

Normally I would have handed over the wheel and taken over map duties right about when we ended up in the same shabby suburb for the third time, instead of on the highway to Szeged. But then I remembered that the last time Mom had rented a car in Hungary she had ended up getting towed out of a ditch, and I thought, hmmm, maybe not.

The southern city of Szeged was our first stop on a two-week road trip that spring, a trip that would take us through two of the country's wine regions, Villány and Tokaj. We were not deterred by the fact that they were at opposite ends of the country. We were planning to taste a lot of wine, from the local varietals like Kadarka, Kékoporto, and Harslevelú, to the international ones like Pinot Noir and Cabernet Franc. But first we were going to take a side trip to Szeged, to talk to the folks at the Szeged Paprika Factory about Hungarian cuisine's main ingredient. But maddeningly, we couldn't find the damn highway.

On the map, the route looked so easy. But the Budapest streets were narrow and busy, the street signs tiny and hard to read, and the Ford Escort's standard transmission new and unfamiliar. There was one directional sign in particular that kept sending us the wrong way and by the time we finally sorted things out, our tempers were somewhat frayed. It didn't help when Mom would say things like "Why did you turn there? I don't think you should have turned there." And it didn't help either when I snapped back, "Well, you're the one who's supposed to be navigating!"

On the map, it looked as though it would take about two hours to get to Szeged. I planned on three, just in case, plus time for lunch. When it took us over an hour just to get out of the city, I began to worry. We had an appointment at 1 p.m. at the factory and, as a good Hungarian, I hate being late. So I pulled another U-turn in the middle of a busy thoroughfare – it was a new skill I learned from getting lost again and again in Hungary, and one I'm mighty proud of – and somehow, somehow we ended up on the M5 to Szeged.

The highway was wide and smooth, the drivers sensible about things like not driving slowly in the fast lane, and gradually the stress of leaving the city faded and we began to enjoy ourselves. Mom told me stories about her family when they were all kids and I talked a bit about the wineries we were going to visit, and it was all very pleasant until Kiskunfélegyháza. Then suddenly the multilane highway ended. We swerved sharply east then sharply south onto an old, single-lane road that was bumper-to-bumper with ancient Trabants, slow-moving farm vehicles, overloaded trucks, and impatient drivers like us. It stayed like that the rest of the way into Szeged.

Under the Soviets, much of Hungary's transportation infrastructure had been left to crumble into obsolescence. Since 1989, though, a massive rebuilding project has gripped the country, as massive as the one at the end of the nineteenth century, though frankly not as beautiful. The roads are a big issue in modern Hungary, especially since it has an enormous number of car fatalities, in spite of all the drunk driving laws that have been passed. One problem is that many projects are not yet complete, although the speed at which roads and other services have been built is astonishing. That's why you'll find yourself driving along a perfect superhighway that suddenly ends and decants the drivers onto narrow, hundred-year-old roadways.

By the time we got into Szeged, we were already late. And then we couldn't find the factory, and no one seemed to know where it was.

Lionel and I had made a quick trip down here the last time I was in Hungary, so I knew a little bit about the layout of the city center. But there was a lot of construction going on, and I quickly became confused. Round and round I drove, until we were so disoriented that we were barely able to take in the beauty of this lovely city.

Szeged is the biggest city in the country's south. It lies at the junction of the Tisza and Maros rivers, transportation routes that brought Szeged into being – and almost destroyed it, too. In 1879, bloated with spring melt and runoff, the two rivers spilled over their banks and destroyed almost the entire city in a single night. More than 5,000 buildings were demolished; only 258 were left standing. When the waters receded, the area for miles and miles around was covered in a rich, black silt. The international community rushed in to help, and the city was rebuilt almost entirely in an Art Nouveau style that has been remarkably well preserved. In gratitude, the city fathers named sections of the ring road that encircles Szeged after the cities that helped: Paris, London, Ottawa, and so on.

Today, the city is a university town famous for its lovely cafés, as well as paprika. Pick salami and, courtesy of the rivers that both give and take away, some of the best fish soup in the country. On our previous visit, Lionel and I had sampled the deliciously spicy fish soup at the Roosevelt Téri Halászcsárda restaurant. It was so good, we went on and had a mixed platter of fried fish – *harcsa* (catfish), *fogas* (pike-perch), and *ponty* (carp). It was a festival of fishy, finny goodness.

Later, we chatted with the chef, Frank Sandor, who brings an innovative approach to even the most traditional of dishes. In Szeged, he pointed out, he has found fresh, flavorful ingredients, and not just the fish from the river. The produce is especially tasty here because the soil is so rich from the flood and because the sun shines more than 2,000 hours a year. The area produces excellent fruit and vegetables, especially corn, which is fed to livestock, producing in turn extra-flavorful pork. When we asked him about the emergence of a modern Magyar cuisine, he uttered what might seem a heresy, especially in the paprika capital itself: "You don't always have to use the paprika," he said. "We have to leave the old Hungarian cuisine behind."

To prove his point, he brought out a spice dictionary and showed us all the spices used in Hungarian cuisine: garlic, dill, caraway, horseradish, capers, chilies, nutmeg, cinnamon, saffron ("I use lots," he says), lemongrass, cloves, anise, liquorice, juniper, bay leaves, curry, pepper, ginger, and vanilla. Paprika is only one among dozens of herbs and spices, many of which can be found in the kitchens of nearby regions that influence the cuisine in Szeged. The herbs, for instance, are used in Transylvania and the Balkans, while the hot spices are popular with the Turks and the Serbs.

Nevertheless, it was paprika that had brought my mother and me to Szeged eight months later, where we were lost in a maze of heavy construction and crowds of students and one-way streets. Eventually, and I'm not at all sure how it happened, we ended up at the Pick Museum, which celebrates the region's famous Pick salami. It was closed, but we found a couple of people in the bar next door. They phoned the Szeged Paprika Factory and got directions for us. The factory, of course, was on the other side of town. We only got lost once on the way over there. Eventually, two hours late and feeling rather flustered, we sat down with the charming factory manager, Tibor Huszka, who told us the story of paprika.

"The history of Szeged paprika is at least 250 years old," he said. "The history of paprika is full of kings, queens, peasants, and scientists."

The story began with Christopher Columbus and his travels to the Americas, which is where the plants of the Capsicum family originated, probably in Brazil or Bolivia. Columbus's doctor, Dr. Chanca, brought back the plants known today as Capsicum anuum, or paprika, as a gift from the New World for Queen Isabella. However, in those days, they were only grown as ornamental plants. The peppers themselves were very, very hot, not at all like the sweet and mild versions available today.

No one is sure when, exactly, people began to use paprika in cooking. It is known that the Turks carried it east from Spain and that it eventually appeared in Morocco, Persia, and throughout Asia. By the seventeenth century, the Turks had brought it with them during their invasion of the Balkans and north into Hungary, where the locals called it "Turkish pepper" or "heathen pepper." Paprika's documented history in Szeged can be traced back to an old shopping account from 1748, which lists, among other things, one kilogram of bacon and half a kilogram of paprika powder. One of the first places it was grown in Szeged was the garden of an old church near the factory.

The Turks used paprika both as food and as medicine for fever and malaria. Capsaicin, the ingredient that makes paprika hot, increases the circulation of the blood, which is why paprika is used in medications that treat frostbite. (Paprika's other major health benefit wasn't discovered until much later: in 1937, a Hungarian chemist named Albert Szent-Györgi – who was, of course, from Szeged – won the Nobel Prize in Medicine for discovering that paprika contains large quantities of vitamin C.) When the Turkish troops left, the paprika stayed behind. Although paprika plants can tolerate almost any climate, they need warmth and sunshine to create the strong aromas that make the spice so valued. Hot, sunny Szeged provided the ideal conditions.

At the end of the eighteenth century, two things happened to popularize paprika throughout Europe: first, there was an improvement in the way it was milled, making the process more efficient; and second, the Naploeonic wars broke out and black pepper became unavailable in much of Europe. (Black pepper is not related to paprika botanically, although both are, well, peppery.)

"Napoleon's troops blockaded the trading lines and this helped the production of paprika because people wanted it as a flavoring," Huszka says. For the first time, paprika became a valuable seasoning in Europe outside the Carpathian basin. Its popularity continued to grow in the nineteenth century, first when traditional peasant dishes like *gulyás* became fashionable on the tables of the Hungarian aristocracy, and later when Hungarian dishes like chicken *paprikás* were exported to France and other countries. By the beginning of the twentieth century, there were twelve to fifteen paprika mills in Szeged.

There are now four mills in the Szeged area and another four or five around Kalocsa, Szeged's competitor for the paprika crown. Many Hungarians will tell you they prefer the Kalocsa paprika "because it's redder," which means that it has more of the carotenoid pigments that give it its rosy hue (and consequently make it more difficult to remove from a white blouse). To me, though, the two paprikas taste very similar – if anything, Szeged seems a bit more subtle and nuanced, though it is true that the Kalocsa paprika has a more robust color.

"In Hungary, we use eight sweet varieties of paprika and two hot," Huszka explained. But, interestingly, until the 1920s, all paprika was hot. Then a Szeged breeder discovered one plant whose fruit was sweet. He grafted it onto other plants, and created more sweet paprika. Now almost all the paprika grown is the sweet variety, Huszka told us. In fact, a paprika fruit contains up to six per cent sugar.

The growing cycle of paprika follows a strict yearly schedule.

"When I started in this business I was told that with paprika, the most important periods belong to the most important holidays," Huszka said with a laugh. Sowing is done from March 15 to April 4; March 15, 1848, was the date Hungary won its independence from Austria while April 4, 1945, was a national holiday commemorating the date Soviet troops liberated Hungary from Germany. The seedlings appear about May 1, the national Workers' Day holiday, and the red fruit by August 20, St. Stephen's Day. The harvest begins in early September and must be finished by October 23, the anniversary of the 1956 Uprising.

"September 28 is the risk day," Huszka pointed out, "because that is traditionally the first day of frost. But in the last twenty years, there was not any frost. But maybe by the twenty-third of October it could happen."

The harvest takes three to four weeks and is done by hand.

"They say paprika likes the shadow. It is completely not true. It likes the sun very much, and the heat, too," Huszka said. "The saying means the paprika likes the shadow of the worker. There is a lot of hard work."

Drying the peppers is a two-stage process. First, the peppers are strung together to ripen in the hot September sun. Throughout the region you can see the bright, red garlands hanging on racks or from rafters. As they ripen, the peppers lose water content, but increase pigment, flavor, and sugars. When the pigments are at their peak, the peppers are perfectly ripe and ready to be dried. They are washed, sliced, and set out to dry until mid-November. Once the peppers are completely dry, they are packed in boxes and bags for up to a year until they are ready to be milled.

The paprika mill has two parts. The first part is a steam sterilizing system that gets rid of dirt, germs, pesticides, or other contaminants without affecting the color, flavor, or nutrients of the paprika. The second part is the actual grinding mill, which uses both artificial and natural stones to grind the dried peppers.

"It's a traditional way of milling paprika," Huszka told us. "As the stones move on each other, the paprika warms up. Then, as the temperature of the paprika is increased, the oils in the seeds are melted and this oil surrounds the parts of the paprika." The powder is made from the walls of the fruit, and when the oil coats the powders, it prevents the pigment from oxidizing. If the millers don't include the seeds and the oil they release, the color becomes dingy brown. "We used to say the color is dead – with oil, it is a bright red color."

The workers also have to be careful to monitor the heat in the tanks where the milling is taking place. If the stones get too hot, the sugars in the paprika will burn and the spice will become bitter.

"We have quite big quantities. We produce approximately 1,200 tonnes per year. One kilogram of powder needs seven kilograms of fresh paprika. And one fruit is about 0.02 kilograms," Huszka said. Doing the math later, I realized that this means it takes 350 peppers to make one kilo of paprika powder.

There are basically four different grades of paprika, the quality based on pigment, pungency, and how finely ground the peppers are. *Különleges* (special) is the best grade, mild and delicate and bright red; *csemege* (delicatesse) is a more common grade with a stronger flavor but no pungency; *édesnemes* (sweet and noble) is the grade preferred by German customers (Germany is a big market for Hungarian paprika); and *rózsa* (rose) is piquant, but has a much lighter color. It is the grade most often exported.

While all the grades come in hot and sweet varieties, sometimes hot paprika is also listed in separate grades – *csipös* (spicy), for instance, is the lowest grade of all. It is made with more of the capsaicin-containing veins and seeds, so it's almost brown in color and though the flavor is hot, it has no depth to it.

In Szeged, paprika is serious business. Local producers have recently sent a petition to the European union in Brussels, applying for a sort of appellation like the controlled wine regions of France and Italy. If they get the approval, they will be able to use the EU symbol for a controlled region, which means that the product's quality, purity, and place of origin are all certified by the international organization.

In the meantime, they are concentrating on other improvements that have become essential in a global economy. One of those is the traceability system.

"Because of the food safety we have to use a traceability system," Huszka explained. "If you buy a kilogram of paprika powder, we have to be able to say who was the farmer who grew it and what kind of pesticides he used." This system is not only essential under EU regulations, but would have helped to prevent the Great Paprika Crisis of 2004.

On October 28 of that year, the Hungarian government banned the sale of paprika after the National Health Service found a toxic fungus called aflatoxin in three brands of the famous Magyar spice. Harmless amounts of aflatoxin occur naturally in foods such as peanuts and potato chips, but in big doses it can cause cancer and liver damage. It's so toxic, reported the *Budapest Sun*, that scientists used it to create chemical weapons in the 1990s. According to other reports, it was supposed to be among Saddam Hussein's weapons of mass destruction.

This was bad news indeed. Hungarians eat more paprika than anyone on the planet – about a pound per person per year. (You'd have to eat a pound of the infected paprika in a week to experience any ill effects from the aflatoxin, so the health risks were actually quite small.) Furthermore, paprika is one of Hungary's biggest exports, at about 5,000 tonnes per year. The timing wasn't very good, either. Only a few months earlier, on May 1, Hungary had finally emerged from its chronic state of isolation to join the European Union and this unfortunately became its first major moment in the international spotlight.

Everything containing paprika, from sauces to sausages, was pulled off store shelves and restaurants were forbidden to serve food containing the spice, which meant they could not offer any of the national dishes: *gulyás*, *pörkölt paprikás*, *halaszlé* or *lecsó* (stewed peppers with sausage).

For a while, it looked as though it would be a bland new world indeed. But then the Hungarians began to stir the pot. The government would fall over this, some said. Hungary would be kicked out of the EU. The entire tourism industry would collapse. Those who hated the leftist government were smug; those who feared the right wingers were in a panic. Meanwhile, everyone continued to eat food made with paprika (what, exactly, were they supposed to do without it?) even as they predicted the disintegration of the country's entire social fabric.

It turned out that the infected paprika had been imported from South America when three Hungarian companies had decided to supplement their own crops, made meager by the previous summer's drought. Once the rogue importers were identified and the contaminated spice seized by the government, the crisis seemed to be over and by November 1, paprika was back on the menu. The government did not fall, tourism didn't die, and Hungary wasn't kicked out of the EU. It turned out to be a tempest in a soup pot after all. The situation was still unfolding in 2005, as some producers began talking about suing the government for lost profits and damage to their reputation.

"The problem last year was in the Kalocsa region," Huszka said, adding that the government still pulled all paprika and products containing paprika – including those from Szeged – out of the marketplace. "They made a big problem from this one sample. I think the government wanted to show their strength. And that's why they pulled all the paprika from the supermarket shelves." He is convinced not only that the government caused unnecessary economic damage to paprika producers, but that the testing itself was not properly done at an authorized laboratory.

On a brighter, spicier note, each year on the first weekend in September, when the harvest begins, Szeged hosts its annual Paprika Days festival. And each year, they try to produce something new and different for Paprika Days. One year it was paprika-based beauty creams; another, it was paprika palinka; and yet another, it was a paprika-flavored chocolate ice cream. (The beauty creams and the palinka have become popular with the general public and are now produced by several companies. The ice cream is taking a little longer to catch on.)

"At Paprika Days, you can buy everything connected to paprika," Huszka told us proudly. There are paprika sweets and paprika oils, drinks made with paprika, and soups, and canned foods, and condiments, and spice mixtures, and sauces, and more. "So you see, paprika can be used in many ways."

With that, he loaded us up with bags and tins of paprika and walked us to the factory gate, waving as we climbed into the car. As Mom and I began the next leg of our journey, we decided that we'd have to come back sometime for Paprika Days. It sounded like delicious fun. Though we weren't entirely sure we were up to trying the paprika ice cream.

CHAPTER 14
Wine-o-rama

From Szeged, Mom and I drove to a village called Villány, where we planned to do a whole lot of wine tasting. I admit, I was a little bit worried about this at first. I am the sort of aficionada who has always refused to vacation in any country that does not have an indigenous wine culture. The rest of my family, however, has a much more casual relationship with wine. They drink a lot of it but tend not to be too fancy about it. "As long as it's red and in a glass" could be the family motto. Or, in my grandfather's case, "As long as it's red and in a gallon jug."

Worse, my mother has in recent years developed a habit of diluting her wine with soda water, and not just at home when she's drinking something cheap and ordinary. She'll take a sip of, say, a lovely Pinot Noir or Brunello di Montalcino, make a face like a six-year-old confronted with a plate of brussels sprouts, then dump half a glass of bubbly water into it with *ice*. It's enough to make you cry.

Of course, in Hungary, the tradition of the spritzer or *fröccs* goes back a long way, back to the nineteenth century and Hungary's revolt against the Austrians. After the Austrian soldiers captured and executed the Hungarian rebel leaders, they reportedly raised their tankards of ale and clinked their glasses in celebration. As a result, beer fell out of favor in Hungary for decades afterwards, and clinking your beer glasses is still frowned upon. But people still needed something refreshing to drink on a hot day. A few years earlier, a Hungarian monk had invented the seltzer bottle, and soon people started splashing a bit of seltzer into their wine. A century and a half later, they're still doing it, though it would be nice if they didn't do it with the good wine.

In addition, as far as I knew, my mom had never been to a winery tasting before, and I was curious to see how that would go. I needn't have worried. She thought the whole thing was a blast, from the swirling to the swishing to the spitting, and she managed to charm every one of the winemakers she met, without a drop of seltzer in sight.

Wine is as important to a Hungarian as air and bread and arguing about politics. Or at least it was before the Second World War, back when Hungary was a major producer of some of the world's best wines, treasured by connoisseurs. After the war, though, the communist regime nationalized the wine industry and almost overnight turned good wine into bad.

If you've had a glass of Hungarian wine in the last few decades, you were probably still in university and the wine was probably Szekszárdi Vörös, which you cleverly nicknamed "Sex on Saturday." (The "i" ending means "from," much as "de" does in French or "di" does in Italian, so the name really means, "Red Wine from Szekszárd.") Back then, you bought it because it was cheap, not because it was good, so you could drink lots and lots of it. That's how it earned its other nickname: "Hangover in a Glass." Even today, most of the Hungarian wine you'll find in North America is of the eight-dollar-a-bottle plonk variety. It isn't horrible, just a bit insipid. The exception is the rare Tokaji Aszú that makes it past all the duties and laws and importers' quotas.

Until the Second World War, Hungary was the third largest producer of wine in the world, after France and Italy. It had a system of wine regulation from 1271 until the communists abolished it in 1949, and it had the first wine appellation region in the world (Tokaj). Even today it has twenty-two wine regions where ninety-three varietals are grown, including more than a dozen unique to Hungary. All this is hard to imagine – unless, that is, you actually go there.

When Lionel and I visited in the fall of 2004, we went crazy for the wonderful wines being produced by small, family-run estates, most of them in the Villány region. We were equally wowed by the beautifully balanced cuvées that blended local varietals such as Kékoporto and Kékfrankos with international varietals. And we were astonished at how good Hungarian Pinot Noir could be – we hadn't expected such subtlety and finesse from Hungarian winemakers. In fact, so impressed were we that right then and there I decided to come back and do a wine tour, which is why Mom and I were driving toward Villány on a sunny afternoon in June.

Back in October, I'd become curious about why the wines in Hungary were so good, while most of the wines exported to Canada were so bad. So my cousin Zsolt called some friends of his at the wine import-export company Monarchia (now Monarchia Matt International), and one afternoon I sat and had a chat about Hungarian wine with András Kató, the company's marketing director.

"So, um," I asked, "how come the wine here is so good, and the wine we get back home is so terrible?"

"Hungary and good wine is not something that goes together in people's minds," Kató said dryly. "After forty-five years of communism, this is not a big surprise."

Under communism, high quantity – not quality – was the goal. Since ownership of land was abolished, the government took over both large and small family estates. The land was amalgamated either into large state-run wineries called *borkombinát* (*bor* is the Hungarian word for wine) or into co-operatives, which in theory were owned by the workers, but in fact operated much the same as the state-run cellars. Rather than make small batches of artisanal wines, the wine factories produced cheap booze for the masses. In fact, many co-operatives made their members add their best must or base wine to the worst to bring up the overall quality of the cheapest wine, thereby ensuring that there would not, could not be an excellent wine.

In addition, because most Hungarian wine was sold to East Germany and the USSR, winemakers had to make wine that appealed to the palates of their best customers: the Russians. After centuries of swilling vodka, the Russkies must have permanently deadened their palates, for they had a taste for wines that were strong (17 per cent alcohol) and sweet (120 grams of sugar per liter). It makes your teeth hurt just thinking about it.

The most productive vineyards were planted in the 1980s. Until then, the wine had still maintained some of its integrity, but once it was produced like so many cans of soda pop, it became undrinkable. In part, that's because the farms became mechanized and production was designed for the machines, not the grapes. To accommodate wide, clumsy Russian-made tractors, vines had to be planted in wide rows on flat, easily accessible, sandy soil. Of course, the best wine-growing areas are on rocky hillsides, which is why a Hungarian winemakers' guild is called a *hegyközség*, or mountain community.

It's no coincidence that during the eighties Hungarians turned from wine to hard spirits and even, shockingly, to beer. And when Hungarians turned to beer and spirits, rates of alcoholism and drunk-driving accidents began to soar. Then in 1989, just before the nation's palate was ruined forever, the communist regime ended.

The time was ripe for a renaissance of Hungarian wine. But it hasn't been without its difficulties. "The first part of the nineties was the privatization of land," Kató said. "Before, only a small amount of arable land was allowed in private hands."

In some areas, such as Villány, the state offered its wine-making employees first crack at the lands it had appropriated. Since many of those employees had come from the great wine-making families and, indeed, had owned the land that had been appropriated, they brought generations of experience to creating good wine. Moreover, most of them had continued growing their own grapes and making their own wine throughout the decades under communism – the plots were small, and the wine just enough for the family, but at least the traditions hadn't died out. (For most of the communist era, individuals were allowed to own 0.3 hectares of land. That was increased to 0.6 hectares of land just before the end of the regime. Members of wine co-operatives and their families could add to that, though, and some winemakers had managed to accrue as much as five hectares of their own land even before privatization.)

Unfortunately, privatization did not go as smoothly or as fairly in other areas, and soon rich foreigners were gobbling up cheap Hungarian vineyards. Laws were passed to prevent this, but not before bitterness and resentment had set in. Not only that, but because of the way the land was divided, many of the parcels were tiny, with plantations broken up and growers forced to tend small plots of land that could be scattered all over a large region – half a hectare here, another half there, yet another across the valley. As another hurdle, in its rush to a market economy, the government didn't provide much assistance to winemakers who suddenly had to invest in expensive infrastructure.

Still, within just a few years, a number of vineyards were already producing good wines, some of which showed the promise of excellence. By the mid-1990s, Kató said, "Restaurants were like, wow, lots of new names and lots of new wines. Looking back, those wines were very much amateur winemaking. The nineties was our learning period."

In the fifteen years since the regime change, a small group of wine lovers around the world has come to appreciate the excellent quality of some Hungarian wines, those from estates such as Takler, Bock, Gere, Vylyan and Tibor Gál, most of it only available in Hungary, though a small amount is exported, mostly to the United Kingdom.

"If we change so much in the next fifteen years, then in fifteen years we will be something very special," Kató told me. "And I'm not talking only about the wine industry." He went on to explain that there were now 90,000 hectares of vineyard in Hungary, of which 65,000 to 70,000 could produce good wines. To put that into context, back in the 1780s, Hungary had more than 570,000 hectares of vineyards.

Hungary's volcanic soil, its south-facing mountain slopes and its mild climate, similar to that of Burgundy, make it ideal for growing vinifera grapes. It has six main wine-producing areas comprising twenty-two official wine regions: the northwest, including Sopron and Somló; Lake Balaton, including Badacsony; the area around Budapest; Alföld (the Great Plain); the south, including Szekszárd and Villány-Siklós; and the northeast, comprising Eger and, farther east, Tokaj-Hegyalja. "We're taking steps towards a terroir-based appellation system," Kató said. The kind of classification system applied to, say, Bordeaux or Chianti, will assure customers of the quality and origin of regional Hungarian wines and help improve their reputation worldwide.

While Hungary produces about three times as much white wine as it does red, Kató believes that its greatest potential is in its reds from Villány, Szekszárd, and Eger. Tokaj, of course, is the country's most famous region, best known for its superb botrytis-affected dessert wine, Tokaji Aszú. And, in a world bored with the same old Chardonnays and Merlots, Hungary also offers its own unique varietals, such as Kékfrankos and Kadarka.

These days, the big challenge is getting the word out to an international market that's flooded with cheap French, Italian, and New World wines and is still skeptical about Hungarian wines. "If you have a good product and a good strategy, you can be successful," Kató told me. "If you want to make a breakthrough success, partly you have to convince a crowd that Hungary can produce high end wines comparable to the world's best. Depending on the quality you don't need to be ashamed of the price."

Inspired by that conversation with András Kató and by the wine tasting that followed it, eight months later I was on my way to Villány with my mother to taste some of Hungary's best wines at their source. Villány is near the Croatian border in the country's southwest, just a few hours' drive from Szeged. The region is properly called Villány-Siklós and it stretches along the hills called the Villányhegy, from the red wine areas around Villány in the east to the white wine area of Siklós in the west. It is the warmest of Hungary's wine regions; its climate is often compared to that of Côtes du Rhône. It comprises eleven communities, the biggest of which are Harkány, Siklós, and Villány, and about 2,200 hectares of grapes. For comparison, Tokaj is five times bigger; Eger, ten times.

Grapes have been grown here since the Romans invaded back in the second century AD. The Magyars conquered in the ninth century and the tribes led by the princes Kár and Bor continued wine growing in the region. Later, Villány's vineyards were the sites of many battles against the Turks and many of the region's first winemakers were Serbs fleeing the Ottoman invasion. They likely brought the Kadarka grape with them. In the eighteenth century, German settlers, the Swabians, moved in, bringing their own grapes – such as Kékoporto and Kékfrankos – as well as their winemaking and architectural styles.

By the end of the nineteenth century, according to Alex Liddell's excellent book *The Wines of Hungary*, Villányi wines were popular in the United States, Brazil, and all over Europe. Then the first of a series of disasters hit the region. Phylloxera, a louse that attacks vine roots, had been making its way through European rootstock, and by the end of the century had destroyed more than half the vines in Hungary. It was a Villányi grape grower named Zsigmond Teleki who saved many of the world's great wine making areas by developing rootstocks that were resistant to the disease.

After the First World War, Villány narrowly escaped being lost during the Trianon treaty talks. Certainly the economy was in no great shape after that, but by the time the Second World War broke out, the wine business was so good that there were twelve full-time wine merchants located on Villány's main street. Today, there are none. Then came the war, the nationalization in 1949, the devastation of the wine industry in the decades that followed, privatization in 1991, and rebirth.

Now some of the best wine in Hungary is once again being produced in Villány. I'd arranged to meet with many of the region's top winemakers, taste their wines, and look at the changes happening in the area. My mother would help with the translation – and with the tasting, of course. We could hardly wait.

As we drove along the pretty country roads from Szeged, red poppies and blue cornflowers bounced in the breeze, cows lazed in the fields, and storks stood in their nests atop telephone poles. Once we crossed the Danube at Mohacs, the terrain became hillier, and soon we could see the first vines striping across the hillsides. The boxy, pastel-colored, stucco houses of the Great Plain gave way to the Swabian style, which is narrower and built of stone and white plaster with black-painted wooden trim. Flowers spilled from every yard and window box.

We were making great time until we got to Boly, or at least I think it was Boly. Suddenly the road split three ways and all the signs to Villány disappeared. Pécs was this way, Mohacs that way and Harkány over here, but where the heck was Villány? Weird, we thought, and took the first turnoff. Nope, not it. We tried another. Nope, still not it. We tried another. Each time, we ended right back in the middle of town. Frustrated, we looked at the map. There was Villány; on paper it was so close we could probably have hit it with a rock, but where the hell was it?

Finally we stopped at a gas station — after all the back-and-forthing, we had to fill up anyway — and Mom went in to ask directions. Eventually, grudgingly, they told us to follow the road to Harkány. "Wasn't that strange?" I said as we got going again. "I mean, Villány has got to be the big attraction in the area and it's almost like they don't want anyone to know about it. Do you think it's some sort of local feud thing?"

We laughed at the absurdity of it, but later in the week when we were talking to the winemaker Attila Gere, he didn't seem to think it was so funny. There used to be signs, it seems, but they've all vanished, as if someone out there really *doesn't* want anyone to find Villány.

"Even the agriculture minister came down here and got lost," he said, shaking his head.

"Maybe they're jealous," I suggested. "Maybe," he agreed.

As we came closer to Villány, the road became crowded with small, narrow tractors on their way home from a long day in the vineyards. Songbirds sang and swooped as we passed, hunting for dinner among the vines. The early evening sky was beginning to glow pink along the horizon, and the air was spicy and still.

Then we were driving past roses and trees and a row of modern-looking houses crowded next to the road, and we were in Villány. At a T-intersection in front of a fancy restaurant called Oporto — named, we would learn later, for the popular Kékoporto grape — we swung left and found ourselves on a street lined with the famous cellars of the region. *Pince* (PEEN-SAY) is what they call wine cellars (thus a *pincér* is a waiter, a *pincemester* a cellar master). There were about two dozen of these cellars, looking like small, whitewashed sheds, with shiny green, red, or black doors and shutters, all cheek by jowl with each other along the main drag. Some had been turned into shops and restaurants; almost all of them were closed for the day.

"Oh, isn't that lovely," we gushed, and then the next minute we were out of town and driving among vines again. I swung the car around in the middle of the narrow road, nimbly avoiding a truck coming one way and a BMW going the other, and back we went to find our panzio. Soon we were inching down a narrow driveway while an old néni in a pinafore waved us into a parking spot.

Accommodation in Villány is all of the bed-and-breakfast sort – if you want to stay in a fancy hotel, you have to go to the spa town of Harkány nearby – so we'd arranged to rent a cottage belonging to the Fejérdi family. (I have to admit I'm not crazy about the whole B&B thing. I have a horror of socializing over breakfast, and in Hungary, the morning *kifli* comes with not only a lot of chit-chat, but also a certain amount of guilt if you don't finish everything on your plate. That's just way too much pressure first thing in the day.)

By the time we got settled in and unpacked and had answered all our landlady's questions, it was getting on to nine in the evening and we'd eaten nothing all day but a stale *pogacsa*. We were not only hungry and tired and a little bit cranky, but we were very, very thirsty. And here we were in the middle of wine country, without a glass in front of us. Luckily, the best restaurant in town was only a block away.

Mom and I walked to Oporto as the last of the sun's rays sank behind the hills. The place was elegant, with high ceilings, white tablecloths, and crystal glasses on the tables. It was also empty. Most of the tourists from Budapest arrive on the weekends; those from more distant places come in the fall during harvest season.

An aproned server was standing at the bar, looking bored and lonely.

"Are you open?" we asked him in Hungarian.

"*Persze*," he said, scooping up a couple of menus. "Of course."

"Oh, thank God," we said.

The menu was filled with interesting dishes, any of which could have qualified as modern Magyar. The wine list was long, filled with wines I didn't know, but names I recognized from my schedule for the days ahead. We could have had ourselves a magnificent feast, but all we wanted was comfort food and an ordinary glass of wine. So we ordered the savory venison *pörkölt*, which came with tender *galuska* sprinkled with fresh dill, and the house wine, a Kékfrankos that came slightly chilled.

The next morning, we started our marathon of wine tasting; by the end of the week, we would taste at least one hundred wines (and add nearly a hundred more the following week in Tokaj).

We began at the Vylyan Winery in the nearby village of Kisharsány. The previous fall, Lionel and I had enjoyed a number of

Vylyan's excellent wines in Budapest. They're not only producing highly drinkable, well-balanced single-varietal and blended wines, but their operation is also one of the most commercially viable in the region.

We had an appointment with the owner, Monika Debreczeni, who welcomed us warmly. She and her husband, Pál, had started the winery in 1988 after making their money manufacturing domestic appliances. Their goal – well, Pál's really, but Monika had gone along with it – was to create the best wines in Hungary, and to put Hungary back on the map of great world wines. He had been well on the way to realizing his dream when he was killed in a car accident just a few months before our visit. (It was in fact a deadly season for Hungary's best winemakers, for not long after that the renowned Tibor Gál, winemaker for Antinori in Italy and owner of his own winery in Eger, was also killed in a car crash, this time in South Africa.)

Monika Debreczeni briskly set us up for a tasting, arranging glasses, spit buckets, and bottles on a long wooden table in a room with a beautiful view over the vineyards. Lined up before us was a row of red wines: the 2003 Kékoporto, 2003 Pinot Noir ("more big-bodied than the Oregon and Burgundian Pinots, a bit spicy"), the 2003 Zwiegelt, 2003 Merlot, 2003 Cabernet Franc ("dark violet aromas"), 1999 Cabernet Sauvignon, and the 2000 Duennium, a big, plummy cuvée of Cabernet Sauvignon, Cabernet Franc, and Merlot created for the millennium celebrations.

Debreczeni told us that Vylyan started planting their 125 hectares of grapes in 1992 and just finished in 2004. Less than 10 per cent of what they grow is white; the rest is red, including local varieties such as Zwiegelt, Kékfrankos, Kadarka, and Kékoporto (which is now called Portugieser because the Portuguese complained that it sounded too much like Port and the European Union agreed) as well as international varietals such as Pinot Noir, Merlot, and a tiny bit of Syrah.

The first vintage for Vylyan – the medieval name for Villány – was in 1994, based on five hectares of old grapes. The region really started to change "productwise, stylewise" in 1998, according to Debreczeni. To repair their reputation from the communist days, local winemakers started setting quality standards. For instance, they established two levels of wines, a basic level and a premium level, with strict rules regarding the production of each. "And we created for ourselves a little super-premium level," Debreczeni added. But, she said, there is still no appellation system in place, although she and other local winemakers had drafted a proposal and sent it to the government, hoping to have it in place by the next vintage.

They had received some grant money from the European Union, though not from the Hungarian government. The process was onerous, "very strict rules, who is able, who is not," but Debreczeni told us they would keep trying to effect change through the EU.

The biggest problem, though, after the ongoing one of the weather, was getting the international market to notice their wines. "We are not yet in the international bloodstream, so to say. I would love to become part of the world wine market," Debreczeni said. The challenge, however, is twofold.

First, Debreczeni pointed out, "There is over-production everywhere. Maybe there is no room for a new entry." Right now the market is glutted with cheap wines from both the New World and the Old. That's a lot of competition for a country that doesn't have the advantage of subsidies and tax breaks the way, say, France and Italy do. Second, and a bigger problem, is letting people know about the wines in the first place. So, with the help of the Monarchia import-export company, Vylyan holds tastings around Hungary and hosts many visitors at the winery, "who are advertising by the tool of the mouth. A lot of tourists are coming. Not yet a lot of wine merchants, but I think that will happen."

Once they come and taste the wines, Monika Debreczeni is sure they will be sold on them. "I think Vylyan wines have a certain personality. We believe that everything starts from the vineyard. So you cannot produce a good wine without serious work in the vineyard. You have to follow the nature of the grape," she said.

But she also knows that the grape sometimes needs some expert help. While many local winemakers are still making their wine with old-fashioned technology, the Debreczenis hired a consultant, Jean-Pierre Confuron of France, to help out in their cellars. Bringing in foreign experts "was crucial at the beginning, but now a new generation of winemakers and viticulturists has grown up," Debreczeni said. "The soil is here, the terroir is here, and we only need to give new life to it."

Those winemakers are, by and large, the younger members of the families that have lived in the region for centuries. In the communist era, most fled to the cities, but now they are finding an exciting future right at home.

One of those people is Nora Becker, the mayor of nearby Palkonya and president of the Villány-Siklós Wine Road. "They call me the mother of the wine road," she said with a laugh. We visited her the next day in Palkonya, a tiny village only a few minutes away from Villány. As we drove into town along the narrow, swooping road, we were greeted by a remarkable sight: dozens of historic whitewashed wine cellars standing row on row. These celebrated cellars are considered a heritage site. Almost all of them are still intact and still in use.

As the daughter and granddaughter of winemakers (though not a winemaker herself), Becker has seen how the changing wine industry has changed her home. "The unemployment rate in 1993 was 32 per cent and the young people disappeared from the villages," she said. "Now the younger generation is staying home because they can see that the family is getting wealthier each year."

One of the things that helped make that possible was the establishment of the wine road or *bor út*, the first in Eastern Europe. It began in 1994 as a partnership between government and private business. Within two years, it had forty members. A decade later, it had 120, including wineries, restaurants, B&Bs and the charming local horse-drawn taxi service. "The wine road is quite a complex project. It's not just tourism, it is also a community rehabilitation project," Becker said.

After privatization, she explained, "We had the knowledge and the huge, big history of wine, but we didn't have anybody who could make the wine." Some of the old families still remembered how, though, and the quality of the wines they made for their own families was very good. So they started making wine commercially, although their vineyards were quite small – most of them only 3 to 4 hectares in size. Soon the women started thinking about "how they could provide a bed and breakfast while the men produced the wine."

In 1995, the wine road organizers won a grant from the EU. It wasn't a lot of money, Becker said, just enough to help get things off the ground. "We were able to help a lot of families establish the first wine businesses," she said. "They just had to change the wine cellars to be open for the tourist business. At the same time, we made a lot of training for them."

So successful was the project that Hungary now has six wine roads. The Villány-Siklós route was based on models from Germany, Austria, and France, especially the one in Alsace. Visitors can go online (www.wineroute.hu or www.borut.hu) or visit the wine route office in Villány to organize a trip that can include wine tastings, cellar tours, a spa visit, trips to the sculpture gardens or the Siklós castle, and a stay in a local bed and breakfast.

"Not everyone is coming here for the top-quality wine. They are coming here for the special atmosphere of a wine-growing region," Becker said. "It's still the beginning, and we don't know what is at the end. The winemakers are getting better and better every year. Now everyone is concentrating on the quality."

We left Palkonya in search of lunch and decided to follow up on Becker's recommendation of a *csarda* called Fölelumet – The Nightingale – on the road back to Villány. By then the weather, which had started out so lovely earlier in the week, had turned nasty. The temperature had dropped to 10° C and it was pouring with freezing rain. It was the perfect weather to be inside with a hot bowl of *gulyás* and a *mezzo* of local Kékoporto, or rather, to give it its new name, Portuguiser.

For the rest of the week, we visited winemaker after winemaker, tasting their luscious wines, wines that were as József Bock put it, "*lágy, bársonyos, robusztus*" – soft, velvety, and robust.

We drank with the winemakers Bock, Zsolt Tiffán, Alajos Wunderlich, Attila Gere and the Fontanyi family in Siklós. We wandered through old cellars with black mold covering the walls like soft velvet, and we checked out huge, new cellars filled with enormous stainless steel tanks. We listened to our hosts talk about the way technology is improving their lives and their wines. "In the last little while, we've learned a lot about creating wine," said Valer Bock, whose father

József is the man behind the remarkable Bock Cuvée. "Thank God, we are fortunate in the last ten years that the machinery has come together, the very best equipment and technology. In the last ten years we've really learned wine-making techniques."

We also listened to these winemakers talk about the old traditions, the old stories that are so important. Zsolt Tiffán told us about how a Roman headstone was discovered in one of their fields in the Kopar district. It was the headstone of a young woman buried there in 260 AD. Carissimae, the headstone read: "Beloved." Twenty years later, Carissimae became the name of Tiffán's premium cuvée of Cabernet Sauvignon, Cabernet Franc, and Merlot. "Carissimae has a big potential," Tiffán said.

The winemakers spoke with pleasure about how Hungarians are finally starting to drink their own wine again. "People didn't drink Hungarian wine because it was so awful – they either drank French wines or whiskey," said Valer Bock. "They've learned to taste wines again, it's part of gastronomy and it's fashionable."

It's becoming increasingly trendy for young people to drink wine – good wine, said Yvette Fontanyi, daughter of Ottó Fontanyi. "Ten years ago there wasn't such a thing because they drank beer. Now lots of university students come here to drink the wine, not to get drunk but to enjoy the wine culture."

We listened to their stories about how they became winemakers. For instance, Attila Gere grew up in Villány, born to a family that had been making wine for years, but left as a young man. He returned and became a winemaker in 1991: "I tasted our wine, enjoyed it and fell into winemaking." He formed a partnership with Austrian winemaker Franz Weninger and opened the first panzio in the area. No so long ago, his Kopar cuvée beat out a Château Petrus, the world's most expensive wine, in a blind tasting.

Alajos Wunderlich was a tinsmith who built the display for Hungarian wine at the 1993 World Expo of Horticulture in Stuttgart. He was so impressed by the wines showcased there, especially those by the Villányi winemakers Attila Gere and Zsoltán Polgár, that he came home and bought himself a small patch of vines. His very first vintage swept the national wine awards.

Zsolt Tiffán's father was a winemaker, but Zsolt left home to become a gym teacher. After privatization he returned, and is now the winery's cellar master.

The brothers József and Ottó Fontanyi say they were "born in the vineyard." So was József Bock, who was one of the first "star" winemakers in the region and has never stopped working to improve his wines – or the lovely panzio where guests can stay and dine in delight.

The winemakers described how they bought their properties, piece by piece, a hectare here, half a hectare there, until they had enough land to start making some money. "It's not just me, but everyone in this neighborhood bought their properties like this. Step by step, each year it became better and better," said Gere, adding that it took an enormous amount of work to get rid of the bad varietals and to fix the soil after forty-five years of communist winemaking. "Even if we don't add any more land, we have thirty-six workers and we have plenty of work for them to do."

After hearing the winemakers' stories, my mother and I tasted their wines, their delicious wines, big and flavorful and rich with fruit and spice. We tasted Pinot Noirs that were sublime and cuvées that were heavenly. We tasted the lightly floral Kékfrankos and Portuguiser, and the darkly floral Cabernet Franc that seems to grow better here than almost anywhere in the world. We sipped and we slurped in cellars and tasting rooms and dining halls and bars all over Villány.

By the end of the week, we felt as if we'd not only been sampling the local winemakers' best vintages, but as if we'd made an entire village full of friends as well. The community of winemakers here is a tightly knit one, and yet one that is generous and welcoming. If it doesn't sound to strange to say it, we felt cherished by all the lovely people we met.

OK. And perhaps just a little bit tipsy, too.

On our last afternoon, our landlord, Gyuci Feyérdi, came home early and took us out to his own cellar. Like most people in the area, he makes his own wine – not enough, perhaps, to make a living from it, but enough for his family and friends and a few favored customers. His cellar was up on a hill on the outskirts of town, one of a number of little white sheds just like the ones in those three perfect rows in

Palkonya and all along the main street of Villány, though not quite as neatly arranged. We parked precariously on a concrete pad outside his *pince*, the car's front wheels almost tipping over the steep edge, and Gyuci unlocked a padlock on the door. Inside, the cellar was small and dark and dusty. At our feet yawned a square gap, stairs leading down into the darkness from which emanated a rich fruity, yeasty, alcoholic aroma. Gyuci flicked a switch and a row of lights flickered dimly on. We walked carefully downstairs on stone steps that had been worn smooth over the years. We found, to our surprise, that though the building upstairs was tiny, the cellar reached back a long, long way, crammed with oak barrels and with brick arches and walls covered in thick black mold. It was cold down there – a constant 12°C, which is great for the wine, but a bit chilly for visitors in summer-weight clothes.

Gyuci told us he didn't have a lot of land, just a couple of hectares, but he had just bought another small patch and was hoping to buy more. Mostly he was growing the local varietals, the Portuguiser and Kékfrankos. He offered us a taste, and we happily accepted. He grabbed a couple of glasses, then popped the bung on one of the barrels. Using a glass pipette, he drew out a sampling of the Kékoporto and splashed it into our glasses. There was no spit bucket, so we drank up.

While the wine didn't have the finesse and subtlety of those we'd been drinking all week, it was perfectly pleasant, light and fruity with a faintly floral characteristic, just like a good Portuguiser should be. It was a wine that would be great with food and also a nice sipping wine for an afternoon on the patio. What a great life, I thought, a small patch of wines, a small cellar, enough wine to keep me and my friends amused . . .

Afterward, Gyuci drove us to the wine bar on the main street where I was scheduled to meet Csaba Malatinszky, possibly the most remarkable winemaker in the region. Malatinszky Kúria is among the best-planned, most professional of the local wineries, and its wines among the most promising in the region. It's all because of its owner-winemaker, the charming, driven, and wine-obsessed Csaba Malatinszky.

Mom, Gyuci, and I were sitting on the wooden benches of the wine bar, sipping some wine from Polgár, when suddenly the door blew open on a gust of stormy air and in walked a man who bore no resemblance to the stocky, weatherbeaten winemakers we'd been drinking with all week. Malatinszky was youngish and tall, with a faint resemblance to Richard Gere. He dressed in designer sweater and jeans, drove a Lexus, and was self-effacing and a little bit shy – until it came to his wines, when his passion blazed forth.

While Mom stayed at the bar and had another round with her new friend Gyuci, Malatinszky drove me up to his winery, a big modern complex at the top of town. He told me that he was the first professional sommelier in modern Hungary, at the famous Gundel Restaurant, and the first to open a private wine store, La Boutique de Vin in Budapest. As long as he could remember, he had felt a passion for wine and a conviction that good wine could be produced in Hungary, especially in Villány. In 1991 and 1992, he studied in the Médoc and got his sommelier's certificate.

"I tasted a lot of very nice wine in Médoc," Malatinszky said with a charming smile. "In Hungary, there wasn't any good red wine at that time. I had the idea that what I saw in Médoc I'd put into production in a co-operative."

He found four partners and they made wine together for four years, until he decided that they had gone as far as they possibly could with the technology they had. In 1996, Malatinszky struck out on his own, even though he didn't have much money. His cellar, built in 1997, was the first truly modern cellar in Villány. From his first vintage, the 1999, his wines have gathered respect and a loyal following. They also command high prices for Hungarian wines, and are worth every forint.

His best wines are his sophisticated Cabernet Francs and his buttery-smooth oak-fermented and aged Chardonnay. (He told me he selects the oak for his barrels himself, a mix of Hungarian and French oak that he then ages for three years.)

We tried the 2002 Noblesse Chardonnay, which had a beautiful balance, with notes of vanilla and green apple; we followed it with the 2003, which was a very hot summer in Villány and produced a bigger wine, round and buttery with strong vanilla flavors. "The Chardonnay is one of the most successful wines at the winery," he told me. "It's no problem to sell it. No marketing, no advertising."

Next we tried his Cabernoir 2002, a softly ripe blend of Cabernet Sauvignon, Cabernet Franc, and Pinot Noir, what Malatinszky called "a wine for gastronomy." Cabernet Franc is a grape with a lot of potential in Villány, he explained, since the climate and growing conditions are ideal for this finicky grape. Certainly, the spectacular 2003 Kúria Cabernet Franc (his "Kúria" label is his highest category of wines) seemed to bear this out. The wine had been getting raves from clients and, Malatinszky said, was used by none other than wineglass master Georg Riedel to demonstrate his Bordeaux glass. Suddenly he laughed. "We put this wine one year ago into a blind tasting in the Médoc. All of them thought it was a St. Emilion vin de garage."

Alex Liddell, in his book, *The Wines of Hungary*, described the young winemaker as "very much the cat who walks alone," and it's true that Malatinszky believes strongly that the greatness of wine rests in the power of the individual. "My life is going always around the wine," he said. "I think always about the wine, how to do it, what to change. The big challenge is that I have my own imagination and my own style in wine." It isn't easy, he said, to preserve his own high standards and yet create wines that will sell.

Malatinszky exports some of his wine to the United States, to the Canary Islands, Australia, and Britain, and is looking for new markets, as long as they're the right markets. Like all the other winemakers I spoke to, Malatinszky believed that if people could just taste the wines from Villány, they'd be convinced that here was something special, something that was worth their money. The problem is getting them to try it when so little of it is available overseas and when so few people have the opportunity to travel to Hungary and taste it there.

Even when I returned home a few weeks later and described the wonderful Villányi wines to the wine importers, marketers, and writers I know, most of them just rolled their eyes and refused to believe that there could be such a thing as good wine coming from the land of "Sex on Saturday." They're flat wrong, but how could I prove it?

The challenge now for these hardworking winemakers isn't creating great wines — that's already happening — but learning how to market them in a world flooded with wine that's cheaper, more familiar, and easier to pronounce. Salesmanship and marketing, unfortunately, aren't high on the list of the average Hungarian's skills, so they're going to need an awful lot of hard work and luck to make it happen.

As for me, after a week in this part of the world, while I'll never say no to "something red, in a glass," I'd prefer something red made by Bock or Gere or Tiffán or Vylyan or Malatinszky. Now, if only someone would start bringing the delicious reds of Villány into Canada, it would make my life so much easier.

On the other hand, I have an excuse to go back to Villány again, and again, and again . . .

CHAPTER 15

The Wine of Kings

A little while later, my mother and I were driving towards a completely different sort of Hungarian wine experience. If Villány is Hungary's unknown gem, then Tokaj is the equivalent of the Hope Diamond. The Tokaj-Hegyalja region, to give it its proper name, is in the country's northeast, close to the border with Slovakia. In fact, after Trianon, part of the Tokaj region ended up on the wrong side of the border, though the Slovaks have yet to create a wine that can compete with the more famous product a few kilometers away.

To get there, we had to drive through a big chunk of the Hortobagy along a wide, straight modern highway. Big trucks whooshed by us on their way to Eger and Debrecen and on to Slovakia, Ukraine, and Romania. The sky hunkered pitilessly above us, hot and dull, while the plain stretched flat and endless on either side, broken occasionally by a stand of trees.

The Hortobagy is where the cowboys once roamed and where the big farming operations are today. It is not a wealthy part of the country, nor is it a part of Hungary I knew at all. Mom, on the other hand, had known it very well at one point. It was not far from here that she'd been *kimenekült* in the early 1950s. Now, *kimenekült* is a word I haven't been able to translate, exactly. Mom insists it was not an internment camp, more like a sort of involuntary exile where you're restricted to a certain area; in her case, it was a village called Tiszabö. She remembers those days with fondness, though, because of the gentle, slow-moving Tisza River, where the young people sailed and swam and her family dreamed about a better future. "I would have died without the river," she said.

I guess I shouldn't have been surprised to learn that even though she'd been living just downriver, Mom had never been to Tokaj. She and her family may not have been "interned," but they clearly weren't allowed to get very far in those days. So this would be a new adventure for the both of us.

By the time we turned off the M3 and onto the country road to Tokaj, it was a little after noon, just enough time to find our panzio, drop off the luggage, and get to our first winery. We were staying at a casual little inn on Tokaj's main street, a couple of blocks down from the pedestrian zone where all the shops and restaurants were. It was not luxurious, but it was bright and clean and had a TV, a kitchen, and a sunny patio where a bunch of kids – Slovakian university students, I think – were hanging out when we arrived. It was surrounded by an explosion of flowers: giant pink roses climbing all over the patio roof, a wall of purple clematis, as well as rows and rows of fruit trees, and herbs, flowers and shrubs everywhere. The owners lived in a house next door and seemed to spend each day puttering around the garden, creating their own little Eden on the Tisza.

The Tisza flows right through Hungary, entering it from the Ukraine at Zólnay and leaving it at Szeged to join the Danube around Belgrade. It is one of the two rivers that flows through Tokaj, the other being the Bodrog. The rivers, along with the south-facing slopes of the foothills of the Zemplén mountains (*hegyalja* is the Hungarian word for "foothills," hence the name of the region) create a unique climate that turns out to be ideal for a tasty little fungus called botrytis cinerea.

Botrytis is the essential ingredient in creating the famous Tokaji Aszú, a dessert wine justly prized by connoisseurs the world over. Even when the rest of the country's wine was reduced to the bottom of the international barrel, Tokaji Aszú maintained its mystique (and its exorbitant price) though perhaps neither its quality nor its popularity.

I have to admit that when we met Laszlo Mészáros, the executive director of the Disznökö winery, later that afternoon, I really didn't know very much about Tokaj or its wines. I mean, I knew that the famous local wine was the aszú and that it had been around forever; that it was made with botrytized grapes, and that it was known as "the wine of kings, the king of wines." This nickname was reportedly bestowed by none other than Louis XIV of France. (I discovered later that other monarchs with a taste for Tokaji Aszú included, according to Alex Liddell's book, *The Wines of Hungary*, Peter the Great, Frederick the Great, Maria-Theresa of Austria, Catherine the Great, Emperor Franz Joseph, and Queen Victoria.) So I knew a couple of basic facts. But the story of Tokaj turned out to be one of the most interesting in all the winemaking world.

"Tokaj is the first appellation, the first delineated wine region in the world," Mészáros told us as we walked around the hilly estate dominated by the big rock for which it is named – the rock or *kö* is said to resemble a large boar or *disznö*. So, Disznökö. "It was probably the most prestigious wine in Europe in the seventeenth, eighteenth, and nineteenth centuries."

There are only certain types of wine that can be produced in the region and can call themselves "Tokaji," all of them white wines. Four styles of wine are produced here: dry whites; Szamorodni, which can be either dry or sweet, but is always made with botrytized grape clusters; a sweet late-harvest wine; and the famous aszú, which is made from dried and botrytized grapes. It's not just the types of wine that are restricted; so are the types of grapes, which must be indigenous to the area. About 60 per cent of the grapes grown here are Furmint and about 30 per cent are Harslevelú ("Linden Tree"). The rest are Yellow Muscat, Zeta, and Köverszölö ("Fat Grape").

"We are not allowed to plant any except these varieties," Mészáros explained. "If someone has Chardonnay, he cannot call it Tokaj and he cannot call it by the names of any of the villages."

But that's not what makes this area so interesting. What makes it so fascinating is its history, and also the story of how the industry is changing with changing times.

According to legend, Tokaji Aszú was discovered in 1630 or perhaps 1633 by a priest named Laczkó Máté Szepsi, who was not only a winemaker but the personal cleric to Zsuzsanna Lorántffy, wife of the Prince of Transylvania, György Rákóczi. (The Rákóczis owned what is now the Disznökö estate well into the nineteenth century.) Worried by rumors of an imminent Turkish attack – or, according to some versions of the story, waiting for those pesky Turks to leave – he kept postponing and postponing the harvest until the berries were shriveled and dried and possibly affected by the botrytis fungus. He made the wine anyway – and the princess loved it so much, they made it every year after that.

"He was a little bit like Dom Perignon for champagne," Mészáros said.

However, the truth seems to be that while Szepsi may have been the first to record the process, wine from desiccated grapes had already been made in the region for some time. No one, however, is entirely sure when winemakers began using the botrytized grapes.

Certainly, making aszú is a unique process in winemaking anywhere. It is similar to sauternes, another botrytis-affected wine, but sauternes is made from grapes better described as "over-ripe," not dried as with the aszú.

Any of the indigenous varietals can be used for the aszú. The grapes are left on the vine as late as possible, well into November, until they've become raisinlike and a few have been infected by the silvery botrytis fungus, which is helped along by the morning mist that rises from the rivers.

"The aszú grapes are handpicked one by one," Mészáros said. One picker can only pick six to ten kilograms a day. "It's a very labor-intensive process. Then, because they are so dried it is not possible to press them. It's skin-to-skin maceration." This means that, because the grapes are so delicate, the pressure of grape against grape is enough to release the juices. "During the skin contact, the aromas and flavors are extracted for the aszú wines into the base must wines."

He explained the process further: Once the aromas and flavors are extracted from the aszú berries, they add it to a base wine and ferment the two together. They always use a set measure of the base wine, a *gönci* barrel, which is 136 liters. The amount of aszú berries varies, however. The aszú are measured in *puttony*, or buckets, each about 25 kilograms.

"The more we use of the aszú grapes, the sweeter the wine," Mészáros said.

A 3 *puttonyos* aszú is semisweet; a 4 is sweeter, 5 even more so, and a 6 *puttonyos* is the sweetest, considered by connoisseurs to be the best. According to legend, in the old days, winemakers would go up to 12 *puttonyos* aszú, but now 6 buckets is the most you'll find. Beyond that is *essencia*, the heady nectar of Tokaj, which is very rare. That sweetness is what makes the Tokaj wines so valued. But it's not a sticky, jammy sweetness with no depth like many icewines and other high-sugar wines. It's spicy, with caramel notes and aromas of tropical fruits and golden sunshine.

"Tokaji is never cloying," Mészáros said, lining up some of Disznökö's delicious wines for Mom and me to taste. "It's well balanced. We have a nice acidity."

However and by whomever the process was discovered, Tokaji Aszú became famous the world over. It was rumored to revive corpses and to age beautifully for centuries. It was a wine associated purely with royalty, aristocracy, and the very wealthy, and not just because its prices were out of reach for the average consumer. The estates where it was made belonged to the most famous nobles in the land, and they managed to get duty and tax concessions unavailable to other wines.

Tokaji survived the Turks and the Austrians, the tax traumas of the 1840s, and the phylloxera outbreak of the 1890s, the First World War, and the devastating peace that followed it. It even survived the communist era, but barely, and badly damaged.

"By the 1990s, there was only one brand in the region and that was the state winery (the Bórkabinet), which had the monopoly on the bottling and marketing. At the same time, there were some very small family vineyards also," Mészáros said. "After the privatization, the first idea was to sell the Bórkabinet to another owner. But fortunately it was canceled, that project. A new idea was to recreate the former historical estates."

And that's what they did. They basically redrew the historic estates and opened them up to foreign and Hungarian investment.

"Since the beginning of the Nineties, Tokaj has become one of the most dynamic wine regions in the world," Mészáros said proudly.

On the one hand, this has preserved an area and a history that is so cherished it has been named a World Heritage Site. On the other, it has offended many of the local people, who are too poor and powerless to bid for land in their own backyard.

Unlike Villány, there are few family winemakers in the region, and their wineries tend to be very small. Perhaps that's why so much of the aszú-making prowess has been lost over the decades – even though the region is so heavily focused on tradition, there is probably more experimentation, guesswork, and seat-of-the-pants winemaking here than anywhere else in Hungary.

One of the few family-owned-and-operated wineries in the region belongs to Zsuzsa Bene, and that's where we were off to the next morning. Bene is a small winery, only about five hectares of vines, in the nearby village of Bodrogkeresztúr. It was a gorgeous day, hot and lazy even before the sun came out in full. Butterflies fluttered and fat bees bumbled happily in the brambles beside the car as we navigated the narrow, single-lane road that led to the winery. It was an excellent day for tasting wine.

Unfortunately, Zsuzsa had been called away to a funeral, so we talked to her business partner and winemaker, Zsolt Tátrai, a young man so full of passion for his wine, he was almost shaking as he talked about it. It's people like this that make wine so much fun – the people who love the soil, the grapes, the tradition so much you'd swear wine ran in their veins instead of blood.

There had been a wine cellar in this location for hundreds of years, Tátrai told us, but after the Second World War and nationalization, the site was used instead for a forestry hut. Then in 1998, after the privatization, Zsuzsa's father Miklos bought the property and started making wine. Tátrai joined Bene right at the beginning. "This entire project grew up with me out of the soil," he said.

Zsuzsa, too, was involved from the beginning. She went to university and got a doctoral degree in oenology, specializing in aszú. They planted more grapes, added to the facility and looked forward to expanding, to maybe 20 hectares one day. (In contrast, Disznökö is 200 hectares.)

In 2000, Zsuzsa's father died and she took over the business. She and Tátrai have continued to expand, to improve the facilities, and to add on to their property, but they still insist on doing things the traditional way. "Miklos Bene believed very much in the traditional methods, and he passed them on to his children," Tátrai said. "It's only in our name that we have money."

During the nationalization of Tokaj, many of those traditional methods were lost, and today some of the winemakers are simply guessing at how to make the aszú. For instance, he said, some of the bigger cellars, which are pressured to make money for their investors, are using newfangled "reductive" technology. "Then it doesn't have this beautiful bronze-gold color," he said, holding up a bottle of aszú to the light.

He took us into the cellar, which was built in 1830. It is made of the local white stone with black mold creeping up the walls. "This is the traditional type of Tokaj wine cellar, 3 meters wide with these old barrels along the side," he said. In the mornings, when the mist creeps up from the valley, the old cellars can look spooky and ghostly; perhaps it's worth remembering that the haunted hills of Transylvania are not that far away.

After our tour, Tátrai opened up several bottles of Bene wines for us to try, including a dry Szamorodni with a lovely aroma of green walnuts. "If a person drinks a deci of this before dinner, it only increases the appetite," he said, adding, "It's very difficult to match the Tokaji wines to the gastronomy because they are so full-bodied and sweet. They are better as dessert wines."

Although the winery is young and small, already its wines – especially its five puttonyos aszú – are winning international awards. "It's not enough, but we are on a good road. We're getting back to where we were," Tátrai said. "These are wines that are just like life, sweet on this hand, bitter on that, sour on the other. It's a living thing, wine."

After Bene, we drove to Tarcal to another family operation, albeit a bigger, richer, and more aristocratic one. The Countess Maria Degenfeld-Schönburg has returned to the region with her husband, German businessman Dr. Thomas Lindner, to recreate something of her family's history. They've opened an elegant castle hotel, gourmet restaurants both in the town of Tokaj and at the castle itself, and the winery, where celebrated local winemaker Zsoltán Demeter is creating wines that are really starting to get noticed.

The Degenfeld history in the region goes back to the thirteenth century. The countess's ancestor, Imre Degenfeld, was one of the founders of the Tokaj Wine Association back in 1857, but until 1964, her family lived in Transylvania. They escaped the Ceausescu regime in 1964, and have been living in Germany ever since. Now, like many other Hungarian expats, she's trying to rebuild something marvelous in her home country, using the family motto "Noble house, noble wine" as her guide.

"This is the renaissance of the Degenfeld family in Tokaj," marketing director Hedwig Petrocki told us during a tour of the winery. "The family tends to have first quality. Whatever they do, the wine or the gastronomy or the accommodation, it's only the best."

This was not the original Degenfeld estate, Petrocki explained. In the nineteenth century, it was a school for oenologists, with a cellar for the students to practise making wine. In 1994, when the countess started building the castle hotel and the winery, she decided to build on to the hundred-year-old cellar instead of building a new one. The builders were instructed to use local wood and stone and amend their construction plans to preserve the trees on the property.

"They wanted to have the feeling that this winery has been here for ages, not just ten years," Petrocki said. "We had the old cellar and the old technology, but the new age requires new technology."

Now their big effort is to get the word out about their wines – and to attract more investors.

"We're looking to develop export," Petrocki told us earnestly. "This decade changed a lot in Tokaj-Hegyalja. It wouldn't be possible without the investors. This wine region wouldn't be able to do it with just Hungarian money. We are faced with the problem every day with the marketing. Some sommeliers and experts know, but most people don't know that the quality is here. It's a mission. It's a real mission. We have to tell people what is here."

Leaving the Old World grace of the Degenfeld Castle, the next morning we plunged into the modern world, with all its big business tactics. We drove to Eger to visit Egervin and see what a truly big operation winery is like in Hungary. Back in the days of communism, this was the state winery for Eger, an area of sixteen wine-producing villages whose climate and terroir are similar to that of Burgundy. It holds huge promise for red wines, which is why both Tibor Gál and the folks at the Monarchia wine import-export company have established their own wineries here. Charming and lovely as those other wineries Mom and I visited had been, this was where the serious money was being made in the Hungarian wine industry.

It took us a while to find Egervin, though. No one in the magnificent baroque center of the historic city of Eger seemed to have a clue what we were talking about, let alone where the winery might actually be. It took the entire staff of young women at the Tour Inform office to get us on the right road. And when we finally found the place, we could see why it's not high on the list of tourist destinations.

Egervin is a huge industrial plant on the outskirts of town, with much of the lingering charm of the Soviet era. It is surrounded by barbed wire fencing, a guard in a booth, and two enormous metal tanks standing sentry in front. They are several stories high, one painted bright blue, the other vivid orange, the colors of chemicals of the more toxic sort.

Surely those aren't filled with wine, I thought. Surely not.

We were met by Ildikó Sófalvi, Egervin's export sales executive, who whisked us through the parts of the property that weren't undergoing renovation and repair. Egervin was established in 1949 as the state winery, she told us. In 1993, after privatization, it was bought by a Hungarian investor group and is still 100 per cent Hungarian owned. It is the second-biggest wine producer in Hungary, after Hungarovin, producing 8.5 million bottles a year, of which 40 per cent is exported. They sell to every country in the EU except France, as well as the United States.

Of course, the story goes back much further than that, to the days of the Turks. Beneath the city of Eger is a three-level, 130-kilometer cellar system that dates back to the fifteenth and sixteenth centuries. In those days, its citizens used the cellars as escape routes from the attacking Turks. This was always a big wine-growing region, though, and in the seventeenth century someone had the bright idea of using the cellars to store wine. Today, Egervin owns about 5 kilometers of that cellar system for storing its wines. In those cellars, they have 400,000 museum wines dating back to the 1960s as well as 800 big oak barrels — some of them more than a hundred years old and monstrously huge — for maturing old wines.

Eger produces both red and white wines, but it is best known for its reds and especially its most famous and popular wine Bikavér, or Bull's Blood. Historically, it was the wine that energized the Hungarians when they fought the Turks during the siege of Eger Castle in 1552. Today, Bikavér gives strength to the whole Hungarian wine industry: the spicy cuvée is probably the country's most lucrative and popular wine export.

Bikavér is a blend of a minimum of three and a maximum of eight different grapes, always including Kadarka and often including Cabernet Sauvignon, Kékfrankos, Merlot, Zweigelt and/or Portuguiser. Unfortunately, even though Bikavér originated in Eger, it is produced in other regions and has over the years lost its uniqueness and much of its quality. Winemakers are attempting to change that, but the process has been a slow one, and there's no telling if Egri Bikavér will ever again be the kind of wine to convince men to kill for it.

As we left, I just had to ask, though I wasn't sure I wanted to know the answer.

"Those two big tanks out front, um, what's in them?" I asked. Wine, of course, was the answer.

Of course.

After our trip to Eger, my mother and I – and our palates – were exhausted. So we decided to take a day and revisit places from my past before heading back to Budapest. We drove over to Sárospatak and checked out the school where Fran and I had gone all those years ago. Mom, of course, had never been there, and was curious to see what it was like.

Funny, I remembered it as so big and yet it seemed so small. I remembered certain details, but not the whole. And I remembered the courtyard as something completely different from what it really was. I walked around fascinated, surprised at how emotional I felt. It was, after all, only a few weeks out of my life, a long time ago. But I could still remember the way the light fell, the way the air smelt, the familiar voices rising and falling, the friends that we made. Where are they now, I wondered; Tom and Tom and Judi and Vali?

And funny, I could remember, too, this one day, when we were coming back from somewhere in an old school bus with the windows open. A late afternoon sun slanted its golden rays across the fields, heavy with barley and wheat. Poppies bobbed between the stalks of grain. Rows of poplar trees rustled as we passed, a warmly spicy scent on the breeze. Then suddenly I was stricken with a wave of emotion, a strange blend of joy and grief. This is where I belong, I thought, and immediately rejected the notion: nah, don't be stupid, I love the mountains and the ocean and the great, big Canadian cities, not this strange foreign place. But still, in years to come, there would be times when I'd sense that light, that air, that aroma, and the feeling would come rushing back – just as it did when Mom an I walked around the old school courtyard that day in June.

Afterwards, we tried to find the old Borostyán restaurant, the place where we stole the flag that got us into so much trouble. "Oh, it's been gone a very long time," we were told again and again. Finally, I decided that it must have crumbled along with the communist regime. But then on the drive out of town, there it was – the same old place, renamed and reborn as the Bodrog. It made me smile to think of it, and I couldn't help but wonder how many other generations of students had walked through its doors and played stupid pranks over the years, and if any of them actually had been sent to Siberia.

That night, we sat and drank Egri Bikavér as we sat on a long, shady patio by the banks of the slow-moving Tisza River. During our time in Tokaj, we'd had some beautiful gourmet meals at the excellent Degenfeld restaurants, but for our last night we decided to go casual and relaxed at a riverside *halaszcsarda*, where we could drink as much cheap wine as we wished and then stumble back to our panzio.

As we sat and sipped the wine, we watched the light fall greenly golden on the water, where river fish leaped up to snap at the clouds of insects hovering over the faint ripples. Boats chugged back and forth, young men waving and shouting to their friends on shore as they passed by. Pelicans swooped down for a bite of dinner, and not far away from us, a fisherman cast his line rhythmically into the water.

Mom sighed a little as she watched the scene.

"That was fun," she said. "All the wine, all those nice people."

"Yes, it was, wasn't it?"

The waiter came by just then and asked us what we wanted.

"Well, I don't know," I said. "What would you suggest? The *halászlé* to start of course, but after that, what should we have?"

"You must have the *süllö*," he said, "fried whole, with parsley potatoes. It's from the river right here."

"I don't know. . ."

"No, you must try it," he said.

OK. We knew when we were beat, so we agreed and we were so glad that we did. The *süllö* is a pike-perch, tender and sweet and flavorful. It is lightly dusted in flour and paprika, then dropped whole into the deep-fryer. It comes out all crisp and golden and curled up like a big smile. We each got one, and it arrived with a mountain of the parsleyed potatoes, the parsley so intense it must have been snipped from the garden mere minutes before landing on our plates. It was simple and simply delicious.

We stayed there talking late into the evening, ordering rounds of artisanal palinka and sharing old family stories, all of which I promptly forgot the next morning. As we gathered up our things to go that night, Mom took one last look at the river and sighed again.

"I should hate this place," she said, "but I don't. I worked so hard on the Tisza. It was such a terrible time, but I love that river."

CHAPTER 16
About That Dead Russian...

There was one last thing Mom and I had to do before leaving Hungary. Well, aside from having one more drink at the Gresham, and picking up bags of paprika for everyone back home, and saying goodbye to the family, and finally getting a chance to experience the supercool wave pool at the Gellért Hotel.

We had to see the house in Balatonalmádi one last time. It was the place my family had come for relaxation and for refuge, the place that was built to withstand war and poverty and family disgrace. It was where a damaged man had once sat by the window for hours, watching the play of light on the water. It was where a disappointed woman had found solace in the kitchen, putting her frustrated energies into her baking and cooking. It was where a young girl had dreamed of a bigger world, a world that was ripe with opportunity and hope. And, years later, it was where two young children met their cousins from a faraway place and got their first taste of the exotic country their parents called home.

Even now, the house at 19 Neptun Utca is what our family thinks of when we consider what home means – a big ochre box by the lake, with stone steps, a red-tiled roof, pots of flowers on the verandah, and trees – willows and poplars – all around it. In all the years of upheaval, all the dislocations, the countries and camps, the apartments and houses, in all the places our far-flung family has lived, this is the closest we've ever been to truly being *home*.

And this was a home we knew we'd never live in again. Even though Luizi had promised to look into the appropriation of the house and what seemed to us its illegal sale, we knew that it was a hopeless quest. At best, we might get a bit more compensation from the government, but even if by some miracle they decided to return our property to us, we would never be able to afford the massive renovations it would need. If I had nurtured any dreams of an *Under the Tuscan Sun*-like renovation – and OK, I admit it, I did, briefly – they were not to be fulfilled.

My uncle Frank drove us – Luizi, Frances, Mom, and I – to Balatonalmádi in his brand-new Mercedes-Benz, a car he'd shipped from Canada at enormous expense and even greater bureaucratic hassle, only to discover that it was too big for Budapest's narrow streets and tiny parking spots. "Bet you wish you'd waited and bought a Trabant over here, huh?" I said. "Yes, yes, I do," he said, his jaw clenched and a vein throbbing on his forehead as he edged nervily through the Buda hills.

On that last Sunday, a day that couldn't decide whether to be hot or cold, sunny or cloudy, we knew in our hearts that we were on our way to say goodbye. Goodbye to the house, to the past and, for now at least, to each other. The car was crowded with memories, with the thought of all the things we'd forgotten to say and do, farewells lingering unspoken in the air.

As we turned off the main highway onto Lake Balaton's northern shore, we passed rose bushes pregnant with blossom and massive shrubs bursting with lavender.

"It's like Provence," I said, breathing deeply. "Do you guys remember there being so much lavender when you lived here before?"

No, they said, they didn't remember any lavender at all, no lavender or rosemary or any of the other herbs and flowers that were making the air smell so sweet. But then, they reminded me, these gardens had been bombed and trampled and abandoned, churned up by soldiers and refugees and neglected through all the sad years that followed. If anyone was growing anything back then, they were growing carrots and cabbages and potatoes to eat, not flowers to look at. Now, though, every bit of soil seemed to be in flower, with birds and butterflies and honeybees buzzing around the vivid blossoms.

It seemed to take no time at all to reach Balatonalmádi. Once there, we took the turn to the lake, then onto Neptun Utca, past the row of lakeside villas hidden behind towering trees and tall fences with locked gates and security systems. We tried to peer through the fences, but we couldn't tell if the houses were new or old; all we could see was that each one had a big motorboat in the driveway, and that the people who owned them must have had plenty of money.

The last house before the playground was ours. It, too, had a big fence around it, but no big boat or elaborate security system. Only a few trees like the neighbors' had been left standing; where the others had been were only stumps that had nearly been swallowed up by the grassy lawn. The fence enclosed not just the house, but the playground to its left where a jaunty sign saying "Neptun Strand" stood over a cash booth with posted rates.

It all looked much as I remembered it from the previous fall: the "for sale" sign, the rusting fence, the broken windows, the missing roof tiles, and the patchy walls. This time, though, the park was open. It was early in the season, but the pier was bustling, with people milling about the fast food stands and the boat launch. Children were playing on the swings and slides, and teenagers in bathing suits were lying optimistically in the weak sunlight that played across the lawn.

We stood around on the street and gazed through the fence for a few minutes, then without saying a word, Mom and I walked away from the others. This we had to do together, just the two of us. We walked up to the cash booth and waited for a young brunette in a bikini top to rise from her lounger and help us.

"Jó napot kivánok," Mom said politely. "Good day. Can we just go in for a moment and see the house?"

"What house?" the attendant said, puzzled.

We were momentarily stunned. Had she not noticed the huge, gloomy building that took up half the property? Was that even possible? Or had it somehow become invisible, like an old lady in a crowd of young hipsters, an embarrassing reminder of the past, a depressing sign of the future?

"That one, that ruin over there," Mom said, pointing, and the woman's face brightened for a moment. "Oh! Of course, go right ahead, just don't let a rock fall on your head," she said, and went back to suntanning.

We walked across the lumpy lawn where some boys were playing with a soccer ball. The teenagers barely glanced at us, two weirdos at the beach in street clothes, as we stopped and stood silently, staring at the sad spectacle before us.

"It's worse than *Dr. Zhivago*," Mom said finally. "Doesn't it make you cry?"

I didn't have to answer, for tears were already standing in my eyes.

From the street, we'd been able to see a hole in the roof, and patches of stucco that had peeled off the walls, and shutters that hung open. As we walked closer, the devastation become more and more apparent. Not only were the shutters hanging open, but the windows were, too. Either that or the glass had been broken out of every one of them. Inside we could see heaps of refuse – old furniture, storm windows, pieces of wood, who knows what it was? Paint was peeling everywhere, and so was the stucco, which had darkened from its original cheerful gold color to a murky shade that can only be described as despondent. The stone steps to the side were crumbling dangerously.

As we walked around to the lakeside front of the house, Mom gave a strangled little cry. "Look, there is a tree growing inside!"

Indeed, there was. It was almost as if the poplar trees that had vanished from the front of the house had relocated to the back. A small copse of them had broken through the floor of the stone verandah. Through the broken panes of the old French doors, we could see several more taking shelter inside, their branches shading the place where the dining table would have been.

From this angle, we could see why the girl at the gate had warned us about falling rocks. Big signs were posted on the house, warning people to keep out. Bars and boards had been put up and a screen erected all around the lower level to prevent adventurous teens from breaking in. Someone had managed to get through one area, though, and through the gap we could see a mound of dusty stones and bricks and what looked like junk from the park. In front of the verandah, a rusted old piece of playground equipment was toppled on its side and rotting boards were piled up in a heap.

We averted our eyes – really, it was the kindest thing to do – and turned to look out at the lake. Or at least we looked out at where the lake should have been. Instead, at the end of the lawn where a stone wall marked the end of the property, a sea of bulrushes began. They towered two, three meters high and stretched as far as we could see. Someone had cut a path through the weeds and a small boat was tied up to the wall, bobbing in the greenly gleaming water. Even gazing along the path we couldn't see to the end of the bulrushes.

We walked down to the water's edge and stared into the silty, weed-choked shallows.

"We used to jump in from here. You could see forever. Now you can't see anything," Mom said. "We had stairs here so you could walk in if you didn't want to jump in."

I remembered those stairs from when we visited during our time at Sárospatak. I also remembered the willow trees whose branches had once swept the lawn all along this shore, and the flowers – pots and pots of flowers everywhere. Now, there was nothing left of its old beauty, just these ugly weeds choking everything.

"It was so beautiful. When the sailboats went by, they all looked at the house because it was so pretty with the flowers and everything," Mom said wistfully, as we started strolling back to the house. "Right here where I'm standing, there was a beautiful willow tree. And there, where the neighbor's tree was – it's gone, too – that's where we buried the Russian soldier in the wardrobe."

I stopped. "The what?"

She began doing this weird twitchy hand thing she does when she's being evasive, a habit that both Fran and I inherited and that makes us want to cut our fingers off with a dull axe.

"Oh, just some dead Russian," she said vaguely.

"Who was he?" I demanded. "When was this? How did he die?"

"Oh, he just died."

"He just died. Of what?"

"I don't know, he was just dead, and we put him in the wardrobe and we buried him, and that's it," she said firmly, and turned back to where the family was waiting.

That's when I realized that despite all I'd learned in the last year, the countless questions I'd asked, the books I'd read, the nights of talking over bottles of wine, the dozens of *gulyáses* and *pörkölts* and *Dobos tortas* I'd made, there would always be things I wouldn't know, questions that wouldn't be answered, stories that would go untold. I took a deep breath and followed her out of the park.

"Where did you go?" Frances asked us a few minutes later as we climbed back in the car. "I didn't see you leave. Where were you?"

"We went to look at the house," I told her. "It was awful."

"Of course it was awful. I don't know why you Wintermantels have to live in the past so much," she said. "You should be thinking about the future."

"I know, I know," I said, "but . . ."

"You know what I know?" my uncle broke in, his patience nearing its end. "I know that we should go for lunch."

And in true Hungarian fashion, we left behind the sad past and went in search of something savory and satisfying instead. We found a little place that served fresh fish from Lake Balaton, fried hot and crispy, and as we sipped our wine and beer in a sunny courtyard, we found we could forget about the house and remember much happier things instead.

Later that night, after we'd taken a dip in the wave pool, I asked my mother, "So, are you heartbroken about the house?" I knew I was.

"Not any more. I got used to it," she said gamely. "But when I came back the first time, I was crying. I loved that place."

I thought about that, and about all the stories she'd ever told us about our past. I thought about the way she could always turn tragedy into farce and humiliation into triumph. I thought about the way she could remember her exile as a holiday, her disgraced father as a hero, her escape as an adventure, and losing everything as a fresh start. I thought about the way she would always embroider the past into something grander, more exciting, less shameful, and how years ago we'd nicknamed her the Queen of Denial. I thought about the dead Russian, whoever he was and however he died.

I'd started this journey thinking about paprika, what it is, where it's from, how to cook with it, and who the people are who made it into their national spice. Along the way, I'd discovered a lot about Hungary, and about my family, and about me.

Like the story of Hungary, the story of paprika is a mysterious one. We know some things, can guess at others and the rest, well, we'll just have to make it up. Paprika is an ornament, a vegetable, a fruit, a spice, and an excellent source of vitamin C. It came home from the New World with Christopher Columbus, traveled in the luggage of the Turkish troops and made its way around Napoleon's blockades. It won a Nobel Prize for Hungary, kept its children healthy during the lean years and, internationally, it has flavored Hungary's reputation as a spicy, exotic place.

Like the Hungarian people themselves, paprika is spicy, sweet, and sometimes bitter. It has another characteristic, too. It's just the thing for covering up an unpleasant taste, the flavor of secrets you don't want to remember.

CHAPTER 17
The Goulash Bash

"You are invited to Joanne and Lionel's inaugural Goulash Bash! Come join the Magyar madness on Saturday, October 8, 2005, at our place...."

It was a year after our first trip to Hungary, a year of cooking with paprika, and I decided it was time to stir up some excitement. I decided it was time for a party.

I planned our first-ever Goulash Bash for Thanksgiving weekend. Once I set the date, I started getting the word out right away since I'd only have a month to get everything organized. I called my mom and my sister on the coast and invited them. I invited old friends and new ones, colleagues from work, and people I'd encountered along the year-long journey through my Hungarian heritage.

I wanted the party to honor the women in my family, the women who'd inspired me with their bravery and determination and handiness with paprika. But I also wanted to put my own personal stamp on the event. And so the planning began.

Obviously, I'd have to serve *gulyás* (for otherwise it could hardly be called a Goulash Bash) but what else? Things had to be impressive and easy and good for feeding a crowd – and not cabbage rolls, no matter how Hungarian they are, because I hate them, and I refuse to cook food I hate. I took to carrying a notebook around with me, jotting down ideas, scratching them out, starting all over again, until I finally came up with a menu.

There would be Mom's cheese straws, of course. Cheese straws are practically the symbol of our family. That coat of arms we have with the man in the red cape and the unicorn? I figure the artist should have skipped the unicorn and replaced it with a plate of cheese straws.

There would have to be other nibbly things, too, like the cream cheese spread called *körözött* and just maybe some *tepertö* (TEP-air-tuh), the deliciously fattening pork cracklings I knew I could get at the Hungarian deli. They're not to everyone's taste, but I figured there would be a couple of people who'd love them, and as it turned out, I was right. In addition, my Hungarian friend Sue offered to bring a cucumber salad, and her mother offered to send over some of her homemade *lángos*.

For the main courses, I decided to have two hot dishes and three cold platters – one of cold cuts, one of cheese, and one of the fancy roast pork stuffed with Debrecen sausage that every woman in my family always makes for parties. The roast would make a beautiful centerpiece for the table, I thought, and it always looked so impressive, whether it was Maju or Luizi or my grandmother or even me who made it.

For the other hot dishes, I decided to make Hortobagyi *palacsinta* with chicken for all my friends who won't eat beef or pork. Now that I'd figured out how to prepare it, it would be a snap. And I was determined to get some use out of the meat grinder I'd bought. I would have loved to make a *bogracs gulyás*, and for a while considered building a firepit in the back yard and getting someone to send me a cauldron from Hungary. But then I decided it would be too cold, too dark, and too difficult to pull off. I'd just have to make it the regular way. Maybe next summer I'd do a proper *bogracsa*. Maybe I could even get Tommi to come out to Canada and cook it. Or maybe not.

There would also have to be some sweets, of course, and for that there was only one choice: *Dobos torta*! I'd also serve some *beigli* and marzipan, just in case there were people who didn't like *Dobos torta*.

I printed up the invitations and glued them onto elegant mossy-green cards, and then hand-delivered them. Right away the RSVPs started coming in: Yes! Yes! Yes, we'll be there, we can hardly wait.

A couple of weeks before the party, I made the base for the *gulyás* and the crêpes – one beef *pörkölt* and one chicken *pörkölt* – and popped them in the freezer. As I chopped and stirred, the aroma of paprika circling through the air, I could sense my grandmother's spirit hovering over my shoulder. "No, not like that, *Csibike*, like this!" If anyone could feed thirty or so people without blinking an eye, it was Aranka néni, so I put myself in her ghostly hands. After that, everything went smoothly, with barely a hiccup along the way.

Closer to Thanksgiving, Lionel and I bought some gypsy music CDs, ordered the balloons, stocked up on candles, and found some funky paper napkins printed with a pattern of red peppers that looked an awful lot like paprika. Meanwhile, Lionel was assigned to cleaning the house and picking up the wine and beer. Of course, the wine had to be Hungarian, and while he couldn't find any of the excellent Villányi wines we drank over there, at least the cheap stuff kept the bar bill down.

The day before the Goulash Bash, my mom flew in from Vancouver. The party wouldn't have meant anything without her and my sister, and they must have sensed how important it was to me because they both dropped everything and got on a plane that weekend. It was even more meaningful because it was the first Thanksgiving we'd spent together in a decade, even if we did have *gulyás* instead of turkey and *Dobos torta* instead of pumpkin pie.

On the way to the airport, I stopped at the local Hungarian deli and picked up three kinds of salami, some dried sausages and *tepertö*. I found some Krisztalyviz sparkling water, too. Then I stopped in at the European bakery next door and picked up a plump *beigli* and some big, fat *tepertös pogacsa* (biscuits made with cracklings) for us to nibble on while we were cooking.

The car redolent with paprika and bacon, I swung up to the airport and gathered Mom and her luggage. From there we stopped first at an Italian deli for cheese and goose liver pâté and other cold cuts, then at a chocolate shop for the marzipan. Then off to the butcher shop, where they not only prepared the pork loin to my specifications, they even stuffed it with the Debrecen sausage, making it just about the easiest fancy food I've ever made in my life.

We swung by the supermarket for everything else we hadn't been able to buy, and finally we arrived home. There we found Lionel in a frenzy of cleaning, the frozen *pörkölt* thawing on the counter, and boxes of wine piled haphazardly on the floor.

And then Mom and I got to work. First, I made the cheese straws as she watched critically.

"You know how you always said you have to use margarine?" I began. "Do you really have to, or were you just saying that?"

She started the hand-twitching thing. "No, I just said that because I was so broke for so long, and I was using the cheapest thing I could find. Luizi always makes it with butter."

"Well then," I said, always the purist and always one to use the most expensive ingredient available. "That's what I'll use, too."

I creamed the butter and added the cheese. Then I poured the flour and salt into a mixing bowl.

'What are you doing? You should be mixing it on the counter."

"I hate mixing things on the counter, it makes such a mess."

"But you'll have to eventually."

"True, but by then it'll all be one dough ball, not a bunch of crumbs."

"Well, whatever works for you," Mom said dubiously.

I rolled out the dough, brushed it with milk, sprinkled cheese on it, and then slid the slicer across its orange expanse, my hands steady and sure, the cheese straws the most perfect I'd ever made.

"You always do things so beautifully," Mom said, then turned to Lionel. "What's it like, living with such a perfectionist?"

"It's not easy, Madge," he said.

"Hey, quit ganging up on me and get back to work," I called.

Next, now that it was finally defrosted, I had to grind the filling for the crêpes. I clamped the old-fashioned meat grinder to the counter and started stuffing the chicken thighs into it, one at a time, while cranking the handle slowly.

"You know, that's just too much work," Mom said. " I just use ground meat in my Hortobagyi *palacsinta*."

"I tried that and it was horrible," I said, remembering the bland, rubber-nubbly filling I'd created for friends who were too kind to say anything mean about it. "The texture was all wrong, and it had no flavor, and the sauce was gross."

"Yes, but this way is so much work."

"But it tastes better!"

"Well, it's your party, dear."

As we debated techniques and ingredients, I paused to realize that I'd always been so critical of Mom's cooking, and yet that was hardly fair. She came from a different generation of cooks than I had, learning to cook when there was no money and few ingredients, when cooks had to make do with what they could find. She also learned to cook at a time when cooking wasn't considered glamorous or important the way it is today, when you have celebrity chefs and twenty-four-hour food television. She didn't care about the origins of her ingredients or Slow Food or any of the trendy culinarianisms of today. She simply had to feed her family after a long day at the office.

Of course, I do care about those things that my mother thinks are too much trouble. I wasn't looking for shortcuts, I was looking for authenticity. On the other hand, I would have happily accepted some shortcuts the next morning, when I was in the middle of crêpe-making hell.

I'd been up since 6 a.m., marinating the pork, boiling eggs, chopping vegetables, setting out the mise en place, and organizing the platters and napkins and serving spoons.

Then I started making the crêpes. I beat together the eggs and milk and flour and set the batter aside for a bit before I started frying the pancakes. God, it took forever. While I was making them, Mom got up and plopped herself in front of CNN, and Lionel got up and drove to the airport. He returned with Fran, who settled in and unpacked her bags, and I was *still* flipping the flipping crêpes. Man, was I sick of that oily-eggy smell by the time they were done.

Luckily, it was time for a break. Fran and I would have almost no other time to visit, so we drove over to the farmer's market and loaded up on armloads of flowers and bags of red, paprika-style hot peppers.

Once we returned home, it was on to the *Dobos*. Quickly, I whipped up two batches of batter and spread it on two rectangular baking sheets covered in parchment paper.

"What are you doing?" Mom asked curiously. "Isn't *Dobos* supposed to be round?"

"Well, technically, I suppose, yes," I said. "But I'm making a *Dobos* slice because it'll work better for serving at a party. And, um, it's easier."

"I can't believe you're making *Dobos* at all."

"I know. Would you believe Luizi says it takes her only twenty-five minutes to make a *Dobos*?"

"That's crazy."

"I know."

We shook our heads in empathy. Or maybe it was sympathy. By then I was certainly starting to feel sorry for myself. I popped the baking sheets into the oven – the cake only takes a few minutes to bake – and mixed up a chocolate pastry cream.

While the cake and the cream cooled, I filled the crêpes and layered them in a large baking dish. Amazingly, the filling and the crêpes worked out perfectly even; how, I have no idea at all. I could sense my Nagymama's spirit nodding at me from across the room. "Well done, *Csibike!*"

Thanks, Grandma.

While I put Mom and Fran to work peeling and chopping the carrots and potatoes for the *gulyás*, I put the pork roast in the oven and started assembling the *Dobos torta*. First I sliced each of the sheets of cake into six even strips. Well, they were kind of even. Then came the tricky part: making the hard caramel top. The last time I'd done this, the caramelized sugar had flowed over the edge of the cake and all over the countertop, which not only made a huge, sticky mess, but was a tragic waste of delicious caramel. This time I made two reservoirs out of well-buttered aluminum foil. I placed the best looking cake slices in the foil frames, caramelized the sugar, then held my breath as I poured it over – it worked! Quickly, I heated a sharp knife and scored the caramel in slices before it could harden. That way, I'd be able to cut easily through all the layers of the cake when it came time to serve it.

I repeated the caramel process with the second cake top; then while it was cooling, I spread the other layers with the chocolate pastry cream and stacked them on top of each other to create two cakes. With a flourish, I topped them with the two caramel layers. I spread the rest of the chocolate cream around the sides of the two cakes and pressed chopped nuts into them. True, they were a little bit wobbly looking, as if Dr. Seuss had tried his hand at pâtisserie, but they were also the most beautiful things I'd ever made.

"Ta-da!" I called, and everyone clustered around, making impressed little noises. I already considered the day a total success, just seeing the looks on Mom's and Fran's faces. I only wished my aunts and my grandmother could have been there, too.

I put the soup on to simmer, took the pork roast out to cool, then stopped and surveyed the kitchen. Everything that needed to be cooked was cooked and I was right on schedule. *Quel* relief! Now it was time for the fun part: the platters. Quickly, I blanched the veggies for the crudité basket and arranged them as well as I could to reflect the colors of the Hungarian flag. I put out the cheeses to get all ripe and runny, and assembled the cold cuts.

While everyone else took a break — Fran to visit a friend, Lionel to pick up the balloons, and Mom to take a nap — I quickly set out the dishes and the glasses. I covered the table with a white cloth, then arranged a vase of flowers in the middle and dotted the candles and peppers about — apparently randomly, though in fact carefully arranged to hide the red wine stains.

Next to the front door, I arranged two platters of wineglasses so guests could pick them up as they came in, sort of like a fancy wine tasting event. As they came in, I planned to pour each guest a precious drop or two of Tokaj Aszú so they'd get to taste at least one great Hungarian wine that night.

I walked around one last time, making sure everything was in place, then went upstairs to change out of my paprika–, chocolate–, and crêpe-batter-spattered sweats.

By 7 p.m., the candles were lit, the gypsy music was playing on the stereo, and clusters of red, white, and green balloons were attractively arranged outside so our guests would know which house was ours. The crêpes were in the oven, the *gulyás* bubbling away on the stove. The roast was sliced, each thin slab with a perfect O of sausage in the middle. The platters were arranged and so were we, each of us with a glass of wine in our hands and our hair and makeup carefully in place.

Guests started arriving at 7 p.m. on the dot, so punctual that they could have been Hungarian themselves. As they entered, I handed each of them a glass of the aszú. "Enjoy it," I told them as they walked in.

"It's the only good Hungarian wine you'll drink all night."

Soon our tiny house – which had always seemed so big until now – was crammed with people. People laughing and talking and drinking and eating, people from different worlds and different places, all coming together with a bit of paprika to spice things up.

Mom and Lionel and Fran kept the glasses and plates filled while I manned "the bridge" of our open-plan kitchen, dishing out *gulyás* and crêpes and taking around the *langos* that Sue had brought over. I was amazed as I watched the food disappear. Everyone actually seemed to be enjoying it. It was a revelation to me – all those years I'd been embarrassed about my culinary history, yet here were all these cool, sophisticated people, digging into the salami and the *tepertö* and the *gulyás*, swilling back the plonk, and having a grand old time.

I could have sworn that somewhere in the crowd I saw my grandmother and she was winking at me.

At one point, I asked people to take notes for me because I was too busy and wanted to remember the events of the evening. Afterwards, I looked at what they wrote. True, some of the scrawls were impossible to decipher – everyone had brought Hungarian wine to honor the theme and were so delighted to discover how cheap it was that they all brought two or three bottles and then proceeded to make merry in a thoroughly Magyar manner. Here's what some of the more legible comments were:

"*Tepertö* should be available at all maternity stores," said my pregnant friend Alex.

"Crêpes were fantastic."

"An incredible Magyar feast. Next year?"

"I felt like I was in late-nineteenth century Budapest, experiencing a decadent meal in a decadent bistro."

"Elegant"

"Lovely."

"Outstanding."

"Delicious!"

"I'll be back for more *Dobos torta*."

As much as people loved the *gulyás* and the crêpes, the *Dobos* was the evening's showstopper. Around 9:30 p.m., I brought it out of the fridge and there was a little intake of breath and a momentary lull in the conversation. "Wow!" I heard someone say. "She didn't make that herself, did she?" And then my mother piped in proudly, "Yes she did!" I couldn't help but smile.

Deftly, I cracked the caramel top, then sliced each cake into pieces. Fran helped me pass it around. Waves of happy little moans followed the cake's passage through the room and within a couple of minutes every crumb, every drop of chocolate cream, and every speck of caramel was gone. If you doubt me when I say it's the best cake in the world, just ask the people who were there that night.

People kept on eating and drinking, laughing and flirting late into the night. The last guest left at 1:30 a.m., with hugs and kisses and a parting comment: "I've had to re-evaluate my entire perception of Hungarian culture!"

Still laughing, we closed the door and blew out the candles.

Lionel and I toasted each other with the last of the Tokaji Aszú. As we sat there in the dark, it occurred to me with a little jolt of sadness that my journey was over. For a year I'd been traveling and searching and asking questions about the whole Hungarian thing, and all that time, all I'd really been looking for was my way back home. What I learned was that while we can dream of a romantic, faraway place, the truth is that home is where we live now, where our friends and family are, where we cook and eat and serve up the gifts from our kitchen. The Goulash Bash was just a way of bringing all my many "homes" together.

I took a deep breath and inhaled the aroma of paprika that still lingered in the air. And then I knew, and I had to laugh. However much I might wish it wasn't so, for me, home is where the paprika is.

THE RECIPES:
Go On, Try It Yourself

What follows is by no means a comprehensive guide to Hungarian cooking. Rather, these are dishes that I love, and have mastered after much trial and error. If you are serious about learning this delicious cuisine, check out the cookbooks by George Lang and Susan Derecskey, listed in my Acknowledgments. In Hungary, authors such as Judit Stahl are hugely popular, presenting a quicker, healthier version of Hungarian cuisine. Unfortunately, they have yet to be translated into English. But when they are, look for another Hungarian revolution — this time in the kitchen.

In the meantime, why not give some of these recipes a whirl? Some are from my family, some are classic dishes updated to modern kitchens and techniques, and some are modern recipes using traditional ingredients.

And if you need an extra bit of inspiration, the full menu from the Goulash Bash is at the very end. What the heck, you can throw your own paprika party!

Sajtos Rúd *(Pintyi's Famous Cheese Straws)*

The best cheese straws ever, handed down from Aranka to Pintyi to me. You can, if you prefer make it the way my aunt Luizi does, with Emmental cheese.

1 lb (454 g) medium cheddar, grated
1/2 lb (1 cup / 250 mL) butter or margarine at room temperature
1 lb (3 1/4 cups / 800 mL) flour

1 tsp (5 mL) baking powder
1/2 tsp (2 mL) salt
about 1/2 cup (125 mL) water at room temperature
milk to brush on top
caraway seeds to sprinkle on top (optional)

Cream butter or margarine. Incorporate cheese handful by handful, setting aside 1 handful to sprinkle on top.

Measure out flour and create mound on board. Sprinkle baking powder and salt on top and mix together. (Or, if you prefer, mix them in a large mixing bowl.)

Using a rubber spatula, scrape cheese and butter out of bowl and on top of flour mixture. Gently knead the cheese mixture together with the flour mixture, adding a little bit of water at a time, scraping up crumbs and stray bits, until it creates a dough. When it's fairly firm but still spongy, cut it in two, form two oblong logs, cover with a tea towel and let stand for 1 hour.

Spray baking sheets with vegetable spray or line them with parchment paper or a silicone liner. Preheat oven to about 310°F (155°C). You don't bake the sticks so much as dry them.

Sprinkle flour on a flat surface and roll out one log until it's about 18 inches (45 cm) long, 5 to 6 inches (12 to 15 cm) wide and about 1/2 inch (1 cm) deep. Brush with milk. Sprinkle with cheese and (if you wish) caraway seeds.

Cut into sticks about 1/2 inch (1 cm) wide. Place on baking sheets about 1 inch (2 cm) apart. Bake 35 to 45 minutes, checking frequently to make sure the cheese straws don't burn. Makes about 3 dozen.

Uborka Salata *(Cucumber Salad and Other Pickly Things)*

I like the simplicity of a cucumber salad with a plain vinegar-based dressing. You can use this dressing on other veggies too: shredded carrots, sliced tomatoes, julienned cabbage, even lettuce (iceberg, not the more flavorful varieties). It is customary to serve it as an arranged salad rather than a tossed one.

Basic dressing:
3/4 cup (175 mL) white vinegar
1/4 cup (60 mL) water
2 tbsp (30 mL) sugar

Mix together until sugar has dissolved. Makes 1 cup (250 mL).

Cucumber salad:
1 long English cucumber
salt
1/4 cup (60 mL) basic dressing
paprika for garnish
1 medium onion (optional)
sour cream to taste (optional)

Slice the cucumber very fine. If you like, you can peel it first for a more delicate salad. Place it in a large bowl and salt it generously. Let it sit for at least 15 minutes while the salt draws the water out of the cucumber and makes it tender. Squeeze as much water out as you can, then rinse the cucumber.

Place cucumber in a serving bowl. If you like, you can add very thinly sliced onions. Toss with about 1/4 cup (60 mL) basic dressing, sprinkle attractively with paprika, and serve. Serves 4.

Alternatively, you can place a dollop of sour cream on top, sprinkle the cream with paprika and let your guests stir it into the salad. Or if you like your dressing really rich and creamy you can mix the sour cream — about 1/2 cup (125 mL) — into the basic dressing and toss it all together.

Borleves (White Wine Soup)

Every year, we make this delicious soup at Christmas. It is at once comforting and decadent, light and rich. Traditionally served on Christmas Eve before a feast that features fish (no meat is eaten at this meal in the Catholic tradition) and Monte Bianco, a mountain of chestnut purée and whipped cream.

6 cups (1.5 L) plus an additional 1 cup (250 mL) dry white wine

1 1/2 cups (375 mL) water
1 cup (250 mL) sugar
8 whole cloves
2 small cinnamon sticks
8 large egg yolks

Put 6 cups (1.5 L) white wine, water, sugar, cloves, and cinnamon into a larger pot and bring to a low boil. (The wine traditionally used is a Harslevelú or Linden Tree, but you can use any light, aromatic white wine as long is it is of a decent quality.)

In a medium-sized bowl, beat egg yolks with remaining 1 cup (250 mL) wine until the mixture is creamy and well blended.

Carefully beat 1 cup (250 mL) of the boiling broth into the egg mixture, adding it slowly and mixing it thoroughly, making sure that the eggs don't cook or curdle. Mix in another cup of broth in the same manner.

Finally, pour the egg mixture into the hot — but not boiling — broth, letting it cook until it's nice and thick. Do not let it boil or else the eggs will curdle.

Strain the soup, pour it into soup cups, and serve. Serves 8.

Pörkölt, Paprikás, Gulyás —The Basic Recipe

Here's how to make the most important dishes in Hungarian cuisine.

Heat some fat in a pot. Lard is good, so are bacon drippings, and vegetable oil will do in a pinch. Best of all is rendered goose fat. Throw in some chopped onions and cook until they're translucent. Next comes the crucial step: Take the pot off the stove and stir in a lot of paprika. And that's it, the basis for an entire nation's cuisine in one easy procedure and one basic spice.

Of course, you go on to add your meat and maybe some vegetables and let it simmer a while. After an hour or so, you have the stew called *pörkölt*.

If you pour in a liter or two of water, you have a soup — *gulyás* if it's beef and potatoes, *halászlé* if it's fish and hot paprika.

If you stir in sour cream instead, the dish becomes a *paprikás*.

There are other options, as well: If you use bell peppers (with or without slices of sausage), it is a dish called *lecso*; if you use potatoes and sausage, it's paprikás *krumpli*. But the basic principle is always the same.

Pörkölt

This recipe works best with cheaper, tougher cuts of meat like ribs, shanks, shoulder, chuck, round, or any cut sold for stew. It is good made with pork, beef, veal, lamb, or mutton, rabbit, chicken, venison, and even tripe, giblets, pork hocks, hearts, or kidneys.

1 large onion
3 tbsp (45 m) oil or melted fat
2 tsp (10 mL) paprika, sweet, hot or a combination of the two
1/2 tsp (5 mL) salt
1 lb (500 g) boneless meat, cut into 1-inch (2 cm) cubes
OR
2 lb (1 kg) of meat with bones, such as chicken pieces

In a large pot or Dutch oven, heat oil or fat over medium heat. Stir in onions, cooking until soft and translucent, but not brown. Remove from heat. Stir in paprika, mixing well. Add meat and salt and mix thoroughly, making sure the meat is completely covered in paprika mixture.

Turn heat to low and replace pot on burner. The lower the heat, the more tender the meat will be. It will need to cook at least one hour, and possibly longer. The meat should release enough juices to keep it tender and moist, but if you need to, you can add a bit of water to keep it from sticking. Serve it with noodles, potatoes, rice, egg barley, or, best of all, the tiny dumplings called *galuska*. Serves 4, but you can double, triple, or quadruple the recipe to feed as many people as you like.

Chicken or Veal Paprikás

This is probably the most famous Hungarian dish aside from *gulyás*. And all it is, is a simple variation on the recipe above. Make the basic *pörkölt* recipe using either 1 lb (500 g) of veal shoulder cut for stew or 2 lb (1 kg) of chicken pieces cut up as for frying. Then just before you serve the dish, stir in 1/2 cup (125 mL) sour cream and heat thoroughly. Serve over egg noodles or *galuska*. Serves 4.

Paprikás Krumpli (Potato Paprikás)

1 large onion
3 tbsp (45 mL) oil or melted fat
1 large green pepper (optional)
OR
2 sweet Hungarian yellow peppers (optional)
2 tsp (10 mL) paprika, sweet, hot or a combination of the two
1 1/2 lb (700 g) boiled potatoes, cut into bite-sized chunks
1 cup (250 mL) sliced spicy sausage such as Debrecen

Prepare onions and paprika in the usual way, then stir in the potatoes, sausages and peppers, cut into 1/2-inch (1 cm) dice, if using. Cook until the potatoes are slightly overcooked and have absorbed most of the sauce.

Gulyás

Make a *pörkölt* with 1 lb (500 g) stewing beef. When the meat is tender (after 2 or more hours of cooking time), add:

3 medium potatoes, peeled and cubed
2 large carrots, peeled and cubed
1/2 tsp (2 mL) salt
1/2 tsp (2 mL) caraway seeds (optional)
4 cups (1 L) water or beef stock

Let simmer for an hour or until potatoes are cooked through, then serve with crusty bread. Serves 4 to 6.

Alternatively, you can prepare this the more traditional way, as a *bogracs gulyás*, in a cauldron over an open fire.

Hortobagyi Palacsinta (Crêpes with Savory Meat Stuffing)

Crêpes – *palacsinta* – are a popular part of Hungarian cuisine, especially as dessert. They can be filled with jam (*lekvar*), or sweetened pot cheese (*túró*), or in the case of the famous Gundel *palacsinta*, filled with ground walnuts, covered in chocolate sauce, drenched with rum and set alight.

But this savory crêpe is one of the most popular of all. It is generally served as an appetizer, but it's so rich and flavorful, I prefer to serve it as a main course. It can be made with a variety of different meats, but I like to use chicken.

Filling and sauce:
2 large onions
6 tbsp (90 mL) oil
4 tsp (20 mL) paprika
2 lb (1 kg) boneless, skinless chicken thighs

Make a *pörkölt*. When it is done, let it cool, then strain off the juices. Mix the juices with sour cream — 1 cup (250 mL) or to taste — to make the sauce. Set aside and reheat when you need it.

Grind the chicken so that it forms a rough paste. You will want to use a hand-operated meat grinder to get the meat just the right texture; an electric grinder or a food processor will make it too smooth and mushy. Stir in 1 cup (250 mL) sour cream.

Crêpes:
4 eggs
1 1/2 cups (375 mL) flour
3 cups (750 mL) milk
1 tbsp (15 mL) neutral-flavored vegetable oil such as canola oil, plus more for frying
1/2 tsp (2 mL) salt

Using a whisk or an electric beater, mix all ingredients thoroughly, then let them sit for about half an hour. If the batter is too thick, add a bit more milk. Once you're ready to prepare the crêpes, stir the batter well. While you're making the crêpes, stir the batter occasionally to prevent it getting lumpy.

Heat 1/3 cup (75 mL) oil in a small pot over medium-low. Heat a crêpe pan over medium heat. Drizzle about 1/2 tsp (2 mL) hot oil on the pan, then swirl around until it covers the entire surface. Working quickly, ladle about 1/4 cup (60 mL) batter into the pan, then swirl it around until it covers the surface of the pan evenly.

When the edges are curled and the top is dry, it's time to flip the crêpe. More confident cooks will toss it into the air; I prefer to use a spatula and stay safe. The second side will take barely a minute to cook. When it's done, slide it on to a plate and repeat the process all over again.

This recipe makes at least two dozen crêpes, which is quite a lot. You can always freeze any leftovers. You can also use these in any other crêpe recipe.

To finish the Hortobagyi *palacsinta*:

Fill each crêpe with about 1/3 cup (75 mL) filling and roll up. If you're not serving them immediately, or you're preparing these for a crowd, place the filled crêpes into a large baking dish and heat for about 30 minutes in an oven on the lowest heat setting. Meanwhile, heat the sauce in a small pot. Serve the crêpes and pour a spoonful of sauce on each. Makes at least 24 crêpes.

Disznó Sült *(Roast Pork Loin Stuffed with Sausage)*

This is one of the easiest and most impressive dishes you will ever serve on a buffet. It can be served either hot or cold, but the important thing is to make sure it's sliced very, very thin. The sausage will flavor the pork, and so will the marinade.

1 boneless pork loin (NOT the tenderloin, but the loin, which is made from two hunks of meat tied together into a nice, round log)

1 or 2 links of Debrecen or farmer's sausage, depending on how long the loin is

1/2 cup (125 mL) chicken stock (approximately)

Marinade:

1/3 cup (75 mL) neutral-flavored oil such as canola

1 tbsp (15 mL) sweet paprika
1 tsp (5 mL) salt
1/2 tsp (2 mL) freshly ground black pepper
any combination of garlic powder, dried thyme, crushed bay leaves or dried sage, to taste.

Ask your butcher to separate the two halves of the loin, place the sausage between them, and tie them back together.

Make the marinade: Mix sweet paprika, salt and freshly ground black pepper into 1/3 cup (75 mL) oil. If you like, you can add other spices as well: garlic powder, dried thyme, crushed bay leaves, or dried sage, to taste.

Mix well, then slather the spice mixture all over the pork. Wrap the pork firmly in plastic wrap and refrigerate for several hours or overnight. Bring the pork loin up to room temperature before you start roasting it.

Preheat the oven to 350°F (175°C). Place pork on a rack in a roasting pan, then pour about half the chicken stock into the pan. Cover with foil and place in the oven. Uncover halfway through cooking time, basting occasionally and making sure the broth doesn't dry out and burn.

Your butcher will give you a pop-up timer to let you know when the meat is done. Expect it to take 2 1/4 to 2 1/2 hours, until the meat reaches an internal temperature of 160°F (71°C). Let it rest for at least 15 minutes before carving. Serves 16 or more people as part of a buffet.

Özgerine Vörösborban *(Roast Venison with Wine Sauce)*
For the marinade:
1 1/4 cups (300 mL) red wine
6 juniper berries, crushed
1 tsp (2 mL) dried rosemary
1 tsp (2 mL) dried thyme leaves
1 tsp (2 mL) dried sage, crumbled

For the venison:

2 lb (1 kg) saddle of venison
1 to 2 tbsp (15 to 30 mL) vegetable oil

For the sauce:

2 shallots, chopped very fine
3 cups mushrooms, quartered (button mushrooms will do, but wild mushrooms such as chanterelle, morel, or porcini would be even better)
1/2 cup (125 mL) light cream
2 tbsp (30 mL) flour
1 tbsp (15 mL) blackcurrant jelly

Make the marinade by mixing together the wine and spices. Place venison in a zip-top bag, them pour marinade over the meat, seal the bag, and place in the fridge. Allow to marinate for at least 6 hours or overnight, turning occasionally.

Take the meat out of the marinade and place on a roasting rack, allowing the surface to dry a little and the meat to come back up to room temperature before roasting. Set the marinade aside; you will use it to create the wine sauce.

Preheat the oven to 400°F (205°C). Heat a little oil in a skillet. When it is hot, sear the venison on all sides. Remove venison from the skillet and set skillet aside. Place meat on a rack in a roasting pan and put it in the oven. Roast it for about 30 minutes, or until it reaches an internal temperature of no more than 130° F (55° C). Because venison is so lean, you never want to cook it more than medium rare. When it is done, remove the meat from the oven and tent it with foil, letting it rest for at least 15 minutes before carving it.

Meanwhile, make the sauce. In a small bowl, stir together the flour and jelly, then thin the mixture with the cream until it forms a liquidy paste.

Put the skillet back on the burner and heat a little oil over medium heat. Sauté the shallots until soft but not browned, then add the mushrooms and cook until softened.

Pour the reserved marinade into the skillet and bring to a low boil. (You might find it easier at this stage to take the mushrooms out of the pan and return them when the sauce is done.) Stir in the jelly mixture to bind the juices and cook until it's thick and rich. Add salt and pepper to taste.

Slice venison and arrange on plates. Pour sauce over meat and serve with roasted potatoes or potato croquettes. Serves 4.

Cseresnyés Kacsa *(Duck Breast with Dried Sour Cherries)*

This is a modern dish based on two of Hungary's most traditional ingredients — duck and sour cherries. It's easy and impressive, the perfect main courses for a dinner when you really want to wow your friends.

1/2 cup (125 mL) dried sour cherries
1/4 cup (60 mL) ruby port or strong red wine
2 to 4 duck breasts (see note below)
salt and pepper to taste
1 shallot chopped very fine
1 tbsp (15 mL) sugar
1/2 cup demiglace (see second note below)

Pour the wine over the cherries and let them soak for at least an hour.

When you're ready to start cooking, preheat the oven to 450° F (230° C). Score the duck's skin several times with a sharp knife and sprinkle with salt and pepper. Heat an oven-proof skillet over medium-high heat, then place the breasts in the skillet, skin side down. Sear them until the skin is a crisp golden brown. (You won't need to add any oil as the duck's skin is already wonderfully fatty.) Flip the breasts and place the skillet in the oven, roasting the duck to medium rare, about 10 minutes. Don't overcook.

Remove the skillet from the oven. Place the breasts on a platter and tent with foil.

If the breasts have released a lot of fat — 1/2 cup (125 mL) or more — drain some of it off, then put the skillet back on the burner. Turn heat to medium. Stir in the shallots and fry until they are soft and translucent. Stir in 1 tbsp (15 mL) sugar and allow it to caramelize.

Deglaze pan with demiglace, then stir in cherries and port. Keep warm while you prepare the duck.

Slice the breasts on the diagonal and arrange attractively on four plates. Drizzle sauce over them, making sure everyone gets their fair share of the cherries. Serve with wild rice or roasted potatoes. Serves 4.

Note #1: This recipe is for four people, but how much duck you want to cook is up to you. Personally, I always find one full duck breast too much and half a breast too little. You could always split three breasts between four people, but that means someone will get stuck with the not-so-attractive end bits, and that's just not fair. Me, I'd splurge on four breasts, then slice off the ends before serving and use them in a salad later in the week.

Note # 2: The best choice here would be to make a demiglace from duck stock — simply boil down 4 cups (1 L) of duck stock to 1/2 cup (125 mL) of thick, flavorful demiglace. Unfortunately, duck stock isn't easily available everywhere so this might not be so easy to accomplish. Instead you can replace it with veal demiglace or, in a pinch, reduced beef stock. Just be careful to use the low-sodium type if you're using a commercial brand.

Töltött Kucsmagomba (Stuffed Morel Mushrooms)

Few dishes could be more Hungarian than stuffed cabbage or cabbage rolls. Unfortunately, I've always hated cabbage rolls. Still, I wanted to include one "stuffed" dish and I was pleased to find a batch of recipes for stuffed morel mushrooms, which take advantage of both the abundance of wild mushrooms in the country and the Hungarian penchant for stuffing things usually better left alone.

The first recipe I found suggested simply blanching the morels, then stuffing them with foie gras, which sounds wonderfully decadent, but I can't imagine it would really highlight the flavor of either. The second recipe I found was for a stuffing of ground veal and bread, which seemed a little bland. Below, you'll find my own personal blend of the two.

Of course, morels are only in season for a few brief weeks in spring and fall, and even then are very rare and expensive. Look for the biggest, most intact ones you can find, and rinse them several times to get rid of all the grit that hides in those little crevices.

1 lb (454 g) morel mushrooms
1/4 cup (60 mL) butter, plus more for baking
2 shallots, very finely chopped
1/2 cup (125 mL) chicken livers
1/2 lb (225 g) ground veal
1/2 cup (125 mL) bread crumbs
1 tbsp (15 mL) chopped fresh parsley
1 egg, beaten
1/4 cup (60 mL) milk
salt and pepper to taste

Once you've cleaned the mushrooms, blanch them in boiling water for 1 minute, then drain them. Cut off the stems, chop them fine, and set them aside.

Heat the butter in a skillet, then stir in the shallots and cook until soft and translucent. Add the chicken livers and cook through. Stir in the veal and chopped mushroom stems, cover, and cook for about 10 minutes.

Take the skillet off the heat. When the liver, mushrooms, and veal are cool, place the meat mixture in a food processor and process until it is finely ground and well-blended, but don't let it become a paste. Scrape into a mixing bowl and stir in bread crumbs, parsley, and beaten egg. Add milk as needed until you get a nicely manageable mixture, then season with salt and pepper.

Heat oven to 375° F (190° C). Stuff the morels, being very, very careful not to break or tear them.

Butter a ceramic or Pyrex baking dish. Put the morels in the dish, then dot each one with a bit of butter. Bake for 15 to 20 minutes, until they are just starting to crisp nicely. Serves 6 as an appetizer or side dish.

Paprika Marinade

Cooking over an open fire is very Hungarian, but it's generally a big production — a day-long endeavor to prepare a whole ox or a pot of *gulyás*. Our North American tradition of flipping on the gas grill and cooking a quick burger is a whole new concept over there. This easy marinade combines the two traditions.

It's ideal for poultry — for instance, chicken breast boned, skinned, and sliced for skewers. It also works well with pork and shrimp for the grill. Alternatively, you could drizzle a bit over root vegetables such as carrots, parsnips, onions, and potatoes, toss the vegetables until they are fully coated with the marinade, then roast them in the oven.

> Mix together:
> 1/4 cup (60 mL) neutral-flavored vegetable oil such as canola
> 1 1/2 tbsp (22 mL) sweet paprika
> 1/2 tbsp (7 mL) hot paprika or 1/2 tsp (2 mL) cayenne, or to taste
> 2 tsp (10mL) kosher salt

Place whatever meat you want to marinade in a zip-top bag. Pour the marinade over and place the meat in the fridge until it's ready too cook, turning every once in a while and moving it around so the paprika doesn't clump up. Then prepare the meat as you prefer, just making sure to bring it up to room temperature before cooking it.

Note: Another popular Hungarian food cooked over an open fire is a bacon pompom. This is not health food, to be sure, but it tastes divine, especially if you let the hot bacony drippings soak into a slice of crusty white bread. Take a slab of sweet bacon, such as white bacon, and cut it into a chunk about 2 inches (5 cm) square. Score the edible side (not the rind side) at least 1/2 inch (1 cm) deep and at approximately 1/4 inch (0.5 cm) intervals. Place it on a skewer and roast it over the flames á la weenie roast. As it cooks, the scored bits will open up to form a delicious pompom.

Grizes Tészta (Grizzly Noodles)

Back when we were little kids, we lived in bear country and we nicknamed this, our favorite dish, "Grizzly Noodles." It's quick, easy, and nutritious, perfect for a light lunch on a cold day.

1/3 cup (75 mL) neutral-flavored vegetable oil, such as canola
1 cup (250 mL) wheatlets (available in the cereal section
   of most grocery stores)
1 cup (250 mL) water (or a little bit less)
1 bag medium-wide dried egg noodles
salt to taste

In a small skillet with a lid, heat oil over medium heat. Stir in wheatlets and cook just until they turn brown. Add water a little at a time, stirring constantly and making sure not to add so much water that it gets really soupy.

Cover and cook for about 15 minutes, stirring occasionally, until the water is fully absorbed and the wheatlets have become plump and nutty.

Cook the noodles according to package instructions and toss with the cooked wheatlets. Salt generously and serve. Serves 4.

Túrós Csuzsa (Noodles with Pot Cheese and Bacon)

Another dish that is a basic in any Hungarian housewife's repertoire. It's what to make when there's nothing else to make — it's cheap and hearty and so very satisfying. Unfortunately, the Hungarian pot cheese known as *túró* is not available in Canada. Instead most cooks use small curd cottage cheese, though I prefer a fine ricotta. *Túrós csuzsa* makes a nice meal on its own with perhaps a bit of salad.

1 package dried egg noodles, square or medium width
1/2 cup (125 mL) ricotta or small-curd cottage cheese
1/3 cup (75 mL) sour cream
salt and pepper to taste
6 thick slices of bacon cut into bits and fried until crispy (optional)

Cook the noodles according to package instructions and drain. Mix ricotta and sour cream together and heat slightly. Toss the noodles with the ricotta mixture. If you wish, stir in bacon bits. Season with salt and pepper. Serves 4.

Galuska *(Tiny Dumplings)*

These toothsome little dumplings are the perfect accompaniment for all the wonderfully saucy stews. Mound them up on a plate, ladle the stew over the dumplings and, if you like, sprinkle them with a bit of fresh dill.

1 1/2 cups (375 mL) flour
1/2 tsp (2 mL) salt
2 eggs
1/2 cup (125 mL) water

Mix flour and salt together in a large mixing bowl. Create a well and, using a wooden spoon, beat in eggs and water. Beat the mixture hard, until it starts to look like ribbons – it doesn't need to be smooth, but it does need to form gluten to get the right texture. Set the mixture aside for 30 minutes to an hour to rest, then stir it well before cooking. If it's too liquidy, add a bit more flour.

Bring a large pot of water to a boil.

You can make the dumplings the old-fashioned way, by pouring the batter onto a cutting board and cutting bean-sized pieces of it into the boiling water. Or you can do it the easy way, by getting yourself a dumpling cutter or spaetzle maker, pouring the batter into the sliding metal compartment and letting the tool do all the cutting for you.

Let the dumplings cook in the boiling water until they float to the top and are firm to the bite. Drain and serve with *pörkölt* or *paprikás*. You can also toss them with a bit of butter or sprinkle them with fresh chopped dill before serving. Serves 4.

Vaniliás Kifli *(Vanilla Crescents)*

A wonderful little cookie, lovely with a morning coffee or as part of the Christmas buffet. This recipe only makes about two dozen cookies, but it can easily be doubled.

1 cup (250 mL) flour
1/2 cup (125 mL) sliced natural almonds
pinch of salt

1/2 cup (125 mL) unsalted butter
1/4 cup (60 mL) sugar
1/2 tsp (2 mL) pure vanilla extract
1 large egg yolk
icing sugar

In a food processor, mix together flour, almonds, and salt until the almonds are processed fine.

In a standing mixer, cream butter, then beat in sugar, vanilla, and egg yolk until fluffy. Slowly stir in flour and almond mixture. Gather together in a disc, cover in plastic wrap and refrigerate 1 hour.

Preheat oven to 350° F (180° C). Form 2-inch (5 cm) cylinders of dough, and then curve to form crescents, pinching ends slightly. Bake on an ungreased cookie sheet, or one lined with a silicone liner, for about 15 minutes or until they are just starting to brown on the edges. Remove cookies from oven and place on racks to cool for a couple of minutes.

Now, here most recipes suggest you roll the cookies in vanilla sugar or icing sugar, but every time I've tried this, I find that cookies crumble into little bits. Instead, I suggest filling a shaker with icing sugar (even better if you stored your icing sugar with a vanilla pod for a couple of days first). Sprinkling it over the cookies twice: the first time when they're still warm so the sugar will melt a bit onto the cookies, the second time when they're completely cool. Makes 24 cookies.

Szilvás Gomboc (Plum Dumplings)

This is as old-fashioned a recipe as you can imagine, but so wonderfully delicious – and the perfect summer afternoon treat when plums are in season. When my grandmother used to make these, the house was rich with plummy sweetness, sugar, and cinnamon.

6 medium potatoes (about 2 lb or just under 1 kg)
3 cups (750 mL) flour
1 tsp (2 mL) salt
3 eggs

1/2 cup (125 mL) unsalted butter at room temperature, divided
18 purple plums, a.k.a. Italian plums
18 sugar cubes
3/4 cup (175 mL) bread crumbs
1 cup (250 mL) granulated sugar
2 tsp (10 mL) cinnamon

The night before: Peel, quarter, and boil the potatoes. When they can be easily pierced with a fork, drain them, let them cool, then either mash them or put them through a ricer. Spread them on a plate or baking sheet and let them dry out overnight. You should have about 3 cups (750 mL) of potato mash.

When you're ready to make the dumplings, first pit the plums and set them aside. Mix sugar and cinnamon together in a small bowl, and set it aside as well.

Place potatoes, flour, and salt in a large bowl and mix together. Make a well, then stir in the eggs, one at a time, using a wooden spoon and if necessary your hands (flour them well first). Then beat in 5 tbsp (75 mL) butter, one spoonful at a time. Knead the dough until it is smooth, then let it rest for 20 to 30 minutes.

Roll the dough out on a floured surface until it is about 1/4 inch (0.5 cm) thick. Cut the dough into 3-inch (7.5 cm) squares.

To make the dumplings: Hold a square of dough in your left hand, place a pitted plum into the middle of it, then place a sugar cube in the middle of the plum. (Alternatively, you could put a teaspoonful of cinnamon sugar inside the pitted plum.) Pinch the dough shut and set the dumplings aside, covered lightly until you're ready to serve them.

To cook the dumplings: Bring a large pot of water to a boil. Drop the dumplings, one at a time, into the pot, making sure they're not too crowded or sticking to the bottom of the pot. They should rise quickly to the surface. Once they've done so, let them cook for about 15 minutes, until the dough is firm and the plum inside is hot and syrupy.

Meanwhile, in a large skillet, heat the remaining 3 tbsp (45 mL) butter and cook the bread crumbs until they are golden brown. Turn the heat way down so the crumbs stay warm but don't burn.

When the dumplings are ready, remove them from the water

with a slotted spoon and roll them in the bread crumbs, keeping them nice and warm until you're ready to serve them. Sprinkle them generously with cinnamon sugar just before serving, and offer more cinnamon sugar on the table. Makes 18.

Dobos Torta

The *Dobos torta* is named for the pastry chef who invented it, not because it looks like and its name sounds like the word for box (*doboz*). It is six layers of dense torte, filled with a chocolate pastry cream and topped with a layer of hard caramel. To make it even prettier and more delicious, you can spread chocolate cream over the sides and press chopped almonds or walnuts into it.

Note: This looks harder and more complicated than it really is, but it's still a lot more work than your average gateau. Plan to spend a good couple of hours at least in the kitchen. Trust me, though – it will be worth it.

For the torte:
6 large eggs, separated
pinch of salt
1 tbsp (15 mL) ice water
2/3 cup (150 mL) granulated sugar
1 cup (250 mL) flour
unsalted butter

Preheat the oven to 400°F (205°C). Line six 9-inch (23 cm) round cake pans with parchment paper and generously butter them.

In a standing mixer, beat egg whites with a pinch of salt and the ice water until they form stiff peaks. With the mixer going, add egg yolks one at a time, beating for about 1 minute after each addition until they are fully incorporated. Turn mixer to low, then add sugar a little at a time. When it is mixed in, repeat with flour.

Divide the batter between cake pans, spreading evenly in each. Bake in the middle of the oven for 10 to 12 minutes, or until golden brown. Unless your oven is especially large and evenly heated, you may want to bake each layer separately. As you remove each layer from the oven, take it out of the pan, carefully strip off the parchment, then set it on a rack to cool.

For the filling:
6 oz (168 g) semisweet chocolate (6 squares)
1 cup (250 mL) unsalted butter
1 cup (250 mL) icing sugar
1/2 tsp (2 mL) vanilla extract
3 tbsp (45 mL) prepared espresso or other strong coffee
2 eggs

Melt the chocolate in a microwave oven or in the top of a double boiler over low heat.

Cream the butter, then add the icing sugar. With the mixer going on medium speed, mix in the vanilla, the chocolate, the coffee, and the eggs, one at a time, beating until the mixture is light and fluffy. Chill for at least 15 minutes before using.

Note: If you have concerns about salmonella and are worried about the raw eggs in this recipe, use pasteurized eggs, which are available at some grocery stores.

For the topping:
3/4 cup (170 mL) granulated sugar

Optional garnish:
1 cup (250 mL) chopped almonds, walnuts or pecans

To assemble: Set aside the most attractive of the cake layers. (If you have concerns about caramel spillage, you might want to set it on a heavily buttered piece of aluminum foil with the edges curled up.)

Spread the other five layers with filling then layer them one on top of the other. Spread filling around the sides of the cake.

Make the topping: In a small saucepan, heat the sugar over medium-low heat, swirling it as it melts and changes color. Do not touch it; it is very, very hot. When it is a rich amber color, but not brown or burnt, remove it from the heat and pour it quickly over the set-aside cake layer. Spread it evenly with a metal spatula.

Using a sharp, buttered knife, quickly score it into 12 even pieces before the caramel hardens. Cutting right through it will make it even easier to slice the cake later on. Arrange the slices on top of the rest of the cake and chill. If you have leftover filling you can pipe it around the edges; you can also press chopped nuts into the sides of the cake if you like. Serves 12.

Joanne and Lionel's Goulash Bash Menu

Recipes included here are marked with an *.

To Start:
* *Sajtos Rúd* (Pintyi's Famous Cheese Straws)
Tepertö (Deep-Fried Pork Bits)
Goose Live Pâté
Crudités with *Körözött* (Creamy Cheese Spread)

To Continue:
Cheese Plate with Fruit
Selection of cold cuts: Hungarian Sausage, Salami, Ham, and Turkey
* *Disznö Sült* (Roast Pork Loin Stuffed with Debrecen Sausage)
* *Gulyás* (Paprika-Flavored Beef Soup)
* Hortobágyi *Palascinta*
* *Uborka Salata* (Sue's Cucumber Salad)
Mrs. Mate's *Langos* (Savory Fritters

To Finish:
* *Dobos Torta*
Beigli (Rolled Pastry filled with Poppy Seeds)
Marzipan Fruits

To Drink:
Selection of red and white wines from British Columbia and Hungary
Big Rock Grasshöpper Wheat Ale

Pronunciation Guide

Hungarian is the most logical, purely phonetic language in the world. However, the language structure is unlike that of other languages, and so is the pronunciation.

For one thing, the stress always goes on the first syllable of a word, not the second as in most languages, unless there's an accent on one of the other vowels. Then the stress goes *there*. Unlike the simple subject-verb-object sentence structure we know so well, verbs come first and comprise the case, tense, and pronoun as well as the action. Subjects and objects come later. Adjectives and nouns often combine to form one word, which means there are a lot of very long words to get your head around.

An accent or umlaut can make all the difference in meaning between, say, *úr*, which means gentleman, and *ür*, which means a void or gap. Not only that, but there are all sorts of double consonants that create sounds foreign to an English speaker's ear, and single consonants that sound different from their English pronunciation.

Here are some of the trickier consonants:

c — like the "ts" in "lets"

cs — like "ch" in "cheap"

g — hard "g" as in "give"

gy — hard "g," hard "y," creating a single-syllable sound sort of like "dya" or like the "dg" in "hedge"

j — like the "y" in young

ly — similar to "j" but a softer, more leisurely sound

ny — the "y" pronounced as a consonant to create a single-syllable "nyuh" as in the Russian word "nyet"

r — rolled just a little bit
s — "sh" like "sugar"
sz — "s" like "sweet"
ty — the "y" pronounced as a consonant to create a single-syllable "tya"
z — like "zero"
zs — a softer, buzzier sound like "azure"

If you think that's tough, try the vowels, which are even more challenging to pronounce:
a — a short "o" sound as in "taut" or "fraught"
á — a flat "a" sound as in "cat" or "bad"
e — short "e" as in "end"
é — a long "a" sound as in "day" or "they"
i — a short "i" sound as in "mitt"
í — a long "e" sound as in teen
o — a long "o" as in bone
ó — the same as above, only longer
ö — a shorter, flatter "o" that's almost a short "u" sound, somewhere between "one" and "sub"
o″ — the same as above, only longer
u — like "book"
ú — like "boot"
ü — like "love"
u″ — the same as above, only longer

All of this, of course, is why we're so happy that almost everyone in Hungary speaks at least a little English.

Thanks, Sources, Credits, and Other Debts of Gratitude

Despite the solitary nature of the craft of writing, no book could exist without the help of many, many other people. *Paprika* would not have come into being without the following people and sources. To them, I owe my deepest thanks:

My partner, Lionel Wild, who is not only the best traveling companion I could imagine, but a brave and willing taste-tester, no matter how outlandish the recipe. Thanks, hon, for accompanying me on this long, strange journey.

My mother, Magdolna Sasvári, a.k.a. Pintyi néni, who generously shared her stories, her time, and her famous cheese straw recipe, and is one of the bravest people I know.

The rest of the family, here in Canada and in Hungary, for sharing their stories, recipes, and opinions: my aunt Luizi Ferenczi, the family historian and our best cook; my aunt Frances Czumpf, the greatest hostess I know; my uncle Frank Ferenczi, for putting up with the Wintermantels and Sasváris for all these years; my sister, Frances Sasvári, for talking me off the ledge when things got too crazy; and the entire Ginter/Wintermantel/Zelinka clan – Maju, Gábor and Támas, Kálmán and Edina, Ístvan and Ildikó, Zsolt and Adrienne, and Tommi, Jolcsi, Cica, and Szilvi. *Köszönöm szépen!*

My colleagues: Shelley Boettcher, who came up with the idea for the book in the first place; Val Berenyi, my editor at the *Calgary Herald*, who has been a great friend and support through all of this; Malcolm Kirk and Monica Zurowski, who helped make it happen; Carole-Ann Hayes at CanWest Books, who believed in the project enough to actually go ahead with it; and my editor, Barbara Hehner,

Thanks, Sources, Credits, and Other Debts of Gratitude

who made me sound good even when, well, I didn't.

Ildikó Vanek and Aniko Sarkozy at the Hungarian National Tourism Office, who helped me find the right people to talk to, the right places to visit, and the right ways to get there. (Go to www.gotohungary.com or www.hungary.com for more information.)

The wonderful folks in Hungary, the restaurateurs, winemakers, spa mangers, and hoteliers, who were never less than kind and generous: Nora Becker, Attila Bicsár and Edit Décsi at Alabárdos, József and Valer Bock, Monika Debrezceni at Vylyan, Gyuci Feyérdi, the Fontányi family, Attila Gere, Tibor Huszka at the Szegedi Paprika Factory, Klára Lukacs and Dr. József Szakonyi at the Danubius Aqua, Csaba Malatinszky, Laszlo Mészáros at Disznökö, Hedwig Petrocki at Degenfeld, József Sandor at the Roosevelt Téri Halászcsarda, Ildikó Sófalvi at Egervin, Zsolt Tátrai at Bene, Zsolt Tiffán, Mihaly Vasony at the Hotel Gellért, Alajos Wunderlich, and all the rest, especially the staff at our home away from home, the Four Seasons Gresham Palace.

For more information, I relied on the following books:

Tokaj: The Wine of Freedom, by Laszlo Alkonyi, Budapest: Borbarát, 2000.

Europe: A History, by Norman Davies, London: Pimlico, 1997 (first published by Oxford University Press, 1996).

The Hungarian Cookbook: The Pleasures of Hungarian Food and Wine, by Susan Derecskey, New York: Harper & Row, 1972.

Culinaria Hungary, by Aniko Gergely, Cologne, Germany: Konemann, 1999 (original title *Ungarische Spezialitäten*)

Eva's Hungarian Kitchen, by Eva M. Kende, Canmore, Alberta, Canada: Try Kay Enterprises, 1984.

A History of Hungary, by László Kontler, Basingstoke, United Kingdom: Palgrave MacMillan, 2002.

The Cuisine of Hungary, by George Lang, New York: Bonanza Books, 1971.

Nobody Knows the Truffles I've Seen, by George Lang, New York: Knopf, 1998.

Villány: The Jewel of Wine Regions, by Dr. József Laposa and Tibor Dékány, Budapest: Aduprint Kiadó és Nyomda Kft, 2001.

The Wines of Hungary, by Alex Liddell, London: Mitchell Beazley Classic Wine Library, 2003.

Paris 1919: Six Months That Changed the World, by Margaret MacMillan, New York: Random House, 2003 (originally published as *Peacemakers*, London: J. Murray, 2001).

A Concise History of Hungary, by Miklós Molnár, Cambridge University Press, 2001 (originally published as *Histoire de la Hongrie*, Paris: Hatier Littérature Générale, 1996).

Hungarian Cookbook: Old World Recipes for New World Cooks by Yolanda Nagy Finto, New York Hippocrene Books, 2001.

The Art of Hungarian Cooking, by Paula Pogany Bennett and Velma R. Clark, New York: Hippocrene Books, 2000 (originally published New York: Doubleday, 1954).

The Storyteller: Memory, Secrets, Magic and Lies, by Anna Porter, Toronto: Doubleday Canada, 2001.

Kaffeehaus: Exquisite Desserts from the Classic Cafés of Vienna, Budapest and Prague, by Rick Rodgers, New York: Potter, 2002.

An Exaltation of Soups: The Soul-Satisfying Story of Soup as Told in More Than 100 Recipes, by Patricia Solley, New York: Three Rivers Press, 2004.

The people and sources above have done their best to set me right on a complex and confusing but tasty history. Any errors, omissions, or things that got lost in translation – those are mine.